CREATION DEVOTIONAL

GENESIS TO REVELATION

Dr. Mark Anderson

Creation Devotional: Genesis to Revelation

© Copyright 2023 by Mark Anderson

ISBN: 978-1-63073-479-4

Faithful Life Publishers
North Fort Myers, FL 33903

FaithfulLifePublishers.com
info@FaithfulLifePublishers.com
888.720.0950

All references come from the New American Standard Bible, 1995 update.

The writings and teachings of this publication are presented by the author and do not necessarily reflect or represent the views, beliefs or opinions held by Faithful Life Publishers.

28 27 26 25   2 3 4 5

DEDICATION

To my wonderful wife (Zelda) who has been an encouragement to me throughout the development of this devotional. My in-laws who I affectionately call my parents-in-love (Richard & Shirley Merrihew) who raised my wonderful wife. To my mother (Leona Anderson) who inspired me to seek God and taught me to appreciate the details of life especially the sun sets and, to my father (Sanford Anderson) who taught me to work hard and use the gifts God gave me. Most of all to our Creator God who is the center of this devotional, without whom we would be nowhere.

ACKNOWLEDGMENTS

The following people have been an enormous help in assisting me in evaluating the material of this devotional. They have encouraged me, given me insights and ideas. They have spent time proofing the text. My thanks to each and every one of my dear friends.

My wonderful wife Zelda who gave me continuous encouragement throughout this process.

Ann Wester who is one of our dear missionary friends while living at Tandala Africa, has gone above and beyond in helping us with this Volume 2 revision in English and in the French edition. Merci Mingi.

Dee Stitt who spent hours proofing the entire document while encouraging me along the way.

Dan Hoselton who went through each devotional with a fine tooth comb pulling out my poor grammar, and my many small but significant errors.

Ken Pittz who spent time going through the entire document correcting and encouraging.

Brian Young who gave me encouragement and insights into the presentation of this devotional.

Roger Eigenberg who gave many hours correcting, challenging, and encouraging.

Dr. David Demick who put forth the forward and giving encouragement.

Our associate pastor Matt & Patti Sass for their many prayers and encouragement.

Deb Lanzen, Don Nelson, Bill & Renee Transburg, Sheryl & Jim Holscher. Our many friends who gave insights into content.

THEME AND PURPOSE
OF THIS DEVOTIONAL

The primary theme of this devotional is the recognition of God as the Creator of the Universe, this planet Earth, and all life including mankind. God has given us provisions through the great variety of plants and animals for food, clothing and shelter. He provided all the elements, the raw materials for our energy needs, our building, our medicines for health and wellbeing. All life forms are diverse and inner dependent, a design quality of God's perfect understanding of His Creation. Man is created for a purpose, to use all the provisions of God's creation to better and improve life on Earth.

The purpose of this devotional is to expand our understanding of God's creative power, to provide **greater clarity in our praise of God**, and His continuing provisions, support, and compassion for Man's wellbeing. In addition, to realize the great potentials God has created within each of us. We have been gifted with the ability to do great things. May this devotional help us reconnect with our Creator God to better implement and use the potential God has given us to serve others, and advance His kingdom on Earth.

God's plan is not limited to history but provided a blueprint for history. The Bible presents an idealist hope for a conclusion that brings all the events of time into a clearer and purposeful end. There is a clear purpose for man and the recorded events of history will conclude as they are intended from the beginning. Creation in this context is still an active series of events that God is working toward a designated ending. That conclusion however will only be the beginning as the continued emphasis on the eternal covenant suggests an ongoing reality that will never end. This is perhaps the most difficult aspect of God's plan to understand. Finite man has little grasped the reality or hope of an eternal existence. Time then reappears to present a dilemma for our finite minds. How can there be an eternity. Time itself would cease to exist but would God's creative work be complete? That is a question for eternity.

GENESIS

The first book of the Bible lays the foundation for the existence of all things, life, the world, language, and the promises of God through the Jewish people. God's creative power is most decisively displayed in this book as He created all things from nothing. Genesis is the most important book in the Bible explaining the existence of sin, right and wrong along with the necessity to resist sin and follow God. Genesis explains flood narrative, and the divergence of races originating from one blood.

January 1: Day 1

CREATION EX NIHILO: GOD CREATES THE UNIVERSE FROM NOTHING

Genesis 1:1 "In the beginning,
God created the heavens and the earth."

The Bible is straight forward in recognizing God as the absolute Creator of the Universe with all matter and energy coming into existence from nothing. Science has little natural explanation for this phenomenon. The 1st law of thermodynamics states: Matter cannot create itself. This idea is compared to a magician pulling a rabbit out of a hat without a rabbit, hat, or magician. Secular science states: every event must have a cause. The God of the Bible constitutes a sufficient cause, something secular science is unable to do. For the creation scientist, God is the only sufficient cause that explains the existence of our universe from nothing. An eternal intelligent Creator lays a rational foundation for how and why we exist.

Many Old Testament passages confirm the essentials of this great event. Proverbs 3:19 *"The LORD by wisdom founded the earth By understanding He established the heavens."* The New Testament of the Bible gives us the same event but through the person of God's Son. John 1:3a *"All things came into being through Him,"* The entire Bible leaves no doubt as to the power behind this great event that brings us to the very beginning of History.

We give praise and thanks to our God for His great power that brought us life, our world, and the universe into existence, Amen!

January 2: Day 2

GOD CREATES BASIC ELEMENTS

Genesis 1:2 "The earth was formless and void, and darkness was over the surface of the deep, and the Spirit of God was moving over the surface of the waters."

God begins the process of organizing His creation. At this point, the text indicates the existence of water H2O, as a natural occurrence of two light elements (Helium and Hydrogen) in the early universe. Water is one of the most common natural structures as nearly 75% of our planet is covered by water. The presence of water reveals God's creative majesty, He designed our planet for life, water being an essential part of God's preparation for life.

The presence of God's Spirit at work is a possible indicator of the power at work in the midst of God's creative act. The presence of God's Spirit throughout the Bible is generally associated with God's power, and His ability to act. The New Testament contributes a bit more information regarding God's control of the basic elements. Colossians 1:17 *"He is before all things, and in Him all things hold together."* God is both the Creator, and sustainer of the elements that make up our world and the universe we see.

Thank you God for Your creative wisdom in ordering the complex structure of the universe, Amen!

January 3: Day 3

THE CREATION OF LIGHT AND DARKNESS
(DAY 1 OF CREATION)

*Genesis 1:3 'Then God said: "**Let there be light**";*

and there was light."

The latter books of the New Testament state plainly that God is light. If God were Himself light, it makes some sense that He would be the ultimate originator of light. Since the primary existence of a light source in our experience is our sun (a star). The absence of stars in this early portion of creation leaves us without a natural light source unless the Creator provides an alternative. The existence of light would also be a necessary step for the creation of life. Life without light would be limited at best, though some creatures exist with little light.

The role of light in Genesis acts as a dividing point in time. To separate the days into nights and to give some illumination toward our understanding of Creation. Geneses 1:4-5 speaks of light as "*good*" and gives God credit for the initiation of the day, night division as a period of time. The most logical conclusion based upon the reference to evening and morning gives us the first indicator that this as most likely a normal, approximately 24 hour day. The nature of light is complex and can be divided into the colors of the rainbow. Without light, we would have no vision. 1 John 1:5 *"God is light, and in Him there is no darkness."* Only in God's light can we know and understand the realities of God's creation.

Thank you Father that You give us light to see.
You have given us day and night and divisions of time,
and to order our world, Amen!

January 4: Day 4

GOD CREATES THE EXPANSE ABOVE
(DAY 2 OF CREATION)

*Genesis 1:6-7 "**God made the expanse**, and separated the waters which were below the expanse from the waters which were above the expanse, and it was so."*

Like Genesis 1:2, water was a critical part of the creation process. The process of organization suggests that matter required progressive development in order to accommodate all living beings that would soon occupy this new world. The expanse may be an indicator of the sky or atmosphere. This expanse would be a necessary step for life to exist. The expanse, if a reference to the skies, offers protection from solar radiation and an atmosphere to breathe.

Genesis One lays the foundation for the creation of our world, and the entire universe we see today. Much debate rages among scholars, theologians, and scientists as to how our universe came into existence. The secular scientists prefer natural explanation for creation, but when the real question of how such an event took place is asked, most will acknowledge, we don't know. Faith carries a great deal of weight both among theologians and scientists in regard to the Creation event. When in doubt, it is wise to go back to the source of all Wisdom, our Creator God. Proverbs 8:27 & 28 *"When He established the heavens, I was there, When He inscribed a circle on the face of the deep. When He made firm the skies above, When the springs of the deep became fixed."* Only God was there to bear witness to His creative work. Moses is God's conduit to us how God initiated His creation.

Thank you Lord for the skies above and the air we breathe, without Your sustaining power, none of us would be here, Amen!

January 5: Day 5

WITHOUT PLANTS, WE HAVE NO FOOD
(DAY 3 OF CREATION)

*Genesis 1:11 "Then God said, "**Let the earth sprout vegetation; plants yielding seed, and fruit trees** on the earth bearing fruit after their kind with seed in them and it was so."*

We have a variety of plants from which we can eat; both vegetables and fruits. Beyond nutrition, plants recycle the carbon dioxide exhaled by animals and convert it to plant material while producing oxygen for animals to breathe. Man and animals could not exist without plant life. Genesis 1 gives us the description of God's creative power introducing the first life forms. Genesis 1:29 adds to this: *"Behold, I have given you every plant yielding seed that is on the surface of all the earth, and every tree which has fruit yielding seed; it shall be food for you."* God is our great provider; without His provisions, there would be no food.

It is an amazing reality we have so many plants that are able to reproduce hundreds of times over. Seed bearing trees give us thousands of fruit in amazing variation. Crops are able to produce sufficient food to feed billions of people. In addition to our need for nourishment, plants in their many varieties throughout the world provide a great many drugs and remedies, sustaining life. God has indeed shown His kindness and grace as we see the abundance of His provision through the plants we often take for granted. Psalm 104:14 continues to show God's provisions: *"He causes the grass to grow for the cattle, And vegetation for the labor of man, so that he may bring forth food from the earth."* All the many varieties of plant life makes possible life on this planet.

Thank you Father for the many types of plant life You have given us to live on. You are the great provider, giving us everything we need to sustain our existence, Amen!

January 6: Day 6

ANIMALS: THE BIRDS AND THE FISH
(DAY 5 OF CREATION)

*Genesis 10:20 "Then God said, **'Let the water teem with swarms of living creatures**, and let birds fly above the earth in the open expanse of the heavens."*

On day 5, God created living animals in the form of fish to live in the sea, and birds in the sky. God's creative work on day 2, made it possible for life to thrive on earth. All animals serve as a valuable service to mankind as they multiply on the earth. Animals were made in many varieties, just as plants. They serve in many capacities for the benefit of man. God brought the quail to Israel while in the dessert for food. Pigeons were used by the poorest Israelites as sacrifices. The dove was used, and is still a symbol for the presence of the Holy Spirit. Scavenger birds such as Hawks, buzzards, and falcons eat and clean up carcasses of dead animals. They eat insects while providing a balance to nature preventing an excess of one population over another.

Fish in the sea provides a necessary means of food for man and his survival. The great diversity of fish also provides us a glimpse into the creative nature of God. The differences between fish and birds gives us an illustration into God's description of man and the differences of one type of flesh to another. I Corinthians 15:39 *"All flesh is not the same flesh, but there is one flesh of men, and another flesh of beasts, and another flesh of birds, and another of fish."* Fish and birds were created in the beginning to serve the needs of Man.

Thank the Lord for the fish and the birds as they provide us understanding into the power of God's creativity, Amen!

January 7: Day 7

CREATION OF LAND ANIMALS
(DAY 6 OF CREATION)

*Genesis 1:24 "Then God said, '**Let the earth bring forth living creatures** after their kind; cattle and creeping things and beasts of the earth after their kind' and it was so."*

The next type of flesh God created was land animals. Both reptiles and mammals were created on day 6. God is progressive in His creative power. After day 3, land animals now had a place to thrive. The great variety of animals (Biodiversity) makes possible the continuation of all life, as animals will depend upon each other for survival. Cattle provide meat along with the hides giving man clothing and protection. Sheep are used for clothing, blankets and food. The many types of animals have symbiont relationships (animals that need each other) without which life would not be possible. The variety of plants and animals within nature maintains a delicate balance of life. Without this balance, man's existence would be unmanageable.

We are dependent upon the animal kingdom for many of our most basic needs. Bees and other insects cross pollinate flowers, trees, and our crops. The worm, one of the lowest of creatures helps break up the soil for our crops. Without the help and existence of these important plants and animals, Man's continued survival would not be possible. Peter is told by God to eat animals: Acts 10:12&15 *"and there were in it all kinds of four-footed animals and crawling creatures of the earth and birds of the air. Again a voice came to him a second time, What God has cleansed, no longer consider unholy."* God created animals for our enjoyment, nourishment and benefit.

Thank you Lord for the provision of the animal kingdom. You have given us food, protection, companionship, and an understanding of Your creative power, Amen!

January 8: Day 8

GOD CREATES MAN AND WOMAN IN HIS IMAGE

*Genesis 1:27 "**God created man** in His own image; **in the image of God He created him; male and female He created them.**"*

The last and greatest of God's creation week was man, to be made in His own image. Man's nature and his flesh was both similar and different from the other land creatures God created on day 6. God's creative power is not limited to the first man and woman. Psalm 139:13 gives us a deeper glimpse into God's continuing creative power. "*For You formed my inward parts; You wove me in my mother's womb.*" Men and women are created for a much higher calling than the rest of creation. Job 33:4 establishes God as creator of every person. "*The Spirit of God has made me, And the breath of the Almighty gives me life.*" Man is also given a soul and spirit, providing man the possibility of eternal life.

God formed man out of the dust of the earth: Genesis 2:7 "*Then the LORD God formed man of the dust from the ground, and breathed into his nostrils the breath of life: and man became a living being.*" God breaths within man life; without God's life giving power, no life could exist. The idea of life coming from spontaneous generation (life from non-life) is impossible. The amazing complexity of life cancels any possibility of life forming by chance.

Thank you God that we breathe and live and have our being. Without You, we have no life. Psalm 139:14 "I will give thanks to You for I am fearfully and wonderfully made." Amen!

January 9: Day 9

WE HAVE A JOB TO MANAGE EARTH'S RESOURCES

Genesis 1:28 "Be fruitful and multiply, and fill the earth, and subdue it; and rule over the fish of the sea and over the birds of the sky and over every living thing that moves on the earth."

God does not leave man and woman without a task to do. Looking at the big picture of man's creative purpose, we are to use the resources of this planet for good. In this passage of Genesis, **God gives man a commission** to populate the earth and to subdue it. We are commanded to take care of this planet and all the creatures within it; to use its resources for our mutual good. In addition, Man is called into a relationship with God; to know Him, and to enter into an eternal relationship with Him.

Ecologically, we are to take care of the earth and to use its resources for our good. God has provided us with the resources to make this earth into a wonderful place to live. The trees give us lumber for housing, furniture, and food. All the resources in the earth such as metal, rock, and fuel provides us the means to build, to create and to establish societies. God did not leave us without the means to construct civilization. Proverbs 27: 18 & 23 *"He who tends the fig tree will eat its fruit, And he who cares for his master will be honored. Know well the condition of your flocks And pay attention to your herds;"* God has given man a job to do, and it is his or her responsibility to do that job to the best of their ability. Most importantly, we to accept our accountability before God, to learn to love and obey Him.

Thank you God for all Your provisions, and resources to make us useful and purposeful in this life, Amen!

January 10: Day 10

THE PROBLEM OF EVIL

Right and wrong, how do we know the difference?

Genesis 3:22 "then the LORD God said, 'Behold, the man has become like one of Us, knowing good and evil; and now, he might stretch out his hand, and take also from the tree of life, and eat, and live forever'"

Genesis three gives the record regarding the origins of sin, explaining the existence of evil in the world and its consequences. The idea of evil is a biblical theme made possible by the existence of a Law giver. Without God, there is no standard of right and wrong. Man would be left to his own preferences. The biblical account puts man squarely in the middle of a battle between good and evil.

The battle for standards is at the very heart of society today. The denial of any absolute standard of morality seeks to place man as his own creation, responsible to no one but himself. The denial of evil gives man autonomy from any Creator. It also places man in a very precarious position of equating Mother Theresa with Hitler, leaving us with no distinction for right and wrong. For those who argue that man can create his own goodness, is short sighted and operating apart from a Jewish-Christian paradigm. Romans 3:23 *"For all have sinned and fall short of the glory of God."* All men know in their hearts that they have done wrong in their lives.

We give thanks to You oh Lord for giving us a standard of morality beyond our own rationale. Only You, our Creator God sets the standard for morality and ethics, Amen!

January 11: Day 11

GOD'S SOLUTION TO OUR PROBLEM OF EVIL

Genesis 3:15 Speaks of a seed coming from woman that will someday crush our advisory. ""And I will put enmity between you and the woman, and between your seed and her seed; He shall bruise you on the head, And you shall bruise him on the heel."

God set a standard for righteousness beyond what any of us is able to keep. There is a tension between God's expectation and our ability to accomplish perfection. Matthew 5:48 *"...you are to be perfect as your heavenly Father is perfect."* It would seem hopeless except that God provided us with a solution. The seed of a woman point to the future coming of the Messiah through a virgin several millennium in the future. The advisory would receive the fatal blow by the death and resurrection of the coming messiah.

The nature of the seed mentioned as coming from woman is given more clarity in Genesis 22:18. *"In your seed all the nations of the earth shall be blessed,"* This reference is to Abraham, the father of the Jewish people. This seed is a reference to the person of Jesus Christ in the New Testament. His death on the cross is the final blow to the adversary and our ultimate victory over sin and death. Acts 3:25 *"It is you who are sons of the prophets and of the covenant which God made with your fathers, saying to Abraham, And in your seed all the families of the earth shall be blessed."* We are blessed by God's gracious pardon of our sins through the vicarious sacrifice of Jesus on the cross.

Thank you Lord for the seed of woman, that we might find fulfillment in Your Son Christ Jesus, Amen!

January 12: Day 12

THE GIFT OF CHILDREN

Genesis 3:16 states: "To the woman He said, I will greatly multiply Your pain in childbirth, In pain you shall bring forth children;"

The Biblical concept of humanity is based on historical documentation through Scripture. Eve is identified as the mother of all humanity. Mitochondria Eve is supported by Modern science, all humanity is derived from a single set of parents. Mitochondrial DMA shows that all have descended from one female. There can be no division among humanity. We are of one blood; God has given us the child bearing process to propagate the human race. This is part of the curse, women will suffer through child bearing. Labor for woman is difficult regardless what medicines we give to reduce the pain.

Despite the difficulty of bearing children, it is still a blessing from God that we can pro-create our posterity. Sexual relations is a beautiful part of the process for creating children. Eve acknowledges that having children is a gift from God. Genesis 4:1 *"Now the man had relations with his wife Eve, and she conceived and gave birth to Cain, and she said, I have gotten a man-child with the help of the LORD."* All children are a blessing from God. Psalm 127:3 *"Behold, children are a gift of the LORD, The fruit of the womb is a reward,"* vs.4 *"Like arrows in the hand of a warrior, So are the children of one's youth."* Just as arrows are valuable to the warrior, so too children are of extreme value to parents.

Thank you Lord for the precious gift of Children, Amen!

January 13: Day 13

WE KNOW OUR ORIGINS

Genesis 5: 1 states: "This is the book of the generations of Adam. ***In the day when God created man, He made him in the likeness of God****."*

It is often said, we cannot know where we are going, unless we know where we have come from. Our origins are important in understanding who we are, where we are headed and what our purpose is. Natural science can give us no insights into these questions. There is no absolute purpose or meaning to life according to the natural sciences. We are only products of blind natural processes that can give us no real meaning in life.

Thankfully, we have a record documenting the origins of life and its meaning. We have a document (The Bible) clearly stating where man came from, and who is responsible for that event. The God who created the universe is one and the same with the creation of man. Genesis 5:2 continues to explain this event. "***He created them male and female****, and He blessed them and named them Man in the day when they were created."* Each of our lives is a gift from God, having purpose and meaning. Psalm 8:4 & 5 *"What is man that You take thought of him, And the son of man that you care for him? Yet Your have made him a little lower than God, And You crown him with glory and majesty!"* We are a product of God's creative power having meaning and purpose.

Thank you Lord for creating us in Your divine image, giving us a purpose to fulfill in this life, Amen!

January 14: Day 14

MALE AND FEMALE
(ONLY TWO)

*Genesis 5:1-2 "**In the day when God created man,** He made him in the likeness of God."*

God progressively reveals His plan for mankind, in spite of the setback created by Adam and Eve's sin. The theme of man being created in the image of God places him in a higher place than all of God's creative works. Genesis 1:27 *"...in the image of God He created him; male and female He created them."* God created man and woman to complement one another in marriage. The husband wife relationship is the basis for pro-creation. This union is the closest human relationship possible, and is a reflection of God's image (Father, Son, and Holy Spirit). Mark 10:6 *"But from the beginning of creation, God made them MALE AND FEMALE."* The marriage relationship reflects God's corporate image.

The quality of mankind is enhanced by the special status given, in that we are a reflection of God's nature. Our ancestors, Adam and Eve were created in the image and likeness of their Creator. That gives mankind special status since that relationship can be restored through the life of Jesus Christ indwelling the regenerate man. This status is in stark contrast to the naturalist's emphasis on man being no more than descending from apes. We are of value with potential far beyond our immediate accomplishments. For this reason, man is held in very high regards by our Creator God. Self-image is a major factor in conduct. When people are taught that they descended from lower animals, that worldview can translate into deviant conduct and attitudes.

Thank you God that we are created male and female as a corporate reflection of Your image, You have given us purpose, meaning, and a much higher calling, Amen!

January 15: Day 15

THE FLOOD

*Genesis 7:4b "**I will send rain** on the earth forty day and forty nights;"*

We can be thankful that God did not completely give up on His creation, even though man had become exceedingly corrupt, God found a way to rescue mankind from his deserved doom. God preserved one family in order to continue the human race, thus to accomplish His purpose in redeeming Mankind. God left us with an account of this world wide event and the circumstances surrounding it. We have other accounts verifying its validity, in addition to hundreds of flood stories around the world from virtually every culture, including flood stories from the western hemisphere.

Noah's ark represents another form of God's grace toward mankind by preserving man, and beast. The preservation of the animals also enabled man's continued survival. We are dependent upon these creatures as mentioned earlier for food, clothing, work, and enjoyment. Thank the Lord for His continued protection and provision as he meets all our needs amidst the conflicts. Genesis 9:13-14 *"God said, This is the sign of the covenant which I am making between Me and you, and every living creature that is with you, for all successive generations, I set My bow in the cloud, and it shall be for a sign of a covenant between Me and the earth."* The rainbow was given as an abiding symbol of God's continuing care and concern for mankind.

Thank you Lord for the promise of never flooding the entire earth again. Your promises are true and abiding. May we learn to be obedient to Your word as Noah was faithful by preparing the ark, Amen!

January 16: Day 16

THE GIFT OF LANGUAGE

Genesis 11:7 "come let Us go down and there confuse their language that they may not understand on another's speech."

Genesis 5:1 speaks of a book documenting the origins of man. Genesis 11 gives us the origins of language going back to post-flood society. We have many forms of writing going back to the 3rd millennium BC. Egyptian hieroglyphics dates back to a little more than 4,000 years. Cuneiform documents placed on clay tablets was a common form of communications between different states going back nearly as far as hieroglyphics. It is quite possible that Adam and his posterity had some forms of writing going back to pre-flood times.

The tower of Babel as recorded in Genesis eleven gives an example of God scattering the people by changing their languages so one group would not understand another. This event would suggest that God is the creator of the world's basic language structures. God has gifted man with the ability to speak and communicate information to others. The ability to speak and to communicate by written word is a gift from God. Colossians 4:6 *"Let your speech always be with grace, as though seasoned with salt, so that you will know how you should respond to each person."* With speech, comes the responsibility to use it wisely.

Thank you Lord for the gift of speech and the ability to learn other languages. While learning other languages is a gift, separate languages separates and protects different cultures, Amen!

January 17: Day 17

GOD WILL PROVIDE

Genesis 22:8 "Abraham said, 'God will provide for Himself the lamb for the burnt offering my son.' So the two of them walked on together."

Just has God provided a way for Noah and his family to escape judgment from the flood, we are given an account of God providing a sacrifice in substitution for Abraham's son Isaac. God gives Abraham a strange and difficult request; He asks Abraham to sacrifice His own son. It was through this son that God promised to provide a future inheritance. This request seems to be in contradiction to what we would consider reasonable. God however is not unreasonable, He has a much greater and deeper purpose for each and every event in our lives.

The willingness of Abraham to sacrifice his own son is a direct parallel of God's willingness to sacrifice His Son for our benefit. God stopped Abraham from following through with sacrificing his son; then provided a substitute for Isaac that was acceptable to God. In the same way, God provided His own Son, Jesus to be a substitute for all our wrongs. God not only provides for all our needs, He provides all that is necessary for our redemption. 2 Corinthians 9:15 should be our daily prayer: *"Thanks be to God for His indescribable gift!"* Christ offered Himself as a substitute for our deserved death and then offered His life to restore the life that was lost in Adam (Romans 5:12), thus restoring our relationship with God.

Thank you Lord for paying our debts. You gave Yourself as the perfect substitute for the debt of our sins, Jehovah-Jireh, God our provider, Amen!

January 18: Day 18

JEWISH PEOPLE ARE A BLESSING THROUGH THE WRITTEN AND LIVING WORD

Genesis 12:3b "And in you all the families of the earth shall be blessed."

God's blessings come in many forms. We are blessed by God's revelation through the written word, The Bible and all its history shows us how God has worked through the Jewish people, the descendants of Abraham. The Bible was written primarily by Jewish writers, both Old and New Testaments. Of the 66 books in the Bible, 33 contain clear acknowledgments of God's creative hand. While the other 33 books make inferences, or paint a compelling picture of the Creator Himself. These descriptions portray God as a sufficient cause for the universe we see today, even in its complexity and grandeur. We are blessed by the written word, giving us a clear understanding of who we are, where we came from, and where we are headed.

God's greatest blessing came through the life of God's living Word, Jesus Christ. All the families of the earth are blessed by the sacrificial death of Jesus Christ on the cross. Jesus was a direct descendant of Abraham, fulfilling God's promise of blessing; without that event, no one would have access to God. Galatians 3:8 *"The Scripture, foreseeing that God would justify the Gentiles by faith, preached the gospel beforehand to Abraham, saying, 'All the nations will be blessed in YOU.'"* We are blessed for eternity, if we have accepted God's unconditional pardon through the death and resurrection of His son Jesus.

Thank you Lord for the blessings of Your written word, and Your living Word. Through the death and resurrection of Your only Son, we are blessed and given eternal life, Amen!

EXODUS

The second book of Moses continues to document the creative abilities of God. God will deliver His people through those we least expect. God is the creator of all our senses; He endows people with wisdom, skills, and abilities to perform specific tasks; without this diversity of skill sets, society as we understand it would be impossible. The seven day creation week is reiterated and confirmed.

January 19: Day 19

THE GIFT OF SIGHT

Exodus 4:11 "The LORD said to him, "Who has made man's mouth? Or who makes him mute or deaf, or seeing or blind? Is it not I, the LORD?

No birth is an accident; even those with disabilities. The details of God creative work is seen in the magnificent structure of the human body. Abilities to perform difficult tasks such as speaking and seeing are testimonies to a magnificent Creator. When a disability shows up, it is easy to question God, as to why. As a future Job would learn, all disabilities and accidents occur with a purpose not seen. We cannot second guess any event. We do not know the reason for anything, until after the fact. We take for granted the abilities to perform these simple tasks, but the reality is just the opposite. We have discovered that enormous amounts of detail and structure goes into the complexities of the human body that science is only beginning to understand.

Psalm 139:14 states: *"We are fearfully and wonderfully made."* The complexities of the body are beyond our complete understanding. We cannot create life except by pro creation, and that also is a design of our Creator God. We may take for granted the astounding ability of our bodies to repair itself, for our senses to detect odors, or to see with such clarity. All our abilities to remember details, to perform specific tasks are gifts from God. Proverbs 20:12 *"The hearing ear and the seeing eye, The LORD has made both of them."* Give thanks to Him for the wonders of our body.

Thank you Lord that You are able to give sight to the blind and hearing to the deaf. You alone do all things well, Amen!

January 20: Day 20

GOD PRESERVES THE JEWISH PEOPLE

Exodus 8:23 "I will put a division between My people and your people, Tomorrow this sign shall occur."

God actively separates peoples and nations. In the context of this passage, God is separating the Jews from the Egyptians. The earth currently has over 200 nation states. Many different languages and cultures exist creating divisions between peoples. We understand from the events of Babel in Genesis, that divisions weaken sin. Man is not able to do all he pleases because of conflicts and divisions. Divisions in the long run preserves and separates. From this perspective, a One World Government would not bring order but chaos and an increase of evil. God is in control of the affairs of man. All men will ultimately submit to God.

In spite of all the chaos, God still loves and preserves His people. The Holocaust is one example of God preserving the Jewish people through unthinkable evil and persecution. Out of this death and destruction, He brought them into the land of Israel. God does the same for His church, as He cares for His body. God loves all people, but He has a special purpose for the Jewish people as a sign of His faithfulness. God cares for all those who call upon His name. Jeremiah 31:37 *"Thus says the LORD, If the heavens above can be measured And the foundations of the earth searched out below, Then I will also cast off the offspring of Israel For all that they have done, declares the LORD."* In other words, God will always be faithful toward the Jewish people.

Thank you Lord for faithfully watching over us. You care for all Your people, both Jew and Gentile, Amen!

January 21: Day 21

GOD IS IN THE DETAILS

*Exodus 9:16 "I have allowed you to remain, in order to show you **My Power** and in order to proclaim My name through all the earth."*

God's ability to deliver what He promises rests upon His power. The Bible presents an image of God that is sufficient to perform the tasks credited to Him. God's power to perform the miracles of Exodus are not confined to the creation event or time, and then withdrawn. God is in an active partnership with man. The Exodus of the Jews from Egypt is but a small token of His power. We get but a glimpse of His majesty, enough to know that He is able to help us deal with our small everyday tasks. As the song goes "He's able to carry you through."

An old TV quote states "Resistance is futile." In the case of the Egyptians fighting the exodus of the Jews, even more so. Exodus 15:7 *"For this reason we cannot resist God. God's creative power is executed in the destruction of the Egyptian."* God is far more powerful than men or nations. God is eternal Power, Knowledge, and Holiness; God is perfect. God is far above all nations, powers or dominions. We cannot resist or fight against God. We can only submit to Him in reverence and awe; we have no other course. Regardless of our actions, God will do His will.

Thank you Lord for watching over every detail of our lives, and for caring about us, Amen!

January 22: Day 22

NO ONE LIKE GOD

Exodus 15:11 "Who is like You among the gods, O LORD? Who is like You, majestic in holiness, Awesome in praises, working wonders?

The wonders of God spoken of by Moses even transcends our grasp in the 21ˢᵗ century. God's power extends well beyond what was displayed in Exodus. He is majestic in power and worthy of praise. His holiness represents His perfection, requiring no improvement. He is awesome in His being, and in His deeds; the universe is a testimony to that majesty.

Chapters 14 and 15 of Exodus presents the story of the Israelites exodus from Egypt. The story includes the parting of the Red sea; a feat demonstrating God's power and control over the elements. Having witnessed this great event, the sons sang a song in praise of God's mighty deliverance: Exodus 15:2-3 *"The LORD is my strength and song, and He has become my salvation; This is my God, and I will praise Him; My father's God, and I will extol Him. The LORD is a warrior; the LORD is His name. Pharaoh's chariots and his army He has cast into the sea;"* Possessing the knowledge we have of God's mighty works, we have even more cause to give God praise today.

Having witnessed Your great wonders in the complexity and life, and the vastness of the universe, we give You praise oh God for all You have done, Amen!

January 23: Day 23

GOD PROVIDES, BUT HOW SOON WE FORGET

Exodus 16:4 "Then the LORD said to Moses, Behold, I will rain bread from heaven for you; and the people shall go out and gather a day's portion every day, that I may test them, whether or not they will walk in My instruction."

Few people like taking major tests, according to this passage, we are living the test of life, day by day in the choices and works we complete. God tested the Israelites to determine their hearts. God's power was manifested to the people in the wilderness in this miraculous act. Moses continually reminded the people of God's power displayed in their deliverance from Egypt. 21st century man is faced with the same problem of forgetting. We forget who we are and why we are here in this world. God is the instructor, we are the students. Just as teachers must continually review the material, we must continually be reminded of God's instructions. Without God's Help, we would fail the test of life.

We are reminded of God's continual prompting through His Spirit. He does not rest, He is actively drawing people toward Him. Those who have become Christians still need God's prompting and reminders. Keep active in His Word; keep active in fellowship with other believers; seek to serve God daily. We are but empty vessels needing God's active presence in our lives to be filled. Joshua 1:8 *"This book of the law shall not depart from your mouth, but you shall meditate on it day and night, so that you may be careful to do according to all that is written in it. For then you will make your way prosperous, and then you will have success."* Our ultimate success depends upon our close fellowship with God.

Thank you Lord for Your many provisions. May we be ever mindful of your grace and kindness toward us. Help us not to forget Your instructions by staying in, and meditating on Your Word, Amen!

January 24: Day 24

GOD'S STANDARD OF MORALITY (THE 10 COMMANDMENTS)

Exodus 20: 3-17 "You shall have no other gods before Me. . ."

Exodus 20 provided a basis for moral absolutes. The 10 commandments according to the biblical text were written by the hand of God; the origins of a moral standard. The rejection of any absolute standard reduces ethics and morals to a relative preference. The Ten Commandments act as a foundation and structure from which to build a moral society, without which chaos would result. God is the creator of our moral and ethical foundation in which to live by. God has also given us a conscience to assist and guide us in our ethical choices.

Our absolute moral code clearly divides right from wrong, giving us a clear understanding of what constitutes righteousness and wickedness. God, our Creator has given us this absolute standard of conduct. We know right from wrong, because of God's standard. No man however can keep God's perfect law to perfection. Matthew 19:17 *"And He said to him, why are you asking Me about what is good? There is only One who is good; if you wish to enter into life, keep the commandments."* Our inability to perfectly keep all the commandment leaves man with a dilemma. Since we are unable to keep the law without failure, God through Jesus Christ kept the law to the letter. He offers His Life to any who will receive it, providing them with His righteousness, giving us access to God. We have a clear list of rights and wrongs to help us establish a solid basis for morality. God however fulfills the absolute standard of the law through Christ's recreated Life in the believer.

Thank you Lord for Your perfect standard for how to be successful in life. You have given us Your Spirit and Your righteousness, that we might live a successful life, Amen!

January 25: Day 25

GOD GIFTS US TO SERVE

*Exodus 28:3 "You shall speak to all the skillful persons **whom I have endowed** with the spirit of wisdom, that they make Aaron's garments to consecrate him, that he may minister as priest to Me."*

Why are some people smarter than others? While some can get 'A's without studying, others labor for hours with marginal success. Some people have special talents for music such as Beethoven and Mozart, while others have extraordinary abilities in Math (Blasé Pascal) or science (Isaac Newton). Prodigies exist today with the ability to do marvelous things. Some people are gifted athletes, while others, have creative skills. Societies all across the globe contain a diverse skill mix that enables cultures and societies to flourish. Exodus 28:3 gives us a hint into the world of unique and extraordinary talents and abilities. God endows man with specific skills and abilities. God endows man; this truth is not limited to the Jews of the 2nd millennium BC, God still endows people today. We may wish to take credit for our abilities or skills, however, the capacity to do extraordinary things is a gift. What we do with it, and how we develop it, is our part.

We are each endowed with potential to do something great. We are God's creation, with a purpose to fulfill. We must learn what we are gifted at doing. How do we translate these gifts into acts of service to others? God made us for a purpose, to serve others and to come to a greater knowledge of God. The Holy Spirit guides us in the process of learning spiritual truth, from which the believer may learn what our talents, gifts, and abilities are, and how to use them for the good of others. I Corinthians 12:7 *"But to each one is given the manifestation of the Spirit for the common good."* All gifts and talents come ultimately come from God.

Thank you Lord for the gifts you have given each of us, may we learn how to use them according to your will, Amen!

January 26: Day 26

GOD IS THE SOURCE OF TALENTS AND ABILITIES

*Exodus 31:3 "**I have filled him with the Spirit of God in wisdom, in understanding, in knowledge, and in all kinds of craftsmanship**.*

God's Spirit is connected to the endowing process. This would reflect upon God's creative nature, just as He was the Creator of all things, he has given men the ability to create on a smaller plane. Exodus 31:6 clarifies: *"I have put skill, that they may make all that I have commanded you:"* God is the originator of all skills and talents from the context of this verse. From the biblical texts, we learn that everyone has talents to differing degrees. It is our responsibility to develop and use them effectively with the guidance of the Holy Spirit. Even our brains are able to do well beyond what anyone has achieved.

When someone tells us we are talented, rather than dismissing the complement, reflect on what that talent is, and give God credit for helping demonstrate that ability. We all have potentials to be good at something. I tell my students to reflect on what classes they like, and what they don't like. God has put within each of us an interest and a talent to be developed; may we find our talents and help our children develop theirs. John 14:12 *"Truly, truly, I say to you, he who believes in Me, the works that I do, he will do also, and greater works than these he will do; because I go to the Father."* God equips His people to do both the spiritual and physical tasks for His glory and purpose.

Thank you Lord for all the gifts you have given to us, that we may be equipped to serve others, Amen!

January 27: Day 27

THE SIX DAY WORK WEEK

*Exodus 31:17 "It is a sign between Me and the sons of Israel forever; **for in six days the LORD made heaven and earth** but on the seventh day He ceased from labor and was refreshed."*

Moses reemphasizes that creation took place in six days. This places the emphasis on the necessity of a day of rest, six days to work and one to rest. From this we learn that man is not meant to work continually; one day out of seven should be set aside for rest and to regroup for the week to come. Sunday, resurrection day, has been observed as a day of worship since that first Easter Sunday. Western culture historically had adopted this philosophy. Unfortunately, much of modern culture today has abandoned this practice.

We all need one day a week to rest; this duplicates the example God set for us. We learn from Exodus 35:2: *"For six days work may be done, but on the seventh day you shall have a holy day, a Sabbath of complete rest to the LORD; whoever does any work on it shall be put to death."* Keeping the Sabbath was one way of honoring God. For the Jews, this was a life and death reality. They took the necessity of keeping the Sabbath very seriously,

Our bodies were not meant to work continuously. We need periodic refreshing from the toils of work, failing to do so over periods of time will result in health issues. God designed us to need a time to recharge and refresh. Mark 2:27 *"Jesus said to them, "The Sabbath was made for man, and not man for the Sabbath."* The Lord gave us at least one day a week to rest and recover from our labors; let's use it!

Thank you Lord for the gift of rest and renewal. Just as You created the world in six days, You have given us six days to work, and preserve one day a week to rest, Amen!

January 28: Day 28

GOD STIRS HEARTS

Exodus 35:21a "Everyone whose heart stirred him and everyone whose spirit moved him came and brought the LORD'S contribution for the work of the tent of meeting. . ."

The following verses brings us to another level of God's endowing work in men's hearts. For specific tasks such as the example given; God gives the energy and motive to move toward a specific task. The will to move is sometimes as difficult as the ability and the task. God's creative work continues with each individual. Verse 35 elaborates: "***He has filled them with skill*** *to perform every work of an engraver and of a designer, and of an embroiderer, in blue and in purple and in scarlet material and in fine linen, and of a weaver, as performers of every work and makers of designs."* We see a specific task that needs to be completed, God will raise the specific people to complete that task; just as God worked through the people of Israel over 3,000 years ago.

Other examples of God stirring hearts: Exodus 35:20-35 *"Everyone whose hearts were stirred. . ."* God enables and gives the motive and the energy to accomplish what He plans. In this case the work of the tabernacle. God's work is not restricted to men, Exodus 35:26 *"All the women whose hearts stirred. . ."* Exodus 35:30-32 God filled Bezalel with *". . . the spirit of God in craftsmanship. . ."* God sets specific individuals apart for a task by name. Each one of us has a task to fulfill from God. It is import that we seek God's wisdom and direction concerning what that task is and to know that we are unable to accomplish anything of value apart from Christ. The Apostle Paul recognized God's moving in his life: I Corinthians 9: 16 & 17 *"For if I preach the gospel, I have nothing to boast of, for I am under compulsion; for woe is me if I do not preach the gospel. For if I do this voluntarily, I have a reward; but if against my will, I have a stewardship entrusted to me."* We each have a stewardship to fulfill, lets do that to the best of our ability in God's strength.

Thank you Lord for moving and stirring hearts to do the good work you have assigned Your people. We are not left alone to accomplish Your work, Amen!

January 29: Day 29

EDUCATION IS A GIFT

Exodus 35:34 "He put into his heart to teach."

Education is not lost in the economy of God's directive plan. Exodus 35:34 demonstrates that teaching, or the ability to be an effective teacher is a gift. As God enabled Bezalel with the gift of craftsmanship. He also bestowed upon him the gift of teaching and training others to become skilled. The value of education is not lost in sight of these passages. Verse 35 goes on to say God also filled them with His Spirit to do these works. God teaches, equips, and directs through His Holy Spirit. The value of skills must be taught and learned, yet God enables all people with the potential to do great things.

I am an educator, often times my wife encourages me that I am a good teacher. I do enjoy seeing people learn, when the light come on in their understanding, it brings me great joy. God has equipped many good teachers, what we teach is equally critical and important. From the Shema in Deuteronomy 6, God through Moses encourages all the Jews to diligently teach their children the way toward God. When we learn to serve God and understand how He has gifted us, we can become the effective stewards of God's many gifts. I Corinthians 12:28 *"And God has appointed in the church, first apostles, second prophets, third teachers,"* We are all teachers in one sense; either to a class of students, or to our own children. Let us be the best teachers we can be with God's help.

Thank You Lord for education, and the gift of learning. You are the One who adequately equips us to serve others, Amen!

January 30: Day 30

GOD DIRECTS OUR COURSE

Exodus 36:1 "every skillful person in whom the LORD has put skill and understanding to know how to perform all the work in the construction of the sanctuary, shall perform in accordance with all that the LORD has commanded."

The LORD put skill within everyone whose heart stirred him. God is not restricted by the events of man. He directs their path, much like steering the rudder of a ship or plane. We are being actively guided by God, yet we must work together in a cooperative path to accomplish not only our plans, but those endowed and directed by God. God is intimately connected to the affairs of man for a much higher purpose.

Discovering what God wants us to do may be as simple as examining yourself. Find out what you are good at, and what you enjoy doing. Some people like math, while others hate it. Others find satisfaction in learning languages while others fail at their own language. We must discover and develop our interests and abilities as we learn to cooperate with God through the Holy Spirit, to discover what direction He wants us to go, and how to serve Him with those talents. Psalm 37:4&5 *"Delight yourself in the Lord; And He will give you the desires of your heart. Commit your way to the Lord, Trust also in Him, and He will do it."* In understanding ourselves, and how we are gifted, we will better understand how to serve God.

Thank you Lord for the gift(s) You have bestowed on each of us to serve You, and others, Amen!

LEVITICUS

Moses makes no specific mention of God's creative power in Leviticus. God however instituted rules for the physical and spiritual health and wellbeing of the Jewish people. God provides the rains and the resources necessary for our survival and prosperity.

January 31: Day 31

PURPOSE FOR CIRCUMCISION

Leviticus 12:3 "On the eighth day the flesh of his foreskin shall be circumcised."

The circumcision of baby boys is very common in western cultures today. Modern science gives us a rationale for this practice. The **8**[th] day is the optimum day for **circumcision** because of the highest presence of the clotting factor vitamin K. This passage demonstrates God's sovereignty and knowledge over His creation. Our Creator God instituted this practice as a sign of obedience, and community. Circumcision has a spiritual connection, giving the Jewish people a sign, identifying them with God. Circumcision also gives an image of man's need to remove sin from their lives; an act of obedience to their Creator.

Today the practice of circumcision is most often performed at birth. Vitamin K can be added to assist with the improved clotting it provides. The benefits of this procedure include: a slight resistance to various diseases including HIV, urinary tack infections, and sexually transmitted diseases. God instituted many of the Levitical Laws not only to secure the obedience of His people, but to protect their health and welfare as well. Jeremiah 4:4 *"Circumcise yourselves to the LORD And remove the foreskins of your heart, Men of Judah and inhabitants of Jerusalem,"* Circumcision carries some physical benefit in preventing diseases. For the Jews it carried a strong spiritual connection. In Christ, circumcision loses some meaning. Galatians 5:6 *"For in Christ Jesus neither circumcision nor uncircumcision means anything."* God does everything for a reason, for our benefit and good. *Thank you Lord, our Designer, for Your understanding and care of our physical bodies, Amen!*

February 1: Day 32

ALL BLESSINGS ARE A GIFT

*Leviticus 25:21 "then **I will so order My blessing for you**, in the sixth year that it will bring forth the crop for three years.*

All blessings are a gift from our Creator God. God's blessing suggests His sovereignty over crops and their success. Leviticus 26:4 "*I shall give you rains in their season, so that the land will yield its produce and the trees will bear their fruit."* Verse 6 "*I shall also grant peace in the land, so that you may lie down with no one making you tremble. I shall also eliminate harmful beasts from the land, and no sword will pass through your land."* The preceding verses demonstrate God's control over all aspects of life. His sovereignty over weather and crop production, peace among their neighbors, and the control of wild beasts. The Jewish people had little to fear when they trusted God and followed His statutes.

We are the beneficiaries of the same God who cares for His people. We still depend upon our God for rains and provisions. We are blessed with resources for life, heat for our homes, fuel for transportation, crops for food. We have been given so much; God gives us blessings that we might be a blessing to others. James 1:17 *"Every good thing given and every perfect gift is from above, coming down from the Father of lights, with whom there is no variation or shifting shadow."* Our Creator God is the source of all blessings.

We thank you Lord for Your continual watchful care over us, and may we remember the many blessings we have received from Your hand, Amen!

NUMBERS

God orders and preserves His people. Our God is the God of order, instructing His people to organize and structure their lives for a greater purpose. God presented the people a medical solution to the plaque of snakes. All medicines originate from God who is the creator of all the sources of our life saving drugs.

February 2: Day 33

ORDER AND PURPOSE

Numbers 2:2 "The sons of Israel shall camp, each by his own standard, with the banners of their father's households; they shall camp around the tent of meeting at a distance."

The book of Numbers gives the reader a demonstration of **God's order and purpose**. Nothing is without a purpose. We see God's instructions on how to order the community around the tabernacle. It is this structure that suggests God's higher plan. In the same vein we witness a very structured and orderly way of life among all creatures among God's creative order. Animals behave in predictable ways. God created instincts to protect the animal world and to enable survival. Chance processes would be very hard pressed to develop the extreme precision of the orderly creation we see today.

The Jewish people were scattered among the nations as a result of their disobedience. All God's warnings were fulfilled; these were carried out in detail among the Jews over the past 3500 years. In spite of the Jews being scattered across the Globe, God was faithful to His promises in returning them to their land. The New Israel in the land of Palestine is a clear demonstration of God's purpose and order being realized today.

Thank you Lord that You are a God of order and purpose. Nothing escapes your notice, as You keep all things in their proper place, Amen!

February 3: Day 34

SALT FOR PRESERVATION

Numbers 18:19 "An everlasting covenant of salt before the Lord to you and your descendants with you."

An everlasting covenant can only be granted by an eternal entity. Salt represented preservation and, was a sign that God would preserve the nation. An everlasting covenant will never come to an end. The Jewish people live on from antiquity through today as a witness to God's faithful promises. God's promise that the Jewish people would survive until the end is reaffirmed in Jeremiah 31:10 *"He who scattered Israel will gather him And keep him as a shepherd keeps his flock."* Only our eternal Creator God can give an absolute promise to preserve. We are witnesses today of that preservation through the reestablishment of the nation of Israel.

In these latter days, God offers the Jews along with all who put their faith in Him a new and better covenant. Hebrews 8:10 *"For this is the covenant that I will make with the house of Israel. After those days, says the LORD; I will put My laws into their minds, And I will write them on their hearts. And I will be their God, And they shall be My people."* As we witness God's faithfulness to His people, the Jews. We can trust Him to keep and preserve His Church. God is faithful to keep His promises to us as a corporate body as well as individuals of faith. Philippians 1:6 *"For I am confident of this very thing, that He who began a good work in you will perfect it until the day of Christ Jesus."* We have a God who will challenge us, discipline us and see us through to the end.

Thank you Lord that You are actively at work preserving and keeping Your people, Amen!

February 4: Day 35

MEDICINES ARE A GIFT

Numbers 21:8-9 "Then the LORD said to Moses, 'Make a fiery serpent, and set it on a standard; and it shall come about, that everyone who is bitten when he looks at it, he shall live."

God provides concerning issues of health and wellbeing. Verse 9 continues *"Moses made a bronze serpent and set it on the standard; and it came about that if a serpent bit any man, when he looked to the bronze serpent, he lived."* God provided the solution for the nation of Israel regarding the curse of snakes. A simple act of faith; by looking at the bronze serpent they would find healing.

Israel's sin brought about the necessity for discipline. The poisonous snakes were the punishment, but God also provided a remedy in the bronze serpent. Miraculous healing from a snake bite was possible when gazing at the fiery Serpent. The same symbol is used today in the medical field as the symbol for healing. In this case, God provided the remedy for the ill. All medicine is a gift from God. All the plants and animals were created for a purpose. Many of these are used to create medicines for our benefit. Thank the Lord for these precious provisions that make healing possible for our many ailments.

This reference to the bronze serpent was used in the New Testament Gospel of John to represent our healing from sin and restoration to God through Jesus' sacrifice on the cross. John 3:14 *"As Moses lifted up the serpent in the wilderness, even so must the Son of Man be lifted up."* Christ's crucifixion on the cross opens the door for our healing from the effects of sin. By a simple act of faith, looking upon the cross, we can be forgiven of our sins. God gave us this symbol to show us the life giving power of God to heal us of sin.

Thank you Lord for providing us with medicines for healing and health. We thank you even more for the healing of our sin condition by the sacrifice of Your Son on the cross, Amen!

February 5: Day 36

WE HAVE A PERFECT CREATOR

Numbers 23:19 "God is not a man, that He should lie, Nor a son of man, that He should repent;

A perfect Being has no need to change. He is already sufficient in all His attributes. The passage continues: *"Has He said, and will He not do it? Or has He spoken, and will He not make it good?"* God will always do as He says. An unchanging (omnipotent) Being has no need for more power, He has all the power necessary to create the universe, and life. God is sufficient in His relationships, and trustworthy in all He does. In the Trinitarian tradition, God has a relationship within the Godhead that is already complete. Like a husband wife relationship, children are a welcome addition to an already complete unity. We are welcome additions to God's sufficient relationship. God's unchanging character is not affected by His love and compassion for mankind.

When God acts, He does so with perfect knowledge. He knows the beginning from the end. God knows every detail of His creation. He knows the number of hairs on our heads. He knows when the sparrow falls from the tree. We can be sure He knows our every need even before we ask of Him. We can have confidence that His judgments are perfect and true. Thank the Lord that He is perfect, and in complete control of His creation. Deuteronomy 32:4 *"The Rock! His work is perfect, For all His ways are just; A God of faithfulness and without injustice, Righteous and upright is He."* We can put our confidence in a loving, all knowing, all powerful God.

We give thanks and praise to You God that You are perfect and complete in all Your dealings with man. Help us to trust You more day by day, Amen!

February 6: Day 37

GOD KEEPS HIS PROMISES TOWARD ISRAEL

Numbers 24:9b "Blessed is everyone who blesses you And cursed is everyone who curses you."

Numbers 24:9 addresses the question of God's continual promise of protection upon Israel and the Jewish people. From the stand point of modern man in the 20th century, this promise is fulfilled in the restoration of the nation of Israel in 1948. For the Arab people, this was seen as a great tragedy. Had the Arab people embraced the Jews rather than fight them, there may have been a great industrial and Cultural Revolution in the Middle East. Instead, we are witnesses to continued war and conflict. A conflict that sees no end in sight. It is often the Arab people, including the native Palestinians who suffer as a result of these conflicts. Except for oil, the Arab nations have never been prosperous, and therefore, many live in destitution and poverty. Blessings still exist for those who will embrace God and His people, while difficulties contrast those who curse Israel and the Jewish people.

As of this writing we are witnessing many changes in the Middle East as Arab nations are making peace treaties with Israel. We are warned however that there will be no real peace until the King of Peace comes. Since God keeps His promises, we can be confident that He will bring peace to the hearts of men. John 14:27 *"Peace I leave, with you; My peace I give to you; not as the world gives do I give to you. Do not let your heart be troubled, nor let it be fearful."* Let's take confidence that God is in control of all conflicts and events.

Thank you Lord for Your precious and eternal promises. You alone are able to bring all circumstance to their proper conclusions, Amen!

February 7: Day 38

PROMISE OF A REDEEMER

Numbers 24:17 "I see him, but not now; I behold him, but not near;
a star shall come forth from Jacob, a scepter shall rise from Israel,
and shall crush through the forehead of Moab,
and tear down all the sons of Sheth."

Numbers gives us a prediction concerning the coming of a redeemer. He will be a descendant of Jacob, later to be named Israel. The Bible plays the part of a very elaborate novel written by many authors over a period of 1500 years by the guiding Hand of the One who created time. The idea of one man descending from one tribe to have a profound influence on all humanity was accurately predicted from this passage. Since Jesus is the one spoken of, His coming brings full circle the completion of this event, and will put Him, the descendant of Jacob, on the throne of Israel, and eventually the supreme ruler of all history and the entire world, including His creation.

The genealogies of this one family are tediously recorded and communicated down through the history of the Jewish people. Matthew 1:17 *"So all the generations from Abraham to David are fourteen generations; from David to the deportation to Babylon, fourteen generations; and from the deportations to Babylon to the Messiah, fourteen generations."* The number 14 represents God's perfect timing in accomplishing His prophetic promises. The greatest irony is the fact that the majority of Jewish people initially rejected their own Messiah because they didn't recognize Him. Yet the continued existence of the Jewish race is a testimony to the faithfulness of God's promises to the Jews. This testimony assures the restoration of the nation of Israel back to their God in fullness.

Thank you Lord that You chose to reveal Yourself to our fallen race. You could have let us die, but You chose to save us, Amen!

DEUTERONOMY

Moses gives us at least three specific references to God as our Creator and Maker. The book reminds us of God's faithfulness concerning His promises but also a warning of curses that will happen if the people turn away from Him.

February 8: Day 39

GOD DESIRES OUR SUCCESS

*Deuteronomy 3:22-24 "Do not fear them, for **the LORD your God is the one fighting for you**."*

Our God is not against us, He is for us and wants our success. vs. 23 *"I also pleaded with the Lord at that time saying, 'O Lord God, You have begun to show your servant, Your greatness, and Your strong hand; for what god is there in heaven or on earth who can do such works and mighty acts as Yours?"* The idea of beginnings from this context suggests an elementary understanding of God and what He is able to do. Without witnessing His miraculous acts, both ancient and modern secular man is skeptical of God. We may doubt God's willingness, and ability to intervene in difficult times. Doubt precedes understanding regarding God's greatness, regardless what age period man is living.

The Bible is a clear testimony to the Creator and His works. Deuteronomy 4:2 God's Word is complete: *"You shall not add to the word which I am commanding you, nor take away from it, that you may keep the commandments of the LORD your God which I command you."* Verses 37-40 Moses makes a prediction of a fall and a restoration of the Jewish people. This cycle has happened numerous times throughout Jewish history. Romans 8:31-22 *"What then shall we say to these things? If God is for us, who is against us? He who did not spare His own Son, but delivered Him over for us all, how will He not also with Him freely give us all things?"* As our Creator, God is in control of the affairs of man; He is fighting for our success.

Thank you Lord that You still care for our revival and success. You created us, You established us, You help us overcome our difficulties, You gave us gifts that we could become partakers with You, Amen!

February 9: Day 40

WHAT IS MAN AND WOMAN

*Deuteronomy 4:32 ". . . **since the day that God created man on the earth**,"*

Man is the product of God's creative power. Man is a very complex creature. He has the abilities to create delicate art, as well as grand structures. Man is also a social creature, who interacts among his own kind. He is created as male and female, capable of reproduction. How this marvelous social creation came about is still a mystery to modern man. Even secular science suggests a mitochondria Adam and Eve; we are all descendants from the same parents. All the human race is One Blood, consistent with the biblical account; we all have our roots from God.

My wife is a labor and delivery nurse, we both marvel at the complexities of the birthing process. We are part of that creative process God has put within the husband wife relationship. As an educator, I see the various talents, skills and interests among my students. Some are good at languages, others at math, while others are extremely good artists or draftsmen. I tell my students to discover their gifts and develop them. God has blessed each of us with abilities to do something well, and to contribute to the good of society. I Corinthians 12: 4&7 *"Now there are varieties of gifts, but the same Spirit, But to each one is given the manifestation of the Spirit for the common good."* Each person is unique, created by God for a unique and special purpose.

Thank you Lord for giving us life; for our families, relatives, friends, and neighbors. We have a community of helpers by God's sustaining grace, Amen!

February 10: Day 41

GOD REMAINS FAITHFUL

Deuteronomy 7:9 "Know therefore that the LORD your God, He is God, the faithful God, who keeps His covenant and His lovingkindness to a thousandth generation with those who love Him and keep His commandments;"

The Lord keeps His promises even to 1000 generations. The longevity of God's nature is displayed in reference to His people. Regardless the time man lives on the Earth, God's presence and His promises will remain. His faithfulness is assured. Natural philosophies can give no such promises or reassurances regarding our future. It would seem pessimism and doom are the more likely responses to the future of civilization. Global warning, asteroids, or self-annihilation from man's own foolish speculations are the rule in today's culture.

Those who know God however, have a future and a hope. We are given God's promises through His revealed Word found in the Bible. God reminds us of His enduring promises through the restoration of the Jewish people back to their homeland. We have the hope of God's presence in this life through His Spirit, and the future hope of eternal life with Him. Thank the Lord for the promise of a future hope that will never fail. Jeremiah 29:11 *"For I know the plans that I have for you, declares the LORD, plans for welfare and not for calamity to give you a future and a hope."* We have a future and a hope because of our faithful Creator.

Thank you Lord for Your faithfulness to Your people. You created us for a purpose, may we be found faithful as You are always faithful, Amen!

February 11: Day 42

WHOSE LAND?

Deuteronomy 10:14 "Behold to the Lord your God belong heaven and the highest heavens, the earth and all that is in it."

God is not only the Creator of all things, He is also the Owner. The ultimate idea of ownership is relative in light of man's limited life span. The same thing is true for power; neither really exists. Man may gain a degree of ownership, and he may pass it on to his children, but there is no guarantee that they will preserve or keep it. From the Jewish perspective in the Old Testament, ownership was always temporary, as property was returned to the original owners or families after the year of Jubilee (every 49 years).

We know that property is fleeting. Jesus warns us on his Sermon on the Mount: Matthew 6:19 *"Do not store up for yourselves treasures on earth where moth and rust destroy and where thieves break in and steal."* One primary objective for serving and helping the poor is to transfer our wealth to heaven. Matthew 25:21 *"His master said to him, 'Well done, good and faithful slave. You were faithful with a few things, I will put you in charge of many things; enter into the joy of your master.'"* We must recognize that we are but stewards of God's possessions here on earth.

Thank you Lord for the privilege of serving You while on this earth. You are the ultimate owner of all things, Amen!

February 12: Day 43

BE KIND TO THE POOR

Deuteronomy 15:11 "For the poor will never cease to be in the land; therefore I command you, saying, You shall freely open your hand to your brother, to your needy and poor in your land."

The prediction is, the poor will always exist among societies. Deuteronomy 15:11 tells us the poor will always be with you, so be generous. Being generous is the expectation for all those who are `called children of God. It is those who know and understand they are a special creation of God. Serving others is the mandate to bring order and stability to society and civilization. A mandate few civilizations are able to follow down through history.

There is one standard that all will follow: God will treat all men alike. He has but one standard of conduct for all, even for the alien and the native among you. Even though the Jews have a high standard, they are also the recipients of both blessings and curses. No one is above God's law; we all fail from time to time. We must consider all people the same, and be willing to help and serve where we can. Proverbs 22:9 *"He who is generous will be blessed, For he gives some of his food to the poor."* God has blessed us, so we can be a blessing to others. John 12:8 *"For you always have the poor with you, but you do not always have* Me." We must learn to be kind to the poor, for in doing so we are serving the Lord.

Thank you Lord for the opportunity to give and serve others. We have been blessed by our Creator God, so we can bless others, Amen!

February 13: Day 44

GOD'S REVELATION & WARNINGS

Deuteronomy 18:15 "The LORD your God will raise up for you a prophet like me from among you, from your countrymen, you shall listen to him."

Many prophets came to Israel during its history. The LORD raises up prophets, in this case the Messiah. It was during the decline of the nation that God sent many of His prophets. He sought restoration and healing to a nation that continually drifted away from His commandments, which were given for their ultimate protection and good. In the same vein today, as societies drift away from standards of moral good, they drift farther away from the knowledge and protection of God. Social decay, conflicts, and war are the result of man's disobedience to God's eternal standards. Prophets were sent to remind the people of their dangerous condition.

From the history of Israel, we learn of God's love for His people. He cared enough to warn them, that their behavior would have dire consequences. He sent messengers to warn them so they could repent and return to their God. Sometimes the people relented and returned resulting in their restoration and blessings. Other times they resisted, ending in death and destruction, or exile and suffering. May we be attentive to God's warning given to us in His revelation and repent of our drifting.

God however is continually reminding us of our total dependence upon Him. We need to stay close to His Word, and His body the Church that we don't drift away from His provisions. John 15:25 *"I am the vine, you are the branches; he who abides in Me and I in him, he bears much fruit, for apart from Me you can do nothing."* We must listen carefully to our Creator God. He is the source of all life; He alone gives purpose, meaning and direction for now, and eternity.

Thank you Lord for making everything known to us. May we be faithful to Your will in our lives, Amen!

February 14: Day 45

PROMISE OF THE LAND

Deuteronomy 19:8-9 "If the LORD your God enlarges your territory, just as He has sworn to your fathers, and gives you all the land which He promised to give your fathers, if you carefully observe all this commandment which I command you today, to love the LORD your God, and to walk in His way always-"

The land of Palestine was given to the Jews as an eternal inheritance. The land of Canaan was given to the Jewish people with the stipulation that they would keep His commandments. Several conditions followed that promise. Those who failed to maintain their relationship with God would forfeit the blessings of that promise; that they would put Him first, and not worship any other gods. God sustains the land for the Jewish people so that they would continue their faithfulness to Him.

God promises to keep and protect us if we abide in Him. We also have an eternal inheritance, one that will never pass away. Although the land of Canaan was given to the Jews on condition of their faithfulness, we have the promise of an eternal inheritance that can never be taken away. God's provision is based upon His faithfulness toward us, all who have accepted His Son Jesus, receive the promise of God's Kingdom.

I Peter 1:4 *"to obtain an inheritance which is imperishable and undefiled and will not fade away, reserved in heaven for you."* God is faithful to keep us by His power until that day.

Thank you Lord for our eternal inheritance that can never be taken away, Amen!

February 15: Day 46

GOD OPENS MINDS

Deuteronomy 29:4 "Yet to this day the LORD has not given you a heart to know, nor eyes, to see, nor ears to hear."

All understanding comes from God. The condition for true knowledge and understanding comes from God and is a result of one's faithful obedience. Even in light of today's science; we know and understand much about the creative order, but still lack understanding. We do not know the 'why' regarding any questions of life. If we reject the God of creation, we reject ultimate solutions and answers to mankind's problems. We work in the blind, even as we discover the mysteries of the universe.

Only God is able to open up our eyes and our hearts to see and understand. Proverbs 1:7 reminds us *"The fear of the LORD is the beginning of knowledge; fools despise wisdom and instruction."* Only as we acknowledge and seek God, can we come to understand the meaning of life, and the *'why'* regarding our purpose. Only God can prompt our hearts to draw us to Himself. We must however respond to His invitation. The Lord offers forgiveness and restoration, that we might know Him and have a relationship with our Creator, the God of the universe. John 6:44 *"No one can come to Me unless the Father who sent Me draws him; and I will raise him up on the last day."*

Thank you Lord that You have opened our eyes that we can see, and opened our ears that we can hear, Amen!

February 16: Day 47

OUR PERFECT GOD

Deuteronomy 32:3 & 4 "Ascribe greatness to our God! The Rock! **His work is perfect***, For all His ways are just;"*

Deuteronomy 32 has several passages reminding us of God's creative power. From the song of Moses, reminding his people they are responsible to their Maker. Deuteronomy 32:6 *"Do you thus repay the LORD, O foolish and unwise people?* **Is not He your Father who has bought you? He has made you and established you.***"* Because of God's blessings, many of the people became comfortable, complacent, and fat. Verse 15 emphasizes: *"You are grown fat, thick, and sleek—**Then he forsook God who made him.** And scorned the Rock of his salvation."* Moses has to continually remind the people to keep their eyes and focus on God, their Creator, their rock and their salvation.

We face the same obstacles today in our culture. Life has become both easier, more comfortable and complex. We have machines to do most of our work. We have access to entertainment and many other distractions that would turn us away from our focus on God. We become busy, just taking care of all the things we have. We must remain in His Word, to be continually reminded of our responsibility to draw near to our God, to avoid the complacency that so easily enters our lives. James 4:8 *"Draw near to God and He will draw near to you. Cleanse your hands, you sinners; and purify your hearts, you double-minded."* Our God is perfect and just in all His works, may we learn to follow in His footsteps.

Thank you Lord for Your perfect Word, and the encouragement of Your people to help us remain faithful in our spiritual journey, Amen!

GOD GIVES PURPOSE

*Deuteronomy 32:6 **"Is not He your Father who has bought you? He has made you and established you."***

Moses again reminds the people of their origins. Our God has brought us into this world for a purpose. We have a direct indication of God's creative power in Deuteronomy 32. We see three events being realized in the context of this passage: we are **created**, purchased, and established. It is God who originally purchased us through His redemptive work on the cross. Even though being our Creator, it was necessary for God to reestablish us into fellowship with Him through the redemptive sacrifice of His Son Jesus.

Many within the sciences would reject the notion of purpose regarding this life. To accept such a condition would require us to accept an absolute reality. God alone is that absolute standard, providing the foundation for purpose and meaning in this life. God has a plan for every person who ever lived. Proverbs 16 reinforces this reality. "*The LORD has made everything for its own purpose,*" God intends to bless us, if we are willing to accept it. I Peter 3:9 *"not returning evil for evil or insult for insult, but giving a blessing instead; for you were called for the very purpose that you might inherit a blessing."* God brought each of us into this world for a reason, to bless others, and to be blessed.

Thank you Lord for Your many blessings. Lord, bless us, that we might fulfill Your purpose for us, to be a blessing to others, Amen!

JOSHUA

Only our Creator God would be capable of overriding planetary motions (stopping the sun). God intervened to fight the battle of Jericho bringing down the walls, giving Joshua the city. God gave the Israelites the inside track to defeating their stronger and greater enemies. God gave the land of Palestine to the Jewish people.

February 18: Day 49

GOD'S POWER

Joshua 3:13 "the Lord of all the earth,"

Joshua was commissioned to take over leadership of Israel following the death of Moses. Joshua was in a sense the military commander and the one responsible for leading Israel into the Promised Land. He was the General in charge of military operations throughout the conquest. He experienced many miraculous events including: the crossing of the Jordan on dry land, the fall of the walls of Jericho, and the cosmic phenomenon of the longest day. He was also confronted by the angel of the Lord in the form of a military commander.

Joshua recognized God's absolute Lordship of earth. Joshua experienced God's power in stopping the Jordan from flowing, thus allowing the people to cross over from Jordan to Canaan just as Moses led the people across the Red Sea. This was a reminder to the people, most of whom had not witnessed the miraculous events of the Exodus, that God would be able to deliver the land just as He promised. Joshua 4:23-24 "***For the LORD your God dried up the waters of the Jordan before you until you had crossed, just as the LORD your God had done to the Red Sea. That all the peoples of the earth may know that the hand of the LORD is mighty.***" This event would have required a great deal of power and timing, at the right moment even as the waters of the Jordan were overflowing and the people gathered at the water's edge. Though most of the peoples of the earth are unaware of these events, the people of those regions surrounding the event quickly learned of God's power.

Thank you Lord for redeeming Israel and delivering them out of Egypt. In the same way, You have redeemed us from the wilderness and will bring us into the promised land, Amen!

February 19: Day 50

GOD CONTROLS NATURE

Joshua 10:12-14 "so the sun stood still, and the moon stopped, until the nation avenged themselves of their enemies."

For the modernist, Joshua 10 is one of the most difficult passages of the Bible to accept. Stopping the sun would have been impossible to stage or create. Only a Creator God could have orchestrated such an event. Stories exist suggesting a missing day in time, along with records of a long day in other cultures. We cannot proof or disprove these stories, we can only speculate at the anomalies that such an event would cause. Arguments against this emphasize the catastrophic results of the earth suddenly stopping. The text gives us few details how the event took place, nor the duration of time for the earth to stop its rotation. It is unlikely the earth stopped suddenly, or that the Earth even slowed, time is relative. A gradual slowing would have left little inertia to cause problems. We can still trust God's Word to be true regarding the events of history.

If God is the Creator of the universe as suggested in Genesis 1:1, there is no reason to believe He would not be able to slow the Earth in order to extend the day light. This miracle is on a cosmic level, giving some proof to God's unlimited power; the power necessary to create the universe we see. Such would have no trouble slowing the earth and returning it to its normal rotation. Matthew 8:27 *"The men were amazed, and said, "What kind of a man is this that even the winds and the sea obey Him?"* Our God is in complete control of His creation.

Thank you Lord for this example of Your power. You have given us a safe habitat on this Earth. We give You thanks and praise that You are in complete control of Your creation, Amen!

February 20: Day 51

GOD STEERS THE HEARTS

Joshua 11:20 "For it was of the LORD to harden their hearts, to meet Israel in battle in order that he might utterly destroy them, that they might receive no mercy, but that he might destroy them, just as the LORD had commanded Moses."

God is just as able to harden a heart as to enable. God demonstrates His mercies and His wrath. As men harden their hearts, God will extend the hardening as a result of His judgments. Man should never be presumptuous regarding what God will or will not do. His mercy, and His wrath are equally characteristic of God's divine work. As demonstrated in this passage, God has complete control over the minds of men. He can enable and harden to accomplish His purpose.

Just as the potter works the clay into a usable vessel, so too does God work in the hearts of men to guide according to His purpose. If we as believers learn to listen and obey, God will strengthen our faith. However we must be careful not to resist God's leading in that we may be guilty of self-hardening, and being led away from God's guiding presence. May we learn to trust Him more each day as we have opportunity to serve God and others. Exodus 4:21 *"The LORD said to Moses, When you go back to Egypt see that you perform before Pharaoh all the wonders which I have put in your power; but I will harden his heart so that he will not let the people go."* Let us not harden our heart that we might serve God more effectively.

Thank you Lord for caring about us. May we learn to listen to your leading, and not harden our hearts toward You, Amen!

JUDGES

God indwells His people, He gives men strength, and demonstrates power over the laws of physics. Though the author of this book is unknown, we are given many examples of God's power enabling His people.

February 21: Day 52

GOD HELPS OUR DOUBTS

Judges 6:37 "behold, I will put a fleece of wool on the threshing floor. If there is dew on the fleece only, and it is dry on all the ground, then I will know that You will deliver Israel through me, as You have spoken."

Gideon tested God's direction concerning a military action. Gideon was bold to ask God to reverse those conditions in verses 38-40, and it was so. God demonstrated His absolute control over the laws of physics and nature. Both conditions demonstrated to Gideon that God was in complete control over the elements. Both conditions would have been impossible to stage. The Bible says in Deuteronomy 6:16 "*You shall not put the LORD your God to the test,*" Why could Gideon get away with it? For Gideon, the results of this proved beyond doubt, God was in control of all the elements of nature. In God's care, Gideon's life was secure. Gideon was for all purposes an ordinary man with little faith. He was raised an idol worshiper, and lived among idol worshipers. His task would require an extraordinary faith, which God seem most willing to supply.

Even Thomas, one of Christ's disciples questioned the resurrection and wanted proof to the reality of this claim. Jesus was more than willing to provide that proof. As we learned from each of these men, both Gideon and Thomas went on to be faithful in the tasks given them by God. May we be faithful in what God has given us; we serve a Creator God who is in absolute control over His creation.

Thank you Lord for the privilege to come before You with all our requests. Grant us faith in your ability to help us in time of need, Amen!

February 22: Day 53

GOD ANOINTS

Judges 11:29 "The Spirit of the LORD came upon Jephthah…13:25 "And the Spirit of the LORD began to stir in Mahanehdan. Judges14:6 "The Spirit of the LORD came upon him mightily."

Numerous examples are given in the Old Testament of God's Spirit descending upon specific people. Each of the preceding verses along with others demonstrated God's work among specific individuals living in Israel. It was God's intention at this point in Israel's history to teach the people the necessity of obedience. By allowing trials at the hands of neighboring states, Israel was pushed back to a condition of dependence upon God. During these periods of difficulty, the people would appeal to God, and He would raise up specific individuals to deliver them. These individuals received an extra measure of God's Spirit in order to accomplish deliverance. It was never God's intention to allow Israel to drift too far from Him during these periods of trial. Israel could be compared to a disobedient child needing discipline. Israel needed constant reminders of their dependence upon God. Just like today, we forget our lessons quickly.

We are constantly reminded through scripture of our complete dependence upon God. John 15:5 *"I am the vine, you are the branches; he who abides in Me and I in him, he bears much fruit, for apart from Me you can do nothing."* He is our Creator and designer; He created each of us for a specific work that we alone can accomplish with God's strength.

Thank you Lord for enabling each of us to accomplish specific tasks designed solely for us, Amen!

February 23: Day 54

GOD GIVES GIFTS, USE THEM WISELY

Judges Chapters 13-16

Sampson: Regardless what one thinks of the story of Sampson, he very nearly takes on the identity of Superman. Until Delilah was able to discover the source of Sampson's strength, the Philistines were unable to confront him. His Kryptonite was Delilah who pestered him until he relented and told her the source of his strength. His long hair was an essential part of his Nazarite vow. The end result of Sampson's foolishness in confessing to Delilah was the loss of His great strength. The ultimate source of his powers was not of his own devices, it was a direct result of God's unique Spirit abiding in him. When his hair was cut, his strength was gone, not because of his hair, but because the Spirit of God had departed from him, leaving him as weak as other men. When God enables someone with a gift, it is prudent to use that gift in the way God instructs, or the gift may indeed be lost.

We are each given gifts for service and ministry. We must however listen to God's leading and direction in order to use our gifts effectively. Sin will sideline the believer and lead in directions that will render our gifts ineffective. We must seek to understand our gifts and use them for God's kingdom. I Corinthians 12:7 *"But to each one is given the manifestation of the spirit for the common good."* We must use our gifts for the good, that we may be good stewards of the gifts God gave us.

Thank you Lord for the example of Sampson that we may learn to remain faithful to Your calling through all our lives. May we use the gifts You have given us, to serve and honor You, Amen!

February 24: Day 55

LISTEN TO GOD'S WARNINGS

Judges 20:28 "Shall I yet again go out to battle against the sons of my brother Benjamin, or shall I cease:" and the LORD said 'Go up for tomorrow I will deliver them into your hand."

God gave specific instructions to the tribes of Israel on how to defeat the lone tribe of Benjamin. Judges 20 highlights the battle for Gibeah and the defeat of Benjamin. One difficult aspect of this event is the harshness of judgment. God allowed the near destruction of the tribe of Benjamin for their un-conditional support for sins committed within her borders. A reminder that in time, God will hold all peoples and nations accountable for unconfessed sin. The necessity for confessions is explained in the New Testament. The need to recognize a condition before God must be realized before forgiveness can be granted; the tribe of Benjamin was unwilling to do so. Judges 20:13 *"But the sons of Benjamin would not listen to the voice of their brothers, the sons of Israel."* The Tribe of Benjamin fiercely defended their territory in disregard of God's earlier instructions against sin.

God will judge His people now or later. Our Creator God made everything for a purpose. Our failure to follow Him, and His plan for our lives can bring some very unpleasant circumstances. God is able to bring about judgment from whomever He wishes, He is in complete control of this world. We cannot run from God, He will find us.

Help us Lord to listen to Your warnings, to learn obedience to Your instructions that we might live a faithful life, Amen!

RUTH

No specific mention is made of God as creator, however; God provides rain for the crops, and endows Ruth with the ability to bear a son. All children are a gift from God.

February 25: Day 56

GOD PROVIDES

Ruth 1:6 "…the Lord had visited His people in giving them food."

Ruth was a Moabitess, a Gentile and a foreigner, yet she fully embraced the God of Israel. She submitted fully to her mother-in-law Naomi, proving to be a faithful provider with her diligence and dignity. She refused to return to her gods which were no gods. She was redeemed by Boaz, becoming his wife, and thus became the great-great-grandmother of King David. Though the book makes no specific reference to God as Creator, it does indicate God's roll as provider for His people. He also provided a kinsman to redeem Ruth along with the land that belonged to her former husband's family. This roll of kinsman redeemer would be one image of God's future role in redeeming all mankind to Himself.

God is our ultimate provider. The Lord is our provider and the One who sends the rain that allows the crops to grow. The ability for crops to grow also rests with how God created photosynthesis. We would have no crops, nor would life be possible without this very complex system of converting sun light into energy for all living things. Jeremiah 14:22 *"Are there any among the idols of the nations who give rain? Or can the heavens grant showers? Is it not You, O LORD our God? Therefore we hope in You, For You are the one who has done all these things."* The reason we celebrate Thanksgiving today is to commemorate the blessings and provisions of our God who gave us a bountiful crop.

Thank you Lord for our crops and for our many blessings, Amen!

February 26: Day 57

GOD CREATED THE BIRTHING PROCESS

Ruth 4:13-14 "the Lord enabled her to conceive, blessed is the LORD who has not left you without a redeemer today."

All births emanate from God; conception is a gift of God. It is for this reason in part, that many Christians are so adamantly against abortion. If conception is a gift of God, how could we reject something so precious? The reproductive process is extremely complex, the combining of genetic information in the form of chromosomes to form a new being cannot be accounted for through chance processes. Conception and the birthing process are a part of God's creative design. The genetic information present in the DNA of each parent will determine the physical characteristics of child.

The labor process is perhaps the most difficult job the woman has. She must bear the majority of pain; for this reason, the husband's roll is also critical to be with her, and to support her. The end result is a precious baby from this difficult labor of love. I Samuel 2:21 *"The LORD visited Hannah; and she conceived and gave birth to three sons and two daughters."* Every child, and every birth is a precious gift from God.

Thank you Lord for every precious child who is born, all children are the product of Your miraculous design, Amen!

I SAMUEL

Samuel establishes the absolute power of God over the affairs of men. The first kings of Israel were by God's choice.

February 27: Day 58

GOD OUR SUSTAINER

I Samuel 2:2 "there is no one holy like the LORD,"

The character of God is very special and set apart from all creation. Holiness is an indicator of perfection. God is presented as holy and perfect. Such a state of being would require all knowledge and all power. He would lack nothing. In such a condition, God would not be limited since He would have no lack. I Samuel 2:8 states *"For the pillars of the earth are the LORD's And He set the world on them."* The establishment of the earth would require a great deal of power. The use of metaphor does not suggest pillars in the absolute sense, only His sustaining grace by which our planet is able to continue. God is the sustaining force behind the continuation of all His creation.

God is not only the Creator of all life, He is also the sustainer of life. He created this world for our habitat. He provided all the conditions and resources for us to live and thrive. It is God who has provided the resources for food, building shelters, and sustaining life. Without God's provisions of life on this planet, we would soon cease to exist. Deuteronomy 8:4 *"Your clothing did not wear out on you, nor did your foot swell these forty years."* Our God is holy, and perfect, lacking nothing and endowed with great power.

Thank you Lord that You are holy, providing us with all our needs. We give thanks to You for Your sustaining grace, Amen!

February 28: Day 59

GOD KNOWS US & REWARDS US

I Samuel 26:23 "The LORD will repay each man for his righteousness and his faithfulness; for the LORD delivered you into my hand today."

Rewards will follow those who honor God in their daily lives. God's system of accounting is absolute and exact. No wrong is committed that God has not taken into account. Proverbs 15:3 tells us that *"God sees the evil and the good."* For billions of lives that would require a super computer, God's system of accounting must be more complex as it misses nothing. The rewards will fit the service. God not only takes into account all the elements in the universe, He also takes account of all the deeds of mankind. God is not lacking in understanding or knowledge; as our Creator, He knows us.

God is not only our **Creator and Maker**, He is our perfect judge who rewards us according to our deeds. Mark 9:41 states *"For whoever gives you a cup of water to drink because of your name as followers of Christ, truly I say to you, he will not lose his reward."* God is the perfect rewarder of those who follow Him. Matthew 10:42 *"And whoever in the name of a disciple gives to one of these little ones even a cup of cold water to drink, truly I say to you, he shall not lose his reward."* Since God knows us and all that we have don, God is perfect in His judgments, and His rewards.

Thank you Lord that all services done for Him will be rewarded and blessed many times over, Amen!

February 29: Leap Day

GOD'S TIME DILATION

II Peter 3:8 "But do not let this one fact escape your notice, beloved, that with the Lord one day is like a thousand years, and a thousand years like one day."

The idea of time dilation was revealed to the ancients long ago. We understand time dilation as a by-product of Einstein's theory of relativity. It took man 1900 years to figure out that time is not an absolute entity, it is subject to laws established by God at the moment of creation. For this reason, God is not bound by the laws that dictate how time will move. It is subject to conditions that modern man is only beginning to understand. It may also give us one example of how God could have created the stars with sufficient time for light to reach the earth.

Our 365 day calendar gives us a standard from which to organize our lives. God revealed to us in Genesis 1:14 the function of the sun, the moon, and the stars. *"then God said, Let there by lights in the expanse of the heavens to separate the day from night, and let them be for seasons and for days and years;"* Even though the creation event was very good in God's sight, we have one flaw that crept into to the precise rotation cycle of the earth. Whether through the curse, or by design, we don't know. We have a few extra minutes a day to account for; this extra time gives us a leap day, or a leap year every four years. Give praise to God, and enjoy the extra day.

Thank you Lord that every minute is accounted for in Your reckoning of time. You are above time and space, and we will one day be with You in a place without clocks or concerns about how much time we have to get things done, we will have all eternity, Amen!

2 SAMUEL

The writer(s) of second Samuel is (are) not known. Even though two names are mentioned as possible candidates. God's creative attributes are not specifically mentioned in II Samuel, however his eternal character is clearly presented. Since matter cannot create itself, (from nothing, nothing comes) something eternal must have existed. God fills that requirement without leaving gaps.

March 1: Day 60

GOD IS EXACTING

2 Samuel 6:6 "The LORD must be treated as holy." Verse 7 states "And the anger of the LORD burned against Uzzah, and God struck him down there for his irreverence; and he died there by the ark of God."

King David sought to move the Ark of the Covenant to a location in Jerusalem. David and the people neglected, or forgot the proper procedure for transporting the Ark. It was essential to treat God with reverence and respect due Him. As a result of this tragic event, the ark was moved to a nearby house until the situation was examined. Verse 11 specifies: "*Thus the ark of the LORD remained in the house of Obed-edom the Gittite three months, and the Lord blessed Obed-Edom and his entire household.*" Uzzah was most likely trying to do the right thing, only it was the wrong thing in the wrong way at the wrong time. God will hold each of us accountable for his own actions. David made the mistake in setting the Ark of the Covenant upon a cart. It was the responsibility of the Levites to carry the Ark according to a specific pattern. 1 Chronicles 15:15 "*The sons of the Levites carried the ark of God on their shoulders with the poles thereon, as Moses had commanded according to the world of the LORD.*"

God is very exacting in His judgments. It is for this reason God needs payment to satisfy all accounts. There is no free lunch even with an eternal God. All accounts must balance. God's perfection is demonstrated unfortunately at Uzzah's expense. God will hold each of us to account unless we accept the pardon He provided for us through His Son Jesus; He paid our debt in full. Revelation 20:12c "*the book of life; and the dead were judged from the things which were written in the books, according to their deeds.*" Our Creator God is the only perfect accountant.

Thank you Lord for the reminder of your exact accounting, and for your perfect provision in your son Jesus. Your work on the cross is sufficient to pay all our debts in full, Amen!

March 2: Day 61

GOD'S ETERNAL NATURE

2 Samuel 22:51 "He (God) shows loving kindness to His anointed, To David and his descendants forever."

According to this promise, God's blessing was upon the House of David. The Davidic covenant is an eternal covenant that a King will always be on the throne of Israel. The promise of the King would be an eternal one: this king must have a divine nature and be in the genetic line of David. The contrast between the kings of Israel and Judah are stark. The kings of Israel changed dynasties and lines continually while the kings of Judah who were subject to God's covenant were maintained. The eventual line is listed in the New Testament, leading to the person of Jesus Christ who would, according to Christian tradition, become the eternal ruler and king of Israel, and the world. God's eternal nature opens the door for the hope of eternal life for all who trust in Him.

Matthew gives us this linage nearly a 1,000 years later. We read this linage in Matthew 1, from Adam to Joseph, the legal heir to the Davidic throne. The years following the exile of the Jews to Babylon were not clearly recorded in the Old Testament, but they were documented in the temple records. Following the fall of Jerusalem around 70 AD, those record would no longer be accessible. God's Son Jesus is the legal heir to the Throne of David and the eternal King of the Israel and the world. Hebrews 1:8 *"But of the Son He says, Your THRONE, O GOD, IS FOREVER AND EVER,"* The promise of eternal life is available to all men.

Thank you Lord for giving us Your Son to rescue us from our sins, and to establish Your eternal Kingdom in glory and power. We acknowledge You Jesus as King of kings, and Lord of lords, Amen!

March 3: Day 62

GOD'S ETERNAL PROMISES

*2 Samuel 23:5 "Truly is not my house so with God? For **He has made an everlasting covenant with me, Ordered in all things,** and secured; For all my salvation and all my desire, Will He not indeed make it grow?"*

The promise made to King David follows a plan set in motion hundreds of years earlier. David is encouraged, that God's promises to him are ordered and secure. The eternal nature of God's covenant with David transcends the physical world whose eventual end is certain. David's kingdom will eventually extend to the heavens with David's descendants, and Jesus upon the throne.

The ordering of all things is one of the attributes of God that indicates why we have an orderly universe, why science and the laws of science make sense. We can make predictions, and we can expect things to happen in predictable ways. This would not be a characteristic of an accidental chance-oriented universe as indicated by current modern science. God's ordered and precise laws make science possible. For David, this eternal promise is sure and secure. We can hold on to God's eternal promises in the same way as did king David. 2 Peter 1:4 *"For by these He has granted to us His precious and magnificent promises, so that by them you may become partakers of the divine nature,"* God is faithful to keep all His promises.

Thank you Lord for your precious and magnificent promises. We know that You are faithful to bring about all those things You promised from long ago, Amen!

I KINGS

Jeremiah is believed to be the author or compiler of Kings I & II. God is credited with orchestrating the establishment of the Kingdom along with the division between Israel & Judah.

March 4: Day 63

GOD'S WARNINGS OF GENERATIONAL CURSES

I Kings 2:33 "So shall their blood return on the head of Joab and on the head of his descendants forever; but to David and his descendants and his house and his throne, May there be peace from the LORD forever."

There may be eternal ramifications to all our actions. For Joab, the consequences of his actions affected his descendants here and now as well as influencing their status in eternity. Our decisions now may have bearing on our children's lives. As the adage goes, "*No man is an island.*" All our actions, good or bad may have eternal consequences. As Creator God, He has dominion over the affairs of men. The cause effect relationship is a reality in time and has played a major role in our understanding of science. Physical as well as moral consequences are a reality of life.

Even though we are responsible for our own sin and our own lives, God has provided a remedy to our sin problem. Consequences however may still follow our behaviors and actions. David's unfaithfulness cost the life of his son by Bathsheba. However, I John 1:9 gives us hope: "*If we confess our sins, He is faithful and righteous to forgive us our sins and to cleanse us from all unrighteousness.*" Another reminder is found in Exodus 34:7b "*He will by no means leave the guilty unpunished, visiting the iniquity of fathers on the children and on the grandchildren to the third and fourth generations.*" May we be faithful, so the consequences of our sins will not pass on to our children.

Thank you Lord that You have cleansed us from all our sins. We pray Your protection on our children. You are still in control of the affairs of our lives and our children's lives, Amen!

March 5: Day 64

GOD GRANTS WISDOM

*I Kings 3:12 To Solomon he says **"I have given you a wise and discerning heart**, so that there has been no one like you before you, nor shall one like you arise after you."*

Solomon, David's son is granted the answer to his prayer for wisdom. Prayers are answered according to God's desire. He can grant requests to those who ask with a right heart. For Solomon, his role as king of Israel placed him in the place of high responsibility. God granted Him his request and more, enabling him to effectively manage the affairs of state. For this same reason, leaders today need to understand their need for wisdom in the same way. Just as God places men in roles of leadership, He also enables them to be good leaders. Those who think they are wise, are only wise in their own eyes.

As God granted wisdom to King Solomon, He will also grant us the tools necessary to live a victorious life. The scriptures tell us specifically to pray for all our needs. John 16:*24* "*. . . ask and you will receive, so that your joy may be made full."* God is the source of all wisdom, and knowledge; we need but ask. James 1:5 *"But if any of you lacks wisdom, let him ask of God, who gives to all generously and without reproach, and it will be given to him."* It is up to us to go before our Lord God and pray, we won't receive unless we ask.

Thank you Lord for the many gifts You have given us. We ask that You grant us wisdom to serve You more effectively through all our days, Amen!

March 6: Day 65

GOD EQUIPS US TO SERVE

*I Kings 4:29 "**Now God gave Solomon wisdom and very great discernment and breadth of mind**, like the sand that is on the seashore."*

God is the giver of all wisdom and understanding. God is able to grant the prayers of men who honestly seek to serve Him. Prayer is not a blank check that can be cashed. It carries conditions that fit according to God's plan and will. It is man's purpose to conform, in order that he can contribute to God's ultimate plan. Prayer is one means by which we can contribute. Solomon in the beginning sought to serve God as a humble servant. He eventually drifted away from God, but Solomon acknowledges God's ultimate control over his destiny and the destiny of Israel.

God equips us with all the provisions necessary to be successful in this life. Our successes however are for a specific purpose; they are to serve God's purpose in bringing others to a saving knowledge of Christ. May we be wise stewards in prayer and in our service for God and others. Matthew 25:23 *"His master said to him, well done, good and faithful slave, You were faithful with a few things. I will put you in charge of many things; enter into the joy of your master."* May we be found faithful in serving God with all the tools He has given us.

Thank you Lord for the gifts of service You have given us. May we be found faithful in the tasks for which You designed us, Amen!

March 7: Day 66

GOD LEADS

*I Kings 8:58 **"God inclines hearts."***

It is God who moves men to act according to His purposes. We are subject to God's ultimate control and purpose. Though man is given a degree of freedom within the confines of this earthly existence. God is the ultimate mover within the hearts of men. He is able to plan the desires, the abilities, and the motives to move and change events, through the lives of both His servants and adversaries. God alone is ultimately in control of the affairs of man.

The Lord will direct our lives as we open our hearts to Him. We can avoid the many pit falls this life presents as we learn to trust Him more. Philippians 2:13 tells us: *"for it is God who is at work in you, both to will and to work for His good pleasure."* As we learn to trust in Him, God will make us into something beyond what we could do in ourselves. Proverbs 16:9 *"The mind of man plans his way, But the LORD directs his steps."* God will bring our plans to fruition as we seek to honor and serve Him.

Thank you Lord for Your faithfulness, may we learn to trust You more to guide and direct our lives that we might accomplish Your purpose in us, Amen!

March 8: Day 67

GOD'S ETERNAL LOVE

I Kings 10:9 ". . . the LORD loved Israel forever,"

We are witnesses to two unshakable aspects of God's character. The eternal nature of God is stressed; God's love according to this passage, never ceases. God is eternal and without end, a condition necessary for a creative power. Second, God loves His creation. Just as God said His creation was 'good'. Genesis 1:31 *"God saw all that He had made, and behold, it was very good."* God also loves His chosen people, Israel. His love for Israel however is not exclusive, John 3:16 states *"For God so loved the world that He gave His only begotten Son that whosoever believeth on Him would not perish but have everlasting life."* His love for Israel is foundational, a beginning step toward God's ultimate love for all people. The entire biblical account rests upon the promise of God, to restore all creation back to its perfect beginnings.

The eternal nature of God gives us a solid hope that we will someday enter into that eternal relationship with God; an unending world, and life without end. Give thanks to God for His unspeakable gift in His Son Jesus whose eternal nature opened the door to eternal life in Him. Romans 9:38-39 *"For I am convinced that neither death, nor life will be able to separate us from the love of God, which is in Christ Jesus our Lord."* We must remember, God loves us with an unending love regardless our circumstances.

Thank you Lord, Your love for Your people will never cease, Amen!

2 KINGS

God made the heavens and the Earth. God cares for and heals Gentiles; He is able to destroy armies. God worked through Elisha to perform miracles in much the same was as He did through Elijah.

March 9: Day 68

THE GOD OF MIRACLES

2 Kings 2:8 "Elijah took his mantle and folded it together and struck the waters, and they were divided here and there, so that the two of them crossed over on dry ground."

Many of the events presented in 2 Kings would seem to read more like myth than reality. Both Elijah and Elisha were wonder workers in the same vein as Moses and Jesus. Few individuals in the biblical account transcend the natural with as much wonder as these two individuals. The problem for modern man is his preference to accept only what can be explained from natural processes. We did not witness the events of 2 Kings and can only take the word of its authors at face value. The few examples given within the Hebrew and Christian scriptures of miracles would indicate their rarity. They are not the common course of events as we would understand them. This leaves us with a question, are miraculous possible? Both the Hebrew and Greek Bibles gives many examples of supernatural events. The Bible makes a clear statement that the Creator God is well capable of miraculous interventions.

How can the God who created the heavens and the earth, not be capable of intervening in His creation? Several Enlightenment philosophers suggested that God created and abandoned His creation; this form of theology is called Deism. The biblical image of God is one of a creator who is intimately connected with His creation. Our Creator God is the God of the miraculous. Praise God that He is concerned enough about His creation that He sent forth His only Son, the greatest miracle of all, to pay our debt of sin, and to put us back into a right relationship with Him. Psalm 8:4 *"What is man that You take thought of him, And the son of man that You care for him?"* God loves His people enough to step out of heaven to perform the greatest miracle of all, the redemptive sacrifice of His only Son.

Thank you Lord that You are a God of miracles, and care intimately for Your people. You are connected to Your creation, even when we can't see it, Amen!

March 10: Day 69

THE GOD OF LIFE

2 Kings 2:9-11"And Elijah went up by a whirlwind to heaven."

The first aircraft was a product of God's construction. The miraculous exit made by Elijah cannot fit into any rational dialogue. We understand from this passage, Elijah did not die, but was translated into a different reality though this vehicle. 2 Kings 4 demonstrates God's power in the healing or raising of the Shunammite woman's dead son. God enabled Elijah to raise to life a dead child. God alone possesses the keys to death and life. Both examples show God's power over death and life. If God is the creator of life, it would be fitting for God to be able to extend life; there is no inconsistency from a biblical perspective.

God's power transcends both death and life. Elijah is the first man in history by the intervention of God, who raised someone from the dead. Jesus raised several people from the dead during his ministry on earth, while Paul raised a young boy from the dead who fell out of a window (Acts 20:10). God's power over death gives us hope for an eternal life. I Corinthians 15:2 *"But now Christ has been raised from the dead, the first fruits of those who are asleep."* We also will someday be raised from the dead as we put our hope in God's Son Jesus.

Give thanks to God that He holds the keys to death and life, extending the promise of eternal life, to everyone who believes, Amen!

March 11: Day 70

GOD LOVES EVERYONE

2 Kings 5:15 "I know that there is no God in all the earth, but in Israel; so please take a present from your servant now."

God's power to heal extends beyond the Jewish people. The captain of the army for the Armenians was healed of leprosy by Elisha. By curing the captain of leprosy, Elisha created a conflict for many Jews years later who heard Jesus' message in his home synagogue. Luke 4:2-27-28 *"And there were many lepers in Israel in the time of Elisha the prophet; and none of them was cleansed, but only Naaman the Syrian. And all the people in the synagogue were filled with rage as they heard these things;"* The reality that God cared about people aside from Israel, did not sit well with the natives. 2 Kings 5:34 gives a second example: *"Elisha stretched himself on him; and the flesh of the child became warm."* The child was raised to life. God is able to heal whomever He wishes by whom He wishes. The Armenian (Syrian) recognized the power behind the healing of his leprosy, giving God full credit. Even though most Israelites had fallen into sin at this point in history, even to the time of Jesus. God showed His compassion on foreigners.

God not only holds the keys to life and death, He chooses by what means to heal and through whom to extend His compassion. All those who seek God will be shown mercy, both Jew and Gentile. We are reminded in 1 Timothy 2:4 God *"desires all men to be saved and to come to the knowledge of the truth."* God loves all His creation. Matthew 26:23 *"that the Christ was to suffer, and that by reason of His resurrection from the dead He would be the first to proclaim light both to the Jewish people and to the Gentiles."*

Thank you Lord for Your compassion and love, for all mankind whom You created, You alone are God, and there is no other, Amen!

March 12: Day 71

HONOR GOD'S NAME

II Kings 19:15 "Hezekiah prayed before the LORD and said, 'O LORD, the God of Israel, who are enthroned above the cherubim, You are the God, You alone, of all the kingdoms of earth. **You have made heaven and earth***."*

God will defend His name among the nations. II Kings 19 is an example of God's absolute power over men and nations. The Assyrian Army along with their King Sennacherib were laying siege to Jerusalem and the nation of Judah. The spokesmen for the Assyrian king made the mistake of blaspheming the name of God, saying their gods were greater, and God would not deliver them. 2 Kings 18:35 *"Who among all the gods of the lands have delivered their land from my hand that the LORD should deliver Jerusalem from my hand?"* Assyria had taken the nation of Israel into captivity over a century earlier. This time God defended His name and preserved the Davidic kingship. King Hezekiah acknowledged God's control over Israel and all His creation. Hezekiah's prayer was answered in the complete destruction of the Assyrian Army by the Angel of the Lord, forcing Sennacherib to return to Assyria where he was assassinated.

We live in a culture today where it seems nearly everyone missuses God's name. Jesus very often is the object of that misuse. We have become complacent in our respect for God, and who He is, the Creator of the Universe. May we learn to guard our words and respect our God by honoring His Name. Exodus 20:7 *"You shall not take the name of the LORD your God in vain, for the LORD will not leave him unpunished who takes His name in vain."* Scriptures are clear, we must honor God in all our speech.

*You Lord are worthy of honor. May we learn to honor
Your holy name in all of our speech, Amen!*

I CHRONICLES

Ezra is considered the compiler of the Chronicles. Chronicles 1 depicts the United Kingdom of Israel in its height. We are given one reference to God as the creator of the heavens. God is also the source of all that exists.

March 13: Day 72

PRESERVATION OF HIS WORD

Chronicles 1-10 list the genealogies from Adam to king David.

While the Chronicles create for the reader a duplicate history, the history brings with it another aspect of God's eternal sovereignty. As is demonstrated by these accounts, errors do appear or rather some contradictions between the histories of Israel, the Kings, and the Chronicles. As is attested by many, these contradictions demonstrate the fallibility of man, but the accuracy of the biblical account. The duplicity of accounts is a safeguard to the accuracy of the texts. Apparent and real errors can be corrected within our knowledge or understanding of the biblical text.

God provided a safeguard for His inspired work through the duplication of events. Though the errors are few and the contradictions minor, they demonstrate the extreme lengths Jewish scribes went to preserve the texts. Even though they had a variant reading, they maintained the integrity before them. The many copies of the Old Testament texts provide us with another safeguard of the work. They demonstrate the preservation of biblical record over thousands of years of recorded history. Variant readings can be quickly identified. For the Jewish scribe, correcting the text was not accepted; their form was heavily established. Matthew 5:18 *"For truly I say to you, until heaven and earth pass away, not the smallest letter or stroke shall pass from the Law until all is accomplished."* God's holy Word is perfect, we would do well to pay attention to it.

Thank you Lord for persevering Your Word so we can receive its benefits today, Amen!

March 14: Day 73

GOD PRESERVES THE LINE OF JUDAH TO KING DAVID

I Chronicles 2:1-15 "The genealogies from Jacob to King David, through the tribe of Judah."

I Chronicles documents many genealogies, but none more important than the connection from Jacob to King David. Though God selected Saul for its first king, he proved to be weak and ineffective, paranoid and a failure. Did God allow Saul to demonstrate to the people, that a king is more than his stature (Saul was a head taller than anyone else). We must note that the ultimate King would come from the tribe of Judah. Genesis 49:10 "*The scepter shall not depart from Judah, Nor the ruler's staff from between his feet, Until Shiloh comes and to him shall be the obedience of the peoples.*" King David became the fulfillment of that prophecy. God was preserving the kingly line through David.

God is also at work preserving His Church. The Church of Christ has been active in this world for nearly 2,000 years. It has grown to over a billion people, at least in name. Few it seems truly follow Christ. Many may attend church but how many are true disciples. We must examine ourselves daily, to follow Christ in serving others that we might be found faithful. All those who confess Christ and seek to follow Him are a remnant being preserved by God. Matthew 7:13 "*Enter through the narrow gate; for the gate is wide and the way is broad that leads to destruction, and there are many who enter through it.*" Our Creator God will preserve those who truly follow Him.

Thank the Lord for preserving the lineage of King David through Christ Jesus, and for watching over Your flock, the household of God, Amen!

March 15: Day 74

GOD REMOVES ISRAEL FROM ITS PROTECTED STATUS

*I Chronicles 5:26 "**So the God of Israel stirred up the spirit of Pul, king of Assyria,** even the spirit of Tilgath-Pilneser king of Assyria, and he carried them away into exile, namely the Reubenites, the Gadites and the half-tribe of Manasseh,"*

God as Creator is God of all the kings on earth. In I Chronicles 5:26 we learn that God is not limited to the affairs of the Jewish people. God is able to move whomever He chooses. In this case the kings of the north (Assyria) were prompted to take the Israelites out of their protected status. God judged these tribes by the means of other rulers. In one sense, the nations and their rulers are but pawns in an elaborate spiritual chess match between the Creator and the powers and principalities of darkness. We know however who is going to win the battle in the end.

God raises up kings and rulers from every nation. All nations are subjected to the supreme ruler-God. In I Timothy 6:15, Paul declares Jesus: *"the King of kings and Lord of lords,"* He alone is the ultimate authority, all other authorities are subject to Him. We are encouraged to pray for those in authority. I Timothy 2:1&2 *"First of all, then, I urge that entreaties and prayers, petitions and thanksgivings, be made on behalf of all men, for kings and all who are in authority, so that we may lead a tranquil and quiet life in all godliness and dignity."* Our Creator God is the ultimate authority.

Thank you Lord that You establish order and tranquility, God You are the ultimate authority over the nations, and the universe, Amen!

March 16: Day 75
FOLLOW GOD'S INSTRUCTIONS, DON'T TOUCH

I Chronicles 13:9-10 "When they came to the threshing floor of Chidon, Uzza put out his hand to hold the ark, because the oxen nearly upset it. The anger of the LORD burned against Uzza, so He struck him down because he put out his hand to the ark; and he died there before God."

Revisiting 2 Samuel 6:6 (Uzzah). God's judgments can be slow or swift. In the case of I Chronicles 15:2 the improper movement of the Ark had consequences. God acted quickly. God chose the Levites to carry the Ark of the Covenant in a specific manner. The events surrounding Uzza's death demonstrated the tragic consequences of not following God's pattern for transporting the Ark of the Covenant. The Ark has eternal significance reflecting our relationship with God, it wasn't to be treated lightly. I Chronicles 15:2 *"Then David said, No one is to carry the ark of God but the Levites; for the LORD chose them to carry the Ark of God and to minister to Him forever."* King David was reminded of his error and corrected the status of transport, The Ark was eventually moved to Jerusalem, and in time to the permanent Temple.

Our Creator God is orderly in all His commands. He expects us to follow Him in obedience with a joyful heart. Those carrying the Ark did not follow protocol in exercising this task. God is to be respected and obeyed in all His commands. Most consequences for bad behaviors are often deferred, or take time to realize. In the case of Uzza, the consequences were immediate; God must be respected and honored. Though we don't often see the immediate effects of our sin, God will ultimately judge. Acts 17:30 & 31a *"Therefore having overlooked the times of ignorance, God is now declaring to men that all people everywhere should repent, because He as fixed a day in which He will judge the world in righteousness."* What God Commands, we must do.

Thank you Lord for Your patience and endurance toward us as we learn to listen and follow Your commands, Amen!

March 17: Day 76

A GENTLE REMINDER

I Chronicles 16:12 "**Remember His wonderful deeds which He has done**, **His marvels** and the judgments from His mouth,"

One purpose for God's creative and supportive works is to give God praise. In I Chronicles 16:9-15, we are reminded to seek God, and admonished to give Him praise for all His works, including His creative acts. Verse 12 reminds us to remember His mighty works. Verse 15 goes on to emphasis the importance of the covenant made between God and His people as an eternal covenant. *"Remember His covenant forever,"* The same symbol for this covenant resides in the Ark of the Covenant. The people must be continually reminded of God's work in redeeming and preserving His people.

We too, often forget the same lessons of who God is, our Creator, and the One whose deeds continually sustain us. Modern man is no different than the Jews of old, we tend to forget who God is, what He did for us, and what is required of us. Even our communion is an event designed to remind us of God's great sacrifice He made on our behalf. Luke 22:19 *"And when He had taken some bread and given thanks, He broke it and gave it to them saying, "This is My body which is given for you; do this in remembrance of Me."* Remember, God still loves you, having died for you on the cross.

Give thanks to God for the greatest deed of all,
His sacrifice on the cross for our sins, Amen!

March 18: Day 77

NO OTHER GODS

I Chronicles 16:26 "For all the gods of the peoples are idols,
But the LORD made the heavens."

All cultures: past, present, and future have no shortages of gods; those things that we come to worship, adore, or idolize. There is no power or purpose in our self-made idols. Whatever man may adore, will give no lasting value, nor provide our means. God alone made the heavens, he alone is the One who provides all our needs, he alone, deserves our praise and worship. God alone created the universe; He gave us our lives, sustains us and preserves our soul. He alone must be worshiped, and no other.

We know from Romans 1 that all men know the one true God. Many suppress that knowledge: Romans 1:18" *For the wrath of God is revealed from heaven against all ungodliness and unrighteousness of men, who suppress the truth in unrighteousness,*" Man would prefer to follow his own desires; none of us are immune to these desires. We create our own gods as diversions from the one true Creator God. But for God's grace in revealing Himself to us, we would all be equally lost. Exodus 20:3 *"You shall have no other gods before Me."* King David recognized the sorrow of those who worshiped other gods. Psalm 16:4 *"The sorrows of those who have bartered for another god will be multiplied."* May we be careful not to put any other gods before us whether that be money, power or prestige.

Thank you Lord for making Yourself known to us,
help us worship You alone in knowledge and truth, Amen!

GOD IS THE CENTER

I Chronicles 16:30 "Tremble before Him, all the earth; Indeed, the world is firmly established, it will not be moved."

Several passages including Psalms 104:5 gives us some support for a geocentric universe (a universe where the universe revolves around the earth). God alone is the One who established the earth. He fixed it in its orbit and path. Does this verse indicated a planet fixed in space, or a safe place under God's protective care? The idea of a fixed earth that does not move has little scientific support. A geocentric universe, one where all the universe revolves around the earth, does not fit with current observational science. Science has demonstrated with some certainty a heliocentric solar system, where all the planets, including the earth revolve around the sun.

Current Scientific man is fixated with end of the world scenarios. Without God as our protector, chance events could destroy all life as we know it. The context of this passage revolves around God's power. If God is Creator and protector, we can trust in His provision to keep the earth. The earth will not falter until God's timing is complete. Thank the Lord that He is in control of all the elements of the universe. We inhabit a safe planet until God's plan is completed.

Thank you Lord that we can rest upon Your protective care. This is a safe planet, fixed in Your faithful arms until the course of this world is complete, Amen!

March 20: Day 79

OUTSIDE OF TIME & SPACE

I Chronicles 16:34 & 36 "For His lovingkindness is everlasting." "From everlasting even to everlasting, Then all the people said, "Amen,"

Our God's love and compassion is never ending. The eternal nature of God is emphasized throughout the biblical record. The idea of an eternal mind, power and substance can be summed up in the person of God as He is presented within the pages of biblical history. The Bible speaks of a God who is not limited by time and space. He is also sufficient in power and strength to create such a universe we are witness to.

Eternity cannot be understood from the small 3-dimensional time space universe in which we live. We are locked into a forward moving time continuum. Only God as our Creator King exists outside this reality. Only He has an eternal nature, and only He can move in and out of time, according to His perfect will. 2 Peter 2:20 " *But do not let this one fact escape your notice, beloved, that with the Lord one day is like a thousand years, and a thousand years like one day."* God's existence extends well beyond this 13 billion light year time locked guppy bowl we call the universe.

Thank you Lord that You are not limited by time and space. You will always be around to help us in time of need, Amen!

March 21: Day 80

GOD OF PROMISE

I Chronicles 22:10 states, David's throne and his kingdom will be established forever. "… I will establish the throne of his kingdom over Israel forever."

The promises made to King David are everlasting promises. Only an eternal God could make and keep such a promise. The Davidic covenant is a promise to David, as well as the entire nation of Israel, that there would always be a king to sit on the throne from the line of David. This promise was given by God through Nathan the prophet to David in 2 Samuel 7:16 *"Your house and your kingdom shall endure before Me forever; your throne shall be established forever."* Our God alone is able to keep all His promises regardless of time, and throughout history.

The return of Israel in 1947 is one reflection of that promise. We do not immediately see the promises fulfilled, God however is not bound by time; His promises will one day be completely fulfilled, just as He faithfully returned the Jewish people to their land. The ultimate fulfillment of that promise is in the person of Jesus Christ who is a direct descendant of David. The Lord is faithful in keeping all His promises, and His Son, a descendant of David, will fulfill that promise into eternity. The fulfillment of this promise was documented in the first chapter of the book of Matthew. Matthew 1:17 *"The record of the genealogy of Jesus the Messiah, the son of David, the son of Abraham:"* The Bible clearly demonstrates God's ability to keep His promises.

Thank you Lord that You are faithful in keeping all Your promises. You are the One sitting on the throne of David and will one day reign over all the affairs of man on this earth, Amen!

March 22: Day 81

GOD'S ETERNAL KINGDOM

*I Chronicles 22:10 "**He shall build a house for My name**, and he shall be My son and I will be his father; and **I will establish the throne of his kingdom over Israel forever."***

Our Creator God is operating on a much higher plane than what we can fully understand. His Kingdom is eternal, and not of this earth. He rules above all the earth, as well as above all the created universe. We cannot fathom such a Kingdom, for it exists far above earthly kingdoms. Speaking of David's son, in this passage; David states: God promises a kingdom that will never end. Since God is the Creator of the Universe, the one who rules over this mighty expanse. There is no concern for any cosmic disaster; no sun firing solar flares or burning out. God is in complete control of His Creation, and promises to establish an eternal Kingdom ruled by the descendant of David, King Jesus.

We know from Revelation, that there will be a new heaven, and a new earth. The old will pass away, being replaced by the new. We believe this new Kingdom will be God's eternal Kingdom on earth, much bigger and better than what we can conceive today. Revelation 21:1 *"Then I saw a new heaven and a new earth; for the first heaven and the first earth passed away, and there is no longer any sea."* This kingdom will be eternal without end, existing beyond our imagination or ability to comprehend. The promise of this Kingdom is given many times in both the Old and New Testaments and is a source of hope for the believer.

Thank you Lord for the promise of an eternal Kingdom that will never pass away, ruled by Your Son Jesus in perfect peace, Amen!

March 23: Day 82

GOD OF ALL

I Chronicles 29:14 "But who am I and who are my people that we should be able to offer as generously as this: **For all things come from You, and from Your hand we have given You***"*

King David, near the close of his life had prepared everything necessary for His Son Solomon to complete the temple of God when he became king. The people of Israel sacrificed much for the building of the temple along with the sacrifices of thousands of animals as an offering to God. King David recognized in this passage that he and the people were privileged to give so great an offering, acknowledging that what they possessed was only returning to God what was already His.

Many within our culture today, live at a very high standard of living. We have been given so much beyond what we really need to live comfortably. We learn from this passage, that all things ultimately come from God. We have so much because God has blessed us. As we see the needs of so many others around us, and around the world; we are challenged to give and bless others with our abundance, just as Israel blessed God. God is the sole possessor of all things; He is the Creator of all that is good. As we recognize, how blessed we are; Luke 6:38 *"Give, and it will be given to you. They will pour into your lap a good measure—pressed down, shaken together, and running over. For by your standard of measure it will be measured to you in return."* This verse gives us the hope of a promise of return. In the same measure we give and serve others, it will be returned to us.

We thank you God for our many blessings, help us remember to use our blessings to serve and bless others, Amen!

II CHRONICLES

God is bigger and greater than the heavens. He knows the hearts of all men, Yet He cares about His creation. He raises up kings, and takes them down. He answers prayers of those who humble themselves before Him. He gives gifts to men, enabling them to do great things. Though no specific mention is given of God as creator in II Chronicles. I & II Chronicles were originally one book; Chronicles One clearly acknowledges God as creator.

March 24: Day 83

GRANDEUR OF GOD
AND HIS CREATION

2 Chronicles 2:6 "But who is able to build a house for Him, for the heavens and the highest heavens cannot contain Him? So who am I, that I should build a house for Him, except to burn incense before Him".

God's eternal attributes are on display as we are witnesses to His grander, even the universe itself, in its immensity cannot contain His presence. This same theme is repeated in 2 Chronicles 6:18 *"Behold, heaven and the highest heaven cannot contain You; how much less this house which I have built."* Solomon realized, even in the construction of the first great temple in Jerusalem, God is much greater than any structure. Modern man should be even more impacted, as astronomy has given us a much larger picture of the universe than Solomon could have known. When we consider the size and scope of the universe, the grandeur of God is unfathomable. His omnipresence is on display through this extreme realization, God is not only the Creator of this universe, but He is also larger and greater than the entire universe.

We cannot comprehend the size and grandeur of the universe, even as we gaze into the farthest reaches of His creation. Only an infinite God would be able to create such a vast and magnificent display, which appears to stretch billions of light years across. Yet amidst such grandeur, God has chosen to reach out to us. Romans 1:20 *"For since the creation of the world His invisible attributes, His eternal power and divine nature, have been clearly seen being understood through what has been made,"* We are the beneficiaries of God's creation. If our Creator God is greater than this universe, He must be infinite.

Thank you God, for creating us and granting us the ability to observe the grandeur of Your Creation, yet, You are even larger and greater than this universe, Amen!

March 25: Day 84

GOD GIVES GIFTS

2 Chronicles 2: 13 "Now I am sending Huram-abi, a skilled man, endowed with understanding."

Chronicles gives us a theme repeated from Leviticus and Numbers regarding the fine craftsmanship required to build the Temple. Special skills are granted to people from every generation through all history for a specific purpose. This idea is not to be limited to the time of the Exile, or the building of Solomon's Temple. God has endowed everyone with special gifts, enabling people to do great things. Throughout history, we can see great men and women endowed with skills to create marvelous structures. Europe has many great cathedrals, churches and works of art that demonstrate men's creative genius; all such skills ultimately come from our Creator.

Each one of us has skills, abilities or aptitudes; the ability to learn certain things better than others. The ability to perform a task well is a combination of study, practice and giftedness. Some people progress with little practice or effort, they are gifted. Ephesians 2:10 *"For we are his workmanship, created in Christ Jesus for good works, which God prepared beforehand so that we would walk in them."* Each of us must discover our gifts and potentials, and use those gifts to the best of our ability to serve our God, and others.

Lord, help us find and appropriate the gifts You have given us, that we may learn to serve others, for Your glory, Amen!

March 26: Day 85

GOD CREATOR & JUDGE

2 Chronicles 6:22-23 "then hear from heaven and act and judge Your servants, punishing the wicked by bringing his way on his own head, and justifying the righteous by giving him according to his righteousness."

God is judge over both the righteous and wicked. The cruelty of life can often result in a bitter spirit. Men respond to adversity in many ways. Some will ignore the consequences and continue on their way; others will take stock of the circumstance and change the path of destruction. Man is still on the outside regarding the events of life. Why do bad things happen to people, good and bad? What we do not understand, is given to us in this passage; we are often our own worst enemy. God allows bad things to happen according to our bad choices. Others receive blessing as a result of wise choices. This is not always apparent; we may not understand all the circumstances surrounding someone's behavior. What is clear, all men are responsible for their behaviors while in this life, it is paramount that we seek God's blessing, and not travel this earthly road on our own.

As our Creator, God is in the ultimate position of judge over the affairs of man. Man will be held responsible for all his choices good and bad. We can take courage that God is not only a righteous judge, but a merciful judge who takes no pleasure in the death of the wicked (Ezekiel 18:23). A full and free pardon is available to all who seek Him. Acts 17:31 "*. . . He has fixed a day in which He will judge the world in righteousness.*" May we judge others fairly and show patience and kindness toward all our neighbors.

Lord thank you that You are a righteous judge who deals with us in our weakness. May we be found faithful, in our dealings with others, and find favor in Your sight, Amen!

March 27: Day 86

GOD'S PLAN FOR OUR LIFE

2 Chronicles 6:30 ". . . render to each according to all his ways, whose heart You know for you alone know the hearts of the sons of men."

God's omnipotence is on display showing God's knowledge of men's hearts (motives). The hearts of men will reflect their inner desires and longings. God knows us from the inner most parts. We cannot fool God; we can only surrender and do His will. Our refusal to follow the path God set before us will only result in a confusing and complicated life. It is our Creator, whose blueprint for our lives will provide a reason and purpose for our existence; a purpose the physical world cannot provide.

We must learn to trust Him in the midst of our circumstances. He not only knows us intimately, He knows our beginning and our end. He has a potential blueprint of what our life can be through His divine wisdom. Let each of us surrender to His perfect plan for our lives and thank Him for His caring guidance. Jeremiah 29:11 *"for I know the plans that I have for you, 'declares the LORD 'plans for welfare and not for calamity to give you a future and a hope."* God alone has the map of our life laid out and ready to guide us through the pitfalls of this life.

Thank you Lord, for a purposeful and meaningful life. You provide the direction according to the blueprint you have for each of us.
May each of us be diligent to find that place you have for us, Amen!

March 28: Day 87

GOD'S OPEN DOOR

*2 Chronicles 7:14 "and My people: who are called by My name humble themselves and pray and seek My face and turn from their wicked ways, then **I will hear from heaven, will forgive their sin and will heal their land**."*

God has set a standard for us to achieve with His help. He does not impose a standard. Yet according to the biblical account, God is near every one of us. Humility is a necessary step toward obedience. We do not have all the answers to life. We must draw near to our Creator God who controls all the strings of life. We will find the solutions to life as we learn to submit to God's ways as opposed to our own foolish choices.

We all want answers to our biggest questions in life. We must be willing to acknowledge our lack of knowledge and understanding; we obviously don't know everything. When we understand that we are limited in knowledge and ability, and turn our lives over to God's absolute control, then our lives can begin to make sense. We were created for a purpose, but we must humble ourselves before God and surrender to Him. Matthew 7:7 *"Ask, and it will be given to you,; seek and you will find, knock and it will be opened to you."* God will provide all the answers we need in life, as we are willing to follow, and ready to receive them.

Thank you Lord that You are always there to help us through the darkness of this life by shining a light onto our path, Amen!

March 29: Day 88

GOD DELIGHTS IN HIS PEOPLE

2 Chronicles 9:8 "Blessed by the LORD your God who delighted in you, setting you on His throne as king for the LORD your God; because your ***God loved Israel establishing then forever,***

This passage is speaking directly to King Solomon, showing God's heart or desire for him to direct his people. God will delight in His people as they learn to follow Him. It is God's desire for justice and righteousness to rule among men. He made Solomon king over them, to do justice and righteousness. King Solomon was given great praise by the Queen of Sheba because of the great wisdom and blessings God had granted him.

God is the author of all things, and the one who bestows wisdom. Just as God granted Solomon wisdom and blessings, so too can we receive such if we will ask of Him. God is the one who equips us for service according to the works He has designed for us. God is the source of all that is good, we must ask for wisdom. 2 Chronicles 1:12 *"wisdom and knowledge have been granted to you. And I (God) will give you riches and wealth and honor, such as none of the kings who were before you has possessed nor those who will come after you."* Knowledge, understanding, and wisdom are available to us as we seek Him, study His Word, and pray. God will delight in us as we learn to serve Him and others.

Thank the Lord for the gift of wisdom. Lord grant us wisdom and knowledge that we may learn to serve You and others more effectively. May we learn to give You delight in our lives, Amen!

March 30: Day 89

GOD PRESERVES HIS PEOPLE

2 Chronicles 11:16 "Those from all the tribes of Israel who set their hearts on seeking the LORD God of Israel followed them to Jerusalem to sacrifice to the LORD God of their fathers."

God preserved a remnant from all the tribes of Israel who set their hearts to follow God. Verse 17 continues "*they strengthened the kingdom of Judah and supported Rehoboam the son of Solomon. For three years they followed Rehoboam until he abandoned God.*" God is actively preserving His people to this day. All the promises to the Jewish people and their descendants are still in effect and will be fulfilled in due time.

God loves all His people today in the same way. He will actively work to preserve both Christians and Jews today, even when we fail Him. God loves each of us in the say way, He will keep and preserve us through the difficulties we face in life. Philippians 1:6 "*For I am confident of this very thing, that He who began a good work in you will perfect it until the day of Christ Jesus.*" God is faithful to keep and bring all those who seek Him through to the end. May we learn to persevere in trusting God till our course is completed.

Thank you Lord God, our Creator for Your preserving hand, You have given us Your promises to help bring us through the fires of this life, Amen!

March 31: Day 90

GOD KNOWS ALL OUR WAYS

2 Chronicles 16:9 "For the eyes of the LORD move to and fro through the earth that He may strongly support those whose heart is completely His."

All events are being witnessed by God. He watches over His own people. He keeps all the peoples of the earth under His protective hand, God knows the thoughts and intentions of all men. As the verse suggests, God is seeking man's success; as we succeed, God succeeds. All men, in one sense are on the same team with God as coach and leader. We are members of His created team, as we conform to His guiding will, it is God's pleasure to guide and bless those whose hearts move into conformity with Him.

God is continually in the process of transforming men into the image of His Son. God has given us a standard to follow by which He grants us the ability to be like Him in attitude and deed. For many of us, we have a long ways to go but God is patient. He knows who we are and what makes us tick. We are His creation from beginning to end. God is not surprised by anything we do, or don't do. Proverbs 5:21 *"For the ways of a man are before the eyes of the LORD, And He watches all his paths."* God directs our paths for our good.

Thank you Lord that You know us, and care for us. Guide us according to Your perfect plan, Amen!

April 1: Day 91

OBEDIENCE IS BLISS

Chronicles 30:9 "Now do not stiffened your neck like your fathers, but yield to the LORD, and enter His sanctuary which He has consecrated forever, and serve the LORD your God, that His burning anger may turn away from you."

God can become our adversary if we refuse to be a team player. 2 Chronicles places all mankind in a precarious situation; we are all accountable to God for our actions. God seeks our good within the context of obedience; we must yield. The passage continues giving those who surrender to the captor's compassion and a future hope. God's anger is directed at those who turn away and refuse to submit to His lordship.

God seeks to bless us in every area of our lives. It is however conditional on our accepting His terms of surrender. We must be willing to obey Him in order to be effective servants. As the old hymn states, "Trust and Obey, for there's no other way, to be happy in Jesus, but to trust and obey." Romans 6:23 *"For the wages of sin is death, but the free gift of God is eternal life in Christ Jesus our Lord."* Obedience through faith in Christ Jesus is the only route to receive God's eternal blessings.

Thank you Lord for Your patience and kindness in drawing us to Yourself. May we learn to surrender into Your gracious arms daily, Amen!

April

April 2: Day 92

GOD WILL DEFEND HIS NAME

2 Chronicles 32:21 "And the LORD sent an angel who destroyed every mighty warrior, commander and officer in the camp of the king of Assyria."

We learned from 2 Kings 6:16, that God will defend His name. It is not wise to taunt our Maker. God is the One who controls completely the affairs of men. The King of Assyria sought to taunt the God of Israel. 2 Chronicles 32:15 *"no god of any nation or kingdom was able to deliver his people from my hand. . ."* God demonstrated otherwise. God is above all nations; He sets up rulers and removes them at His will. All nations exist at His calling.

We have a greater purpose in this life. To serve the Maker of heaven and earth, the One who is over the nations, but who still cares about each of us. God numbers the hairs of our heads, He alone knows us. He is the author of all living things. God is in complete control over His creation. We must however honor God before man, never to disrespect Him. Isaiah 40:15 *"Behold, the nations are like a drop from a bucket, And are regarded as a speck of dust on the scales Behold, He lifts up the island like fine dust."* God knows us, and will defend us, and His Holy name.

Thank you Lord for Your grace and mercy, and for caring for us. May we learn to honor and respect your holy name before others, Amen!

April 3: Day 93

GOD MEETS US AT OUR GREATEST NEED

2 Chronicles 33:13 "When he prayed to Him, He was moved by his entreaty and heard his supplication, and brought him again to Jerusalem to his kingdom. Then Manasseh knew that the LORD was God."

Manasseh was a very wicked king, He put idols inside the temple; he moved the nation farther away from God. Why would God heed his prayers? What we can learn from this passage is, God listens, even to the prayers of the wicked when they beseech Him in humility. Because of this prayer, Manasseh moved from being a wicked king, to a good king. We must humble ourselves enough to come before God with our requests.

God beseeches us to come before Him in prayer when we have needs. God desires to help us in times of our greatest need. We have a heavenly Father who is not disconnected from His creation. He cares about every detail of our lives. Hebrews 4:16 states: "*Therefore let us draw near with confidence to the throne of grace, so that we may receive mercy and find grace to help in time of need.*" God is willing to help us, however we must have enough faith to ask. John 16:24 "*Until now you have asked for nothing in My name; ask and you will receive, so that your joy may be made full.*" When we have a need, go to God in prayer first.

Thank you Lord for keeping the door of access always open before You, Amen!

April 4: Day 94

ONLY GOD CAN ADD YEARS TO YOUR LIFE

2 Chronicles 34:27 "Because your heart was tender and you humbled yourself before God when you heard His words against this place and against its inhabitants, and because you humbled yourself before Me, tore your clothes and wept before Me, I truly have heard you," declares the LORD"

When we have problems, as is often the case, we try to fix them ourselves. Prayer is often the last course of action in solving difficulties. In King Josiah's case, he was told the nation of Judah was about to be taken into captivity. Like Manasseh before him, when King Josiah was confronted with captivity of his nation, he humbled himself before God and prayed; God delayed the calamity for his sake.

We do not necessarily have to tear our clothes every time we come before God in prayer. We must humble ourselves enough to realize we can't solve many or most of our problems in our own strength. Our ultimate destination is in God's hand, He controls our destiny and no other. Only God has the keys to life and death. Proverbs 9:11 *"For by me your days will be multiplied, And years of life will be added to you."* God desires fruitful servants. If we are productive, according to this passage, God may indeed add years to our life. Another way of looking at it, God may not subtract years as we humble ourselves and follow Him.

Thank you Lord, that You alone are in control of our life, and the lives of those around us. May we be faithful stewards that years of service be added to our life, Amen!

EZRA

God is the ultimate causal agent of all events in history. God moves the hearts of Kings and men to accomplish His purpose. God's blessing rests upon those who acknowledge Him. God's creative power is made evident in the hearts of men. Ezra being credited for compiling I Chronicles makes a clear reference to God as creator.

April 5: Day 95

GOD GIVES US JOY

Ezra 6:22 ". . . for the LORD had caused them to rejoice, and had turned the heart of the king of Assyria toward them to encourage them in the work of the house of God, the God of Israel."

The Lord causes the people to rejoice. God can turn whoever He wishes. God brings rejoicing to those who are faithful. This passage brings us to the heart of what our purpose in life is. We are created for a purpose: to rejoice in our Lord and Creator. We are created to enjoy the life God has given us. God helps us to be joyful, to see the good in life as well as to recognize the evil.

We have a God who loves us enough to desire our good. God can turn any heart to accomplish His work. However, He desires that we willingly come to Him, for He is the source of all joy. He gives us reason to be joyful, but we must turn to Him in to find that joy. When we surrender our wills to God, we will find our ultimate purpose in life: To enjoy Him forever. John 15:11 *"These things I have spoken to you so that My joy may be in you, and that your joy may be made full."* We can rejoice, knowing that God can make even our enemies be at peace with us.

Thank you Lord, for the gracious gift of Joy; this joy is made available when we draw near to You, Amen!

April 6: Day 96

GOD GIVES BLESSINGS

Ezra 7:6 & 9 Ezra was blessed "because the hand of the LORD his God was upon him."

Verse 9 continues, "because the good hand of his God was upon him."

Blessings and successes come from God the creator of all that is good. God is the source of all blessing. This passage makes a distinction between those who seek their own devices, and those who seek God's plan. God will bless all those who position themselves according to God's plan and purpose. Those who would deny God's plan, purposely place themselves in a dangerous way.

God is the source of blessings, blessings being God's favor. God desires our successes and gives us abundant blessing as we draw near to Him and seek His favor. As we learn to walk nearer our Lord, we will experience more blessings. Our experiences may not always be easy to bear, but God promises us His grace and strength through the difficult as well as the good. Genesis 1:28 *"And God blessed them, and said to them, Be fruitful and multiply and fill the earth. . ."* God's blessing will follow those who serve God, even through times of trouble.

Thank You Lord for Your blessings that You will bestow upon each of us as we seek to follow and serve You, Amen!

April 7: Day 97

NO MAN IS A FOOL WHO SEEKS GOD

Ezra 8:22 "The hand of our God is favorably disposed to all those who seek Him,"

God's blessing is available to everyone who is willing to seek Him. The promise of blessing is available to everyone who truly seeks to follow in God's way. We must be willing to lay aside our own wants and interests to follow Christ. Luke 9:23 tells us: *"If anyone wishes to come after Me, he must deny himself, and take up his cross daily and follow Me."* That is often the most difficult step, self-denial. The promises however are much greater, God's blessings are far greater than any hardships we may face. The greatest blessing being eternal life with our Creator God, made possible through the sacrifice of His only son, Jesus.

God has already blessed us; we have the opportunity to follow after Christ. We have His word at our fingertips to give us encouragement and direction. We have fellowship with His people, the saints of God to support us in our own difficulties. Many people around the world do not have these same blessings. We do however have the privilege to come boldly before God's throne in prayer on behalf of others and their needs. John 1:12 *"But as many as received him, to them He gave the right to become children of God even to those who believe in His name."* God's blessing truly follows those who honestly seek Him.

May we learn to follow You Lord more diligently, not only for the hope of blessings, but because of the many blessings we have already received, along with the hope of eternal life, Amen!

NEHEMIAH

The people are reminded of all the blessings from God. Nehemiah reminded the people that God is their creator, admonishing the people to rebuild the temple. God moved Nehemiah and directed Him what to do. Nehemiah makes a clear reference to God as creator.

April 8: Day 98

GOD GIVES SUCCESS

Nehemiah 2:8 "The good hand of my God was upon me."

Nehemiah follows the same theme as Ezra, as we seek God's plan, God will bless and enable success. Verse 20 affirms: "The God of heaven will give success." For our lives to be successful in this life, we must align ourselves according to God's heart and plan. As we move toward conformity to His way, we can expect to receive blessings and success. At the same time, we can also expect trials and resistance. Nehemiah encounter much resistance in his effort to rebuild the walls of Jerusalem. In spite of the barriers, he was able to overcome all of them through God's hand. It is more often through the conflicts and trials that we recognize God's hand, moving through the circumstances.

Each one of us will encounter resistance as we seek to serve and honor God. God however promises to give us success if we will follow Him and trust him with all our circumstances. God is sovereign over all the circumstances of our lives. All real success is from God, the creator of all things. Isaiah 48:15 *"I have brought him, and He (God) will make his ways successful."* God will lead in our lives, as we learn to trust in Him.

Thank You Lord for our successes. May we be blessed with more successes and victories as we seek to serve You each day, Amen!

April 9: Day 99

GOD INSPIRES MEN

Nehemiah 7:5 "Then my God put it into my heart to assemble the nobles, and officials and the people to be enrolled by genealogies."

Nehemiah repeats Ezra's acknowledgment. ". . . *the good hand of my God was on me*." God first directed Nehemiah to rebuild the wall against fierce resistance. He was now directed to keep accurate genealogies, necessary for preserving the integrity of Christ's lineage. Nehemiah had much responsibility handed to Him, but by God's guiding hand, he was able to accomplish both tasks. God still requires of us to trust, and to keep faith. Nehemiah knew he must do the work of God; in this case, to rebuild the wall and to restore the genealogical record. *God inspires men* to write, to work and to build.

We are each assigned a task(s) to complete in our lifetime. We are given a passion and a talent to accomplish these tasks. It is up to us to discover what God has put within each of us, and to develop it. Like Nehemiah, He was given a burden by God for his city Jerusalem. So too, we each have been given a burden or passion. Let us discover the burden God has put within each of us. Use the talents and skills God has put within you to accomplish His purposes. God will grant us success as we use the abilities He has given us to serve Him. 2 Timothy 3:16 *"All Scripture is inspired by God and profitable for teaching, for reproof, for correction, for training in righteousness;"* God can inspire us through His Spirit and His inspired Word.

Thank you Lord, for the work You have given use to do. May Your hand guide and direct our lives in such a way as to accomplish these tasks. God grant us success, Amen!

April 10: Day 100

GOD IS OUR GREAT CONDUCTOR

*Nehemiah 9:6 "**You alone are the LORD. You have made the heavens, The heaven of heavens with all their host, The earth and all that is on it, The seas and all that is in them. You give life to all of them, And the heavenly host bows down before You.**"*

The creative powers of God are again recognized. Nehemiah gives praise to God for His creative work. He continues on, giving credit to God for orchestrating all the events surrounding the Jews and the nation of Israel. God is not only the Creator; He is the Conductor of all history. All life on earth is by God's design, and all the events of history move according to His divine plan.

God is not only the Creator of all we see and don't see; He is also the great Conductor of His creation. He is in charge of all life. He knows all the affairs of men and their works. We can trust God to orchestrate in our own lives. He knows our beginning and our end. Romans 8:28 *"And we know that God causes all things to work together for good to those who love God, to those who are called according to His purpose."* God will complete His creation in the hearts and minds of all those who call upon Him.

Thank you Lord, that You not only created us and the world we live in, You are the One true operator who truly cares for us and You alone are able to bring us through to the end, Amen!

April 11: Day 101

GOD GIVES JOY & STRENGTH

Nehemiah 8:10 "The joy of the LORD is our strength."

There is a purposeful joy in living a godly life. We were created to be joyful in our relationship with God in that we were created in His image. Our strength comes from our connection to God, through our faithful obedience, the faithful follower of God has the strength to overcome the circumstances of life. The Joy of the LORD is the fruit of a life devoted and committed to serving Him. God's strength will follow those who find their joy in serving the Lord.

God seeks for our joy because a joyful heart helps us have a healthy life. Proverbs 17:22 *"A joyful heart is good medicine."* When we have joy in our lives, and are content with our circumstances, we tend to be at peace with ourselves and others. It is God's desire that we get along with others. Joy and strength are a direct result of our faithfulness in serving others and obeying God in our daily lives. Philippians 4:13 *"I can do all things through Him who strengthens me."* God is the source of both our joy and our strength.

Thank you Lord, for providing the way for a joyful and productive life as we learn to serve You, Amen!

April 12: Day 102

GOD RULES OVER ENTROPY

Nehemiah 9:21 "Their clothes did not wear out, nor did their feet swell."

God alone is able to overrule the laws of entropy. The Law of Entropy states that all of nature is in a state of decline, things wear out. Nehemiah speaks about how God preserved the People of Israel during their wanderings in the wilderness. Our Creator God is able to rule over all the laws of nature. Entropy lays in direct conflict with evolutionary theory, a theory that all things ordered themselves, and are becoming more complex. Evolution has very little sustaining substance in light of the power of Entropy to destroy. The One who created this order is also the only one who can overrule it. It is by God's sustaining power that man's existence can even continue. We are not above the laws of physics, only God can rule over His own creative work.

Everything around us is running down. Buildings deteriorate and must be maintained. Our cars last only a few years unless we put a lot of work into keeping them running. Even our bodies get old and run down. However, God can and does intervene to prolong and preserve life for those who serve and honor Him. Romans 8:21 "*. . . the creation itself also will be set free from its slavery to corruption into the freedom of the glory of the children of God.*" These years are a time of fearing and honoring God. God is the author of all the laws of physics; He alone is able to overrule any scientific law.

Thank you Lord, for enabling provisions to last longer and to prolong our lives as we diligently learn to serve You, Amen!

ESTHER

God places people in the right place at the right time, to accomplish His purpose and to preserve His people. God delivers His people through the tribe of Benjamin whose remnant was preserved in Judges 20-21. Though God is not mentioned by name, He was clearly working behind the scenes through Esther to rescue the Jewish people from destruction.

April 13: Day 103

GOD PROVIDES THROUGH OTHERS

Esther 4:14a "For if you remain silent at this time, relief and deliverance will arise for the Jews from another place and you and your father's house will perish."

Esther's decision to go before king Xerxes without summoning was made simple as a result of this warning. "And who knows whether you have not attained royalty for such a time as this?" Esther's obedience resulted in deliverance for the Jews. God places people where He wishes to accomplish the greatest good. Mordecai understood God's capacity to preserve and restore, God can use people strategically located for His purposes. This principle is not confined to leadership. God can use whosoever is willing to serve in whatever capacity they are willing to commit to God; our willing obedience is key to useful service.

We all have a purpose in life: to accomplish specific tasks that we are equipped to handle. Each of us has been given gifts to serve as stated in I Corinthians 12:7 *"But to each one is given the manifestation of the Spirit for the common good."* God desires each one of us to serve in some capacity to save and help others. Esther was given the extremely high task of intervention on behalf of the Jewish people. In much the same way God sent His Son to save and rescue His people. Ephesians 2:10 *"For we are His workmanship, created in Christ Jesus for good works, which God prepared beforehand that we would walk in them."* God has equipped each of us for a specific purpose. May we be faithful to accomplish that for which we were designed.

Thank you Lord, for sending people into our lives to encourage, and in some cases to rescue us from difficult circumstances, Amen!

April 14: Day 104

GOD'S PERFECT TIMING

Esther 4:14b ". . .And who knows whether you have not attained royalty for such a time as this?"

Esther presents a remarkable attribute of God, His timing. He places people in strategic places to accomplish His bidding at the appropriate time. For Esther, she became queen of Persia for one very critical purpose, to save her people from destruction. By her faithfulness, she was rewarded with both her life, and the lives of her people, the Jews. God orchestrated the events with foreknowledge of the tragic events that were to come. God is not bound by the constraints of time. He knows the beginning from the end.

God knows the beginning from the end of His-Story. He was able to put Esther in the best place to help her people. God knew the events which were about to transpire against the Jews. God is also in control of the events that transpire in our lives. He knows our beginnings and our ends. He loves us as His dear children. We can trust God to put people into our lives to help and encourage us in our difficulties. Like Esther, God uses Paul to rescue others. Acts 9:15 *"Go, for he is a chosen instrument of Mine, to bear My name before the Gentiles and kings and the sons of Israel;"* God can use anyone who is willing, to help save others.

Thank you Lord, for the example of Esther and for giving us the hope of Your continuous watchful care, even through the faithfulness of others, Amen!

JOB

Job and his friends give us many reference to God as creator. We are given a behind the scenes look at the battle between good and evil on the spiritual level. Job and his friends are confronted by God with the complexities of God's creative power; we don't have a clue.

April 15: Day 105

GOD'S PURPOSES ARE ACCOMPLISHED EVEN IN SUFFERING

The book of Job: overview

Job brings us to a unique place in the Biblical text. We do not know for certain the time or place of Job's life. Most commentators assume Job belongs to the same period as the patriarchs; this would be about the same era as Abraham, Isaac and Jacob. We seldom get an inside peek into the spiritual battles behind the scenes surrounding God's people, but Job fills us in on the events we do not see. The issue of suffering brings front and center the conflict between God's goodness and His possessing all power. The logical question comes to the front of all discussions regarding evil. How can God be all powerful and all good, why does evil exist? For secular man, this suggests a contradiction. Job and his friends also misread the reasons for Job's trials. It was thought that either Job had sinned, or that God was not fair. In the conclusion, we learn otherwise.

Job confronts us with our own battles with evil and suffering. No one escapes all the difficulties life presents. We will all encounter family and friends who are taken away in death. Accidents and illness happen. Some may experience more problems than others, but we are confronted with the difficulty in understanding why a good God would allow evil in this world. Ephesians 6:12 *"For our struggle is not against flesh and blood, but against the rulers, against the powers, against the world forces of this darkness, against the spiritual forces of wickedness in the heavenly places."* God is in control, even in our distress.

Thank you Lord, that You give us a peek behind the curtain, that we may see the spiritual battle raging behind the scenes; even amidst evil, You are still in control, Amen!

April 16: Day 106

GOD OUR DELIVERER

Job 1:21 "Naked I came from my mother's womb, And naked I shall return there. The LORD gave and the LORD has taken away. Blessed be the name of the LORD."

Every man's destiny is the same. God is the source of all blessing but allows suffering for a purpose. This is perhaps the most difficult question asked during any time in history. Why do good people suffer? The question has no easy answers. If God is good and all powerful, why would He allow suffering? For the rationalist, God cannot be all good and all powerful. In times of extreme conflict or war, it becomes easier for some to dismiss God as unreasonable, while others will be pushed closer to God. For Job, he remained faithful in spite of the cruelty of his suffering. God's purposes transcend our understanding. We do not see the entire picture. The Bible carries another message in contrast to the events of Job. God places a special hand upon those who suffer most, for no fault of their own.

All men suffer, some more than others. We are all to bear burdens for ourselves and for others. We must learn, as Job did, our suffering carries with it a greater purpose; to teach us endurance, and patience through hard and difficult times. We must learn to trust in the Lord through those times. Our faith is strengthened, and God will be shown to be faithful and true. James 1:2 & 3 *"Consider it all joy my brethren when you encounter various trials, knowing that the testing of your faith produces endurance."* God will deliver us through all our difficult times.

Thank you Lord, for Your grace and mercy, as You deliver us from the hardships of life, Amen!

April 17: Day 107

GOD'S SOVEREIGNTY OVER THE AFFAIRS OF MAN

Job 4:11-12 "The humble are lifted up, while the proud are brought down. He frustrates the plotting of the shrewd, so that their hands cannot attain success. He captures the wise by their own shrewdness, and the advice of the cunning is quickly thwarted."

Understanding the nature of God and how he relates to man goes well beyond our current understanding. Job's friend Eliphaz communicates a relatively solid understanding of God's sovereignty. Eliphaz assumed Job was suffering because of sin and pride. The Bible however reveals a much deeper reality. Though misunderstood in this context, the passage reveals God's ability to control, direct, to guide, and protect the affairs of man as He chooses. God is the ultimate arbiter of man, working in the midst of our lives to bring about His perfect plan in each of us. Let us praise God that He cares about every detail of our lives, even to protect us from evil and to deliver us ultimately into His presence.

We have a God who is intimately involved in our daily lives. Every detail of our lives is ultimately in His control, guiding and directing according to His pleasure for our good. As we submit and humble ourselves to His guiding hand, He will lift us up and keep us through the difficulties, and eventually into His presence. Romans 1:27a "*God has chosen the foolish things of the world to shame the wise,*" So we must humble ourselves knowing we cannot fool God.

Thank you Lord, for You are in complete control, over our lives. May we learn to trust You in everything, Amen!

April 18: Day 108
GOD IS ALWAYS AT WORK

*Job 4:17 "**Can a man be pure before his Maker?***

Job had several friends who came to comfort him during his trial. Even those who were friends of Job, recognized God's hand as Creator. Their advice however was less than admirable. Job's friend Eliphaz gives a direct acknowledgment of God as his Maker and Creator. Eliphaz had no better understanding of why Job is suffering than Job himself. In Job 5:9 Eliphaz continues to expound his understanding of God's ways. "*Who does great and unsearchable things, Wonders without number, He gives rain on the earth and sends water on the fields.*" Eliphaz communicates a solid understanding of God's sovereignty. In verse 11 Eliphaz supports a common biblical theme. "*So that He sets on high those who are lowly, And those who mourn are lifted to safety.*" The humble are lifted up, while the proud are brought down. He furthers this idea in verse 12 "*He frustrates the plotting of the shrewd, So that their hands cannot attain success. He captures the wise by their own shrewdness, and the advice of the cunning is quickly thwarted.*" Eliphaz assumed Job was suffering as a result of pride. A man's good works would result in God's blessing, while acts of wickedness would have the opposite outcome. As the friends of Job would later learn, God is not bound by our actions. He may do what He desired for a greater cause, regardless of our conduct. Bad things may indeed happen to good people.

We may not understand everything God is doing in our lives, but God is always at work, accomplishing a greater purpose. Even though Eliphaz rightly understood the power of God as his Maker, he failed to understand along with Job the greater matter that was being played, Jeremiah 18:6 "*Can I not, O house of Israel, deal with you as this potter does*" declares the Lord, "*Behold, like the clay in the potter's hand, so are you in My hand, O house of Israel.*" The first matter is that we are all flawed individuals. God is actively forming us into new people.

Thank you Lord, that You are ultimately in control and working for our good to the very end, Amen!

127

April 19: Day 109

GOD DISCIPLINES HIS OWN

Job 5:17 "Behold, how happy is the man whom God reproves,
so do not despise the discipline of the Almighty."

Eliphaz assumes God is disciplining Job for some misdeeds. Eliphaz's statement is generally true, however God may have other more pressing issues that would require sacrifice as Job and his friends later learned. God may indeed discipline those whom He desires. None of us are immune to correction; God will disciple those who need it. The lesson here was not about discipline; it is about trust in the Almighty that He has our best interests, even through the difficult times.

We must also learn to trust God through hard times, knowing that God is working in us for our own good. We must continue to be diligent in doing what is right, trusting God to be at work for our best. We must also keep in mind; we don't have all the facts; God is at work on a much higher plane. Thank the Lord for His discipline and compassion, knowing that He is bringing our lives into harmony with Him, even through trials. Hebrews 12:10 *"For they disciplined us for a short time as seemed best to them, but He disciplined us for our good, so that we may share His holiness."* Our God is continually in the process of correcting His children for our own good.

Thank you Lord, that You care enough about us to discipline and correct us for our good and according to Your good purpose, Amen!

April 20: Day 110

GOD IS INTIMATELY CONCERNED ABOUT HIS CREATION

*Job 7:17 "What is man that You magnify him,
and that You are concerned about him."*

Job asks a very probing question concerning God's interest in man. God knows every detail of our lives. This may be disconcerting to some but comforting to others. God knows our every need and want. He knows our needs and our requests before we ask. The contrast between the smallness of man the greatness of God is so stark, why indeed would an all-powerful God bother. If God is so great, why does He demonstrate so much concern for man? Proverbs 27:23 gives us similar advice, to pay attention to our affairs to be successful. *"Know well the condition of your flocks and pay attention to your herds."*

Since we are created in God's image, it makes sense that God would be attentive to all aspects of his creation. He is the perfect guide to our life as we wonder so helplessly through the darkness of this world. Let's praise God that He is concerned about man, and cares for our success. Romans 8:21 *". . . that the creation itself also will be set free from its slavery to corruption into the freedom of the glory of the children of God."* God is in the process of restoring His Kingdom. He cares for us, because He wants us to accurately reflect His image in our lives.

Thank you Lord, for creating us, and for caring about us. You gave Your Son to restore us into a right relationship with You, Amen!

April 21: Day 111

GOD IS THE ALMIGHTY

*Job 8:3 "Does God pervert justice? Or does the Almighty
pervert what is right?*

Job's friend Bildad follows much the same reasoning as Eliphaz, seeing God as just and punishment based solely on conduct. While Bildad makes no direct reference to God as Creator, He refers to Him as the Almighty in verses 3, 5 and 6. God solely possesses all power to do according to His purpose. The big picture as to the why this is happening was still missing in this conversation. If God was all powerful and good, why would He allow such suffering?

We do not know all the circumstances around events in our world, or what is happening in our own lives. God moves according to His purposes. We must only learn to trust Him, for the outcome will be for His glory and our own good. God's ways are far above our ways. Isaiah 55:8 *"For My thoughts are not your thoughts, neither are your ways My ways, declares the LORD."* Our God will bring about justice on the earth. He will always do what is right; even the existence of evil will one day be understood.

Thank you Lord, that You are in complete control of Your creation. You have a greater purpose and will always do what is right, Amen!

April 22: Day 112

GOD STRETCHES THE HEAVENS

*Job 9:8 "**Who alone stretches out the heavens** . . ."*

In Job's response to his friends, He gives us more details regarding God's relationship with the universe. Current science suggests our universe is expanding. Bodies seem to be moving away from each other as we observe the red shift in the stars and galaxies. Verse nine gives us more details: "Who makes the Bear, Orion and the Pleiades, And the chambers of the south; Verse 10 "who does great things, unfathomable, And wondrous works without number." Modern science is discovering a more complex and marvelous universe than Job or his friends could comprehend. Yet with all our knowledge, we are still clueless as to its origins and function when we dismiss the possibility of a Creator.

What is most astounding regarding the complexities of God's universe, is its size and vast distances. God tells us in Psalms 19:1 "*The heavens are telling of the glory of God, And their expanse is declaring the work of His hands.*" What we know now from current science gives us a clearer understanding of the marvels of the universe. Yet even today, we wonder at the vastness of God's heavenly creations. This gives us cause to wonder and give thanks to such a mighty God who has created such an immense universe, while still caring about us. Psalm 147:4 "*He counts the number of the stars; He gives names to all of them.*" Only our Creator God has the power to stretch out the heavens. Just has God knows all the stars by name, He knows each one of us completely.

Thank You Lord that You are powerful and able to create the universe. You stretched out the heavens. You know all Your creation, even caring for us, Amen!

April 23: Day 113

GOD REVEALS HIMSELF TO THOSE WHO SEEK HIM

Job 9:11 "Were he to pass by me, I would not see Him; Were He to move past me, I would not perceive Him."

We cannot see God, for He transcends our perceptions. Were He to snatch us away, who could restrain Him? Who could say to Him, what are You doing?" The idea that God is hidden from man is consistent throughout scripture. God will reveal Himself to those who honestly seek to find Him. For those who would deny God in their ignorance, God will remain obscure. For those who acknowledge Him, He will reveal Himself to them.

We must continually seek Him throughout our lives. God encompasses the entire universe, for He is its Creator. We are so small, insignificant in comparison. Even the Psalmist ponders the question of God's concern for man. Psalm 8:4 "*What is man that You take thought of him,*" We have the promise that God would reveal Himself to us, if we seek Him. We must continually seek God, that we might experience His presence daily. James 4:8 "*Draw near to God and He will draw near to you. Cleanse your hands, you sinners, and purify your hearts, you double-minded.*" In some ways, God works in stealth. However, He has clearly revealed Himself to those who seek Him through His word (Bible) and His creation.

Thank you Lord that You were willing to reveal Yourself to us as we seek and honor You, Amen!

April 24: Day 114

OUR BODIES ARE THE PRODUCT OF INTELLIGENT DESIGN

Job 10:8 **"Your hands fashioned and made me altogether."**

Even though the ID (Intelligent Design) movement is maligned by the secular science community, there can be no mistake that our bodies are a marvelous creation. Man is a product of God's creative design. Man is not an accident, nor a product of chance events. Verse 11 continues: You (God) "***Clothe me with skin and flesh, And knit me together with bones and sinews***" Man is wondrously designed. We are able to self-repair when injured. Our bodies are able to reproduce through the union of male and female. We have unique talents and skills that are able to perform marvelous acts or build magnificent structures. We are social beings capable of much love and creativity.

We were created for a purpose to fulfill, that purpose by God's design. Our bodies are extremely complex. The genetic code is a blueprint filled with information ordering our development from conception, ordering all our bodies characteristics; we are not an accident. Let us praise God that we are so well designed, and that we are created for a purpose. Psalms 139:14 *"I will give thanks to You, For I am fearfully and wonderfully made; Wonderful are Your works, And my soul knows it very well."* There is no mistake, we are not an accident. We are designed for a purpose, to give glory and honor to God.

Thank you Lord, for creating me with ability to think, remember, to fight infections and to heal myself. We are created by Your intelligent design, Amen!

April 25: Day 115

GOD REVEALS HIMSELF TO US

Job 11:7-8 "Can you discover the depths of God? Can you discover the limits of the Almighty? They are high as the heavens, what can you do?"

Zohar: Job's third friend speaks up, revealing his thoughts on God. Job's friend Zophar acknowledges that God is above our understanding. Our capacity to understand the things of God is limited. He basically accuses Job of acting presumptuously in assuming his innocence. All three friends of Job acknowledge God's power while assuming Job's guilt. The book of Job reveals a much deeper understanding of God's nature and His working. Unless God reveals Himself to us through the Biblical accounts and through the vast wonders of His magnificent creation. Without God's intervention, we would have little to no understanding of where we came from or why we are here.

Modern man seeks to understand our reality solely through the tools of natural science. Man seeks to observe, test, and then create models that seem to fit the observation. These tools are useful in understanding many of the mechanics of life, and the workings of the cosmos, but wholly inadequate in understanding the nature of God, or spiritual reality. So much of nature is still a mystery and defies natural explanations. Let us praise God for revealing Himself to us through His revelations. Jeremiah 55:9 *"for as the heavens are higher than the earth, So are My ways higher than your ways And My thoughts than your thoughts."* If not through God's revelation through His word, man would have no way of knowing Him. We can now know God in part, through His Son Jesus, and the spirit He has given us.

Thank you Lord, for all the wonders of your creation, and for your written revelation that we may begin to know You, Amen!

April 26: Day 116

GOD GIVES US BREATH AND LIFE

*Job 12:10 **"In whose hand is the life of every living thing, And the breath of all mankind?"***

Job recognizes God's hand in his suffering. He also recognizes his dependence upon God for life and breath. Job 12:9 ". . . *who among all these does not know that the hand of the LORD has done this.*" Job acknowledges God's sovereignty over the lives of men. Job agrees with his friends regarding God's absolute power, while still questioning God's motive. They acknowledge, God gives breath and life; our continuing existence depends entirely upon God's gracious hand.

The complexities of life, boggles the mind of man. We are extremely complex creatures, having the ability to procreate, our bodies heal themselves, and we have the capacity to think and create marvelous wonders. Yet the origins of life are still a mystery. Job and his friends recognize this truth; God is the originator of life and breath of all creatures on earth. Job 33:4 *"The spirit of God has made me, And the breath of the Almighty gives me life."* God has given to each person alive, the breath of life. All living things, and all life originates from our Creator God.

Thank you Lord, for the breath of life, You have given us the ability to breath, and a suitable habitat to support us on the Earth. You sustain us by Your power and grace, Amen!

April 27: Day 117

OUR DAYS ARE NUMBERED

Job 14:5 "since his days are determined, The number of his months is with You; And his limits You have set so that he cannot pass."

Job contemplates his day; he knows his days are numbered by God. God knows the numbers of days allotted each person that walks on the face of the earth. His days are determined well in advance of his birth. Job continues in 14:16: *"For now You number my steps, You do not observe my sin."* God is exacting in all His works, His accounting also includes my sins, for this, Job recognizes God's grace in overlooking his wrongdoing. Even though this appears to be the case, God does a reckoning with sin at a future date; through the vicarious atonement of His Son (Jesus) on the cross who paid our debt of sin.

Our Creator God has allotted each of us a number of days to accomplish our tasks. Most jobs allot us a specified period of time to accomplish our work. So too, God has given a period of time to accomplish the work He has given each of us on earth. Psalm 90:10 *"As for the days of our life, they contain seventy years, Or if due to strength, eighty years."* Psalms 90:12 presents to us a challenge, to make each day count: *"LORD, teach us to number our days, That we may present to you a heart of wisdom."* We have all been granted a time on this earth; let us be faithful to make the most of our allotted days.

Thank you Lord, that all our days are accounted for; even in death, we can rest upon Your continuous mercy and grace throughout the days You have given us, Amen!

April 28: Day 118

GOD OPENS THE DOOR TO SCIENCE

*Job 26:7 "**He stretches out the north over empty space and hangs the earth on nothing.**"*

Job displays some insight into science. Even though ancient man would not be privy to many of these specific details, they are accurate. This empty space to the north is called Boötes Void; a region of space where very few objects exist. The earth hangs on nothing would be an accurate description; the concept of gravity or space distortion would not be understood by the ancients. The earth resting on nothing, questions one interpretation of I Samuel 2:8 *"For the pillars of the earth are the LORD's and He set the world on them."* How do we define pillars, obviously, they are not literal.

Job 26:8 describes how water vapor is held in clouds until they are released in the form of rain. *"He wraps up the waters in His clouds, and the cloud does not burst under them."* God is the creator of the water cycle and the weather. In addition to the earth being hung on nothing, we are given an accurate description of the earth as a sphere. Verse 10 *"He has inscribed a circle on the surface of the waters."* Several other biblical writers use this description (Proverbs 8:27 & Isaiah 40:22) The circle translated as vault could also indicate a sphere. The curvature of the earth was understood by the ancients. The scientific method allows man to explore the wonders of God's creation. Psalms 19:1 *"The heavens are telling of the glory of God; And their expanse is declaring the work of His hands."* Our Creator God has given Man the tools for the exploration of His creative work through science.

We give praise to You, Oh God, that You have given us the means by which to understand the marvels of Your creation, Amen!

April 29: Day 119

GOD IS PERFECT IN KNOWLEDGE

Job 36:4b **"One who is perfect in knowledge is with you."**

Job looks to God as the one who alone is all knowing. To be perfect in knowledge is to lack nothing in understanding. God alone knows all things. He knows all His creation: He knows the thoughts of men. He knows the beginning from the end. He is not bound by the restrictions of time and space. He is aware of all that happens on the face of the earth. He even knows our inner thoughts. We are His creation designated for a specific job. To be perfect in knowledge is to lack nothing in understanding the operation of all nature, the behaviors of all creatures.

Man is only scratching the surface in his desire to explore the wonders of God's creative knowledge. God not only designed the universe, He designed us, and knows us completely. Intelligent Design is an understatement; we all know who the Intelligent Designer is. I Kings 8:39 *"then hear in heaven Your dwelling place and forgive and act and render to each according to all his ways, whose heart You know, for You alone know the hearts of all the sons of men,"* We can hide nothing from our Creator God. Our God knows our heart and our thoughts. May we learn to fear and honor Him every day.

Thank you Lord, that you designed me, you know me,
and you have given me a purpose, Amen!

April 30: Day 120

WE ARE PART OF GOD'S GREATER PURPOSE

Job 38:4 **"***Where were you when I laid the earth's foundation?***"**

Job accepts God's rebuke for his misrepresentation of God's purpose. A sobering question, no one in history can respond to that statement with an intelligent response. Chapter 38 examines the wonders of God's creation from His point of view. The intricacies of the created order go well beyond the capacities of man, even into the 21st century. Man in his ability to learn, can to understand much of how the universe operates, the details however are still very blurred as science seeks to unravel the mysteries of creation and life. For Job the questions are well above his ability to grasp.

We must accept God's gentle corrections, knowing we too understand only in part. The bigger questions of purpose most likely will never be answered in this lifetime. As Job experienced, we can only accept God's response to the origins of our universe. I Corinthians 13:12 *"For now we look into a mirror dimly . . . but then, I will know fully just as I have been known."* We can have confidence in God's Word, that He is the Creator of our world, and the universe.

We give You praise Lord that You know the beginning from the end, You know each one of us fully, You laid the foundation of the world, Amen!

May 1: Day 121

GOD IS CREATOR
OF ANIMAL INSTINCTS

Job 39:17 **"Because God has made her forget wisdom, And has not given her a share of understanding."**

God further explains to Job some of the mysteries of nature and the behaviors of the animal world. Job 39 summarizes a list of animals, and their behaviors. God awards each creature with a measure of knowledge as it relates to each of their needs. Instincts carry much of the weight concerning why animals behave as they do. For man however, the ability to reason and make choices sets him apart.

We must not descend to carnal instincts that will lead only to nihilism and destruction; we were created to be much more. Man has been given part of God's nature. We have the ability of rational thought; we can communicate in language through text and speech. Man is given the ability to create much beauty and complexity. Man in the form of male and female was created a little lower than the angels (Psalm 8:5), with the potential to create much good. We must learn to recognize our potential and make wise choices. Unlike the animals, man is not limited to instincts. Matthew 6:26 *"Look at the birds of the air, that they do not sow, nor reap nor gather into barns, and yet your heavenly Father feeds them. Are you not worth much more than they?"* May we learn to live our lives according to God's spirit in us, and not the carnal instincts of our flesh.

Thank you Lord, for the diversity of the animal kingdom, and for placing part of Your nature within us, Amen!

May 2: Day 122

GOD CREATED THE DINOSAURS

*Job 40:15 **"Behold now, Behemoth, which I made as well as you.""***

Job 40 delves into some strange creatures; concerning the Behemoth, this passage raising questions regarding who or what this animal was. Many within the schools of theology since the middle and late 1800s sought to explain this creature as an elephant or hippo, even though the descriptions fell far short of the realities. Job 40:15 establishes God as the creator of all life. All animals, including the largest and most powerful known to Job were products of God's creation. The passage gives a description of this animal. The tail ". . . *like a cedar.*" Does not mesh with any known animal today. What we have learned regarding ancient dinosaurs would fit into this description suggesting that Job may have lived alongside these giant creatures.

According to the Bible, God is the creator of all life, even the dinosaurs. The extinction of this group of living creatures does not diminish the magnificence of God's creative abilities. God establishes His proprietorship. Job 41:11 *"Whatever is under the whole heaven is Mine."* We are only Stewards of God's ultimate possession. The Creator is also the owner and landlord. We must take responsibility for the things entrusted to us as tenants. God's covenants with Israel and the nations allow us temporary responsibility. Power and wealth are but commodities given with the expectation of returns. We must however keep the covenant tasks in order to maintain our stewardship. Job 41:1 *"Can you draw out Leviathan with a fishhook? Or press down his tongue with a cord?* The size and power of these creatures is only a tiny glimpse into God's creative power. God is author, owner, and proprietor of all His creation.

Thank the Lord, for these amazing creatures that lived within the lifetime of man. You are far beyond even these great creatures. We give you praise as we consider all of Your marvelous works, Amen!

PSALMS

The Psalms carries more reference to God as creator, than any other book in the Bible. God gives us blessings, gladness, and a reason to give Him praise. Psalms is a book of praise, recognizing God's creative works.

KING DAVID ACKNOWLEDGES GOD AS THE SOURCE OF ALL GOOD

*Psalm 4:7 "**You have put gladness in my heart.**"*

Many of David's psalms are songs of praise to his Maker. Psalms are designed to give a larger perspective of God through His creation, through all His mighty works, and protective hand. David recognized the source of his joy and gladness as coming directly from God. For David, God was intimately connected to every phase of his life. His gladness is dependent upon God and His integration with finite man. David's joy comes from God and is the source of his strength. Psalms 81:1 *"Sing for joy to God our strength."*

King David recognizes the source of his righteousness. Psalms 4:1 *"O God of my righteousness."* A theme persisting from Abraham on to the New Testament. Since man has no righteousness within himself, He must receive his righteousness from God in order to have any hope in a resurrection and future life in the spiritual realm. Going back to Abraham, Genesis 15:6 states: *"Abraham believed God, and it was credited to him as righteousness."* Abraham's obedience was also credited to him as righteousness. We are completely dependent upon God for the capacity to enter into His presence, He provides us with His righteousness that we may enter into His presence. Our Creator God is the one who ultimately clothes us and makes us acceptable. Proverbs 17:22 *"A joyful heart is good medicine,"* All real joy, comes for God.

Thank you God, for our joy, and Your everlasting provisions.
You are the author of all things good, Amen!

May 4: Day 124

OUR SAFETY IS IN GOD'S HANDS

Psalm 4:8 "O LORD, make me to dwell in safety."

Our security does not depend upon chance or luck. Our lives as well as our safety rides squarely within God's hands. Those however who live outside the protective arm of God are not safe. Our only safety is to repent and turn to God. Jesus extends this warning to all those outside of God's protective hand. In Luke 13:4-5 Jesus tells his followers about the tower of Siloam that killed 18 people: *"Or do you suppose that those eighteen on whom the tower of Siloam fell and killed them were worse culprits than all the men who live in Jerusalem? I tell you, no, but unless you repent, you will all likewise perish."* God is our rock, our fortress and our protector. Our ultimate safety rests upon Him.

God knows His own, those who have repented, and those whom He calls to repent; we however must respond. God is in control of our destinies just as He is in control of the entire universe. The safest place for each individual is in the center of God's will and plan, Just as General Stonewall Jackson once stated, "My religious beliefs teach me to feel as safe in battle as in bed." Even though Jackson was killed in battle; he was secure in his knowledge of God. True security rests solely in living at the center of God's perfect will. Thank the Lord that nothing can happen by accident, unless by God's design. Ephesians 1:5 *"He predestined us to adoption as sons through Jesus Christ to Himself, according to the kind intention of His will."* God alone is our ultimate security; He alone is able to protect us and to bring us through the difficulties of this world.

Thank you, Lord for Your watch care over us, we are most secure within the context of Your protective hands, Amen!

May 5: Day 125

WHY ME GOD?

Psalm 8:1 "O LORD, our Lord, How majestic is Your name in all the earth, **Who have displayed Your splendor above the heavens***!"*

Psalm 8 is David's Psalm of praise concerning God's creative work. As David seeks to give God honor for His creation, he compares man with God, and finds God's interest in finite man a bit puzzling. Psalm 8:4 *"What is man that You take thought of him, And the son of man, that You care for him?"* How or why would God take an interest in man, let alone make the effort to create him. The Bible reminds us that we are of value to God because we are created in His image. Genesis 1:26 *"Then God said, Let Us make man in Our image, according to Our likeness;"*

It is truly amazing that God would take an interest in every detail of our lives. God's love for Man, His greatest creation extends even to His willingness to sacrifice His only Son to pay the debt of our sin; that debt we could not begin to pay. God will extend His grace to all those who would acknowledge their need for His forgiveness and to follow Him, even in the darkest times. Thank the Lord that He loves His creation, and that He loves man, whom He created in His image. Luke 15:7 *"I tell you that in the same way, there will be more joy in heaven over one sinner who repents, than over ninety-nine who need no repentance."* God's power and splendor is so far above Man, yet God cares about us.

Thank you Father, that You care about us, Your creation. Your splendor is far above this world, yet You love us, Amen!

May 6: Day 126

GOD WORKS THROUGH
THE LEAST OF US

. *Psalm 8:2 "From the mouth of infants and nursing babes You have established strength."*

Biblical lessons in contrasts and extremes, in short God uses the smallest and weakest among us to communicate His power. We too often expect to perform great tasks in our own strength, then expect to give God credit. The life of Gideon is a good illustration: God sent home 32,000 soldiers and Gideon was able to defeat the Midianites with only 300 warriors. In that case, God needed only a few good men. That victory showed, God was in complete control.

We must learn as king David understood 3,000 years ago, God is able to raise praise for Himself from those least able to give it. God will ultimately do His work through those whom He chooses, both great and small. May we learn to expect God to work in the least likely places. Judges 7:2 *"The LORD said to Gideon, The people that are with you are too many for Me to give Midian into their hands, for Israel would become boastful, saying, My own power has delivered Me."* God's power is more than sufficient to help us through any difficulties this life presents.

Thank you Lord, that you love us and abide with us, giving us the strength to do the work You assign to us, Amen!

May 7: Day 127

GOD OUR MASTER BUILDER

Psalm 8:3 **"When I consider Your heavens, the work of Your fingers, The moon and the stars, which You have ordained."**

David reflects upon God's creative work; David's comprehension of the heavens is only a tiny sliver in contrast to the image we have through our telescopes today. The vastness of the universe is mind boggling in contrast to the limited understanding possessed by King David. He had only a small glimpse of God's wondrous creation; the implications of this passage are far more profound today than they were in David's day.

When we consider the immensity of the universe, along with the complexities of life. Our God is indeed a Master Builder. The amount of energy and power necessary to create the septillion or more stars and galaxies is beyond comprehension. Not only the size and grandeur of the universe, but the precision of time as orchestrated by the orbits of the sun, and moon. Our God is indeed a Master Builder, infinite in knowledge and power. Proverbs 8:30-31 *"then I was beside Him, as a master workman; And I was daily His delight, Rejoicing always before Him, Rejoicing in the world, His earth, and having my delight in the sons of men."* It is hard to imagine the size of our universe, let alone contemplate the power necessary to create all the stars and galaxies. Our God is indeed worthy of honor and praise.

Thank you Lord, for the wonders of your creation, You are excellent in all your works, You are both faithful and powerful, Amen!

May 8: Day 128

CARE FOR MY WORLD

*Psalm 8:6 "You make him to rule over **the works of Your hands**; You have put all things under his feet,"*

Man is placed in a position of caretaker over the earth. Our place is to take care of the world God has given us. We are responsible to use the resources God created for the good; to preserve God's creation with care and diligence. The environmentalist is correct in one sense, we must take care of the planet in which we are entrusted. God gave the Jewish people specific instructions on how to take care of their land. Numbers 35:34 "*You shall not defile the land in which you live, in the midst of which I dwell for I the LORD am dwelling in the midst of the sons of Israel.*" God's instructions were clear, to care for the land, and to live in harmony with it.

God removed Israel from the land of Palestine for their sins, including their failure to give the land rest. We too are also responsible to care for the land we live in. We have environmental protections to protect our land for generations to come. Our land and our animals are precious and must be properly cared for. Genesis 2:15 "*then the LORD God took the man and put him into the Garden of Eden to cultivate it and keep it.*" We all have a stewardship to care for all that God has given us. Let us be faithful in all things God has entrusted to us.

Thank you Lord, for the wonders of Your creation and for the responsibility to care for it. We are Your stewards in this world, Amen!

May 9: Day 129

GOD'S PRECIOUS NAME

Psalm 8:9 "O LORD, our Lord, How majestic is Your name in all the earth!"

David gives a special honor to God's holy name; the name which is above every name. The names of God, as referenced through the Bible gives the reader a different perspective on God's nature and His holy attributes. God is not confined to one name; He is far too complex to be limited to a simple description. We must learn to understand God as the One who is far more diverse than any one stereotype or image. God cannot be placed in a box or limited in His nature. The majesty of God's name(s) is found in the many different ways He is worshiped throughout the world by those who seek Him.

We worship God in many ways. He is our Creator and we acknowledge Him by the name ELOHIM: God "Creator, Mighty and Strong". The people of Israel recognized God as El SHADDAI: "*God Almighty, and ADONAI "LORD"* We recognize Jesus in much that same way: He is Lord, Savior, Redeemer, and our soon coming King. Philippians 2:10 *"so that at the name of Jesus every knee will bow, of those who are in heaven and on earth and under the earth,"* Our God's name is holy, and He is worthy to be praised. Let us honor the name of our Lord, this day and every day.

Thank you Lord, for revealing yourself to us and giving us a glimpse of Your Glory, may we learn to honor Your holy name each and every day, Amen!

May 10: Day 130

GOD'S ETERNAL KINGDOM

Psalm 10:16 "The LORD is King forever and ever; Nations have perished from His land.

God is absolute ruler of all His creation. Most kingships last fewer than 40 years. Queen Elizabeth celebrated 70 years as ruler of Great Britain, ending her reign at the age of 96. Even though, kings and queens die and relinquish their power; God will never relinquish His Kingship. The Bible gives us many references to His eternal kingdom. God is not only eternal but He is also above His creation, and outside of time and space. He cannot be confined to any one place. He is eternal and absolute in His position as King.

All those who call upon the Lord are part of God's eternal kingdom. One thousand years after this passage was written, Jesus ushers in the beginning of God's Kingdom on earth. This kingdom is not built on brick and mortar; it is established in the hearts and lives of His followers. Luke 17:20-21 *"The Kingdom of God is not coming with signs to be observed; nor will they say, 'Look here it is!' or, 'There it is!' For behold, the kingdom of God is in your midst."* Jesus brings us into God's Kingdom through His death and resurrection. 2 Peter 1:11 *"For in this way the entrance into the eternal kingdom of our Lord and Savior Jesus Christ will be abundantly supplied to you."* We are given the promise of an eternal Kingdom in Psalm 145:13: *"Your kingdom is an everlasting kingdom; And Your dominion endures through all generations."* Though the nations of this earth will pass away, God' Kingdom will endure forever.

Thank you Lord, for the hope of an eternal kingdom through Your Son, Jesus Christ, Amen!

May 11: Day 131

GOD SHINES A LIGHT

Psalm 18:28 "For You light my lamp; The LORD my God illumines my darkness" "We see as in a mirror darkly."

We do not see our place in this vast creation unless through the ordered pages of the Bible. Without a revelatory source, man is confined to his ignorance. As much as we discover about the complexities of life and the universe, we can never know, nor prove any detail. We can only speculate. History is past, we are bound by our finiteness. We cannot go back to the beginning and see, we must take someone else's word for how the universe came into being, since no one living today, but God was witness. We have a source that makes claim to be a witness. The question then becomes, is it trustworthy?

Jesus makes the claim that He is the light of the world. "John 8:12 *"Then Jesus again spoke to them saying, "I am the Light of the world; he who follows Me will not walk in the darkness, but will have the Light of life."* The Bible clarifies to the world, how our universe began, who was the cause, and our purpose for being here. We know we were created in the image of God, yet man sinned and fell out of fellowship with his Creator. The final piece of this puzzle is God's redeeming grace, showing Man the way to God through His Son Jesus. We are restored, so we can walk as sons and daughters of God. How do we know this is true: He has given His Spirit, we have His Word, and the many proofs within His Word confirming its reliability. The final proof is the death and resurrection of God's Son Jesus Christ. I Corinthians 13:12 *"For now we see in a mirror dimly, but then face to face, now I know in part, but then I will know fully just as I also have been fully known."* Our lives on this earth are only a reflection of God's presence, we will one day see Him face to face.

Thank you Lord, for shining a light unto our path, revealing yourself to us, and providing a way for us to enter into Your presence, Amen!

May 12: Day 132

GOD'S POWER IS INFINITE

*Psalm 19:1 "The heavens declare the glory of God; **And the firmament showeth his handiwork.**"*

The depth and magnitude of that statement pales when put in contrast to the universe seen today through the Hubble telescope, and now the James Web Telescope, along with other astronomical devices. We cannot comprehend the vastness of the universe we perceive; we can only speculate as to its depth and size. The complexities continue to stagger the imagination as well as conflict with attempts to harmonize its structure. Many contradictions rise to the surface as modern secular science seeks to solve the confusion of its own theories. The entire universe defies any attempts at a natural solution, we still need a Creator to complete the full picture.

This verse challenges man to look directly into the heavens and to contemplate their wonders, and its vastness. What we know today about the heavens, far surpasses knowledge of the ancients. Even then, King David understood in part the vastness of God's creative hand. The more we understand concerning the universe today, the more we should be in awe of how big God is. According to the Bible, God's power is infinite. We could not even begin to understand how great God is. Yet, man is His greatest creation, we are made in His image. Psalm 147:5 *"Great is our Lord and abundant in strength; His understanding is infinite."* God has revealed Himself not only in His written word, but through the grandeur of His creative works.

Thank you Lord, for revealing some of your great power through the wonders of your magnificent creation, Amen!

May 13: Day 133

THE SUN STILL MOVES

Psalm 19:6 "Its rising from one end of the heavens, And its circuit to the other end of them."

The Sun is not stagnant, a description of the sun running its course. Though science proved that the Sun does not move in the sky in relation to the earth. The rotation of the earth gives us our earthly perspective on the sun's course. This statement of Psalms still holds true as we consider the circuit of our sun's movement within the context of our galaxy. Even though the perspective on this reality has changed since the ancients, the biblical truth still holds true. A Creator God can still direct the thoughts and ideas of men into truth, providing a double fulfillment as our knowledge is increased, God's truth remains.

All objects in the universe are in a state of constant motion. The planets revolve around the sun, including the earth. The sun moves in its course around the galaxy, and galaxies move within the expanding universe. Yet, in spite of what we know to be true, our newscasts still refer to sunrise, and sunset. How we observe our creation is still one of convenience. It is easy to forget, God is the one who creates the sun rises and the sunsets. Isaiah 38:8 gives us another perspective of God's control over the heavenly bodies: *"Behold, I will cause the shadow on the stairway, which has gone down with the sun on the stairway of Ahaz, to go back ten steps, so the sun's shadow went back ten steps on the stairway on which it had gone down."* All heavenly bodies move in their respective relationships to other bodies in space. Our planet however is kept safe in the caring hands of our heavenly Father.

Thank the Lord, that we are able to enjoy the beauty of Your wondrous creation without fear, Amen!

May 14: Day 134

WE ARE STEWARDS OF GOD'S CREATION

*Psalm 24:1 "The earth is the LORD's and all it contains, The world and those who dwell in it. **For He has founded it upon the seas, And established it upon the rivers.**"*

God is the possessor of the heavens and the earth. The idea of God's ownership is repeated many times in the Bible. We are but tenants to the builder, who gives men a short period of ownership and power. Absolute power and ownership belong to our Creator God. As David ascended to the throne as king of Israel, he still recognized his place as a steward of God's possession.

We too are God's stewards of His wonderful creation. We possess many things, houses, cars, bank accounts; but at the end of our lives, we must pass all our possessions on to others. We create a will or some documents stating how we want our possessions used, but in the end, all things belong to God. Lord help us be good stewards of all you have given us. I Corinthians 4: 1&2 *"Let a man regard us in this manner, as servants of Christ and stewards of the mysteries of God. In this case, moreover, it is required of stewards that one be found trustworthy,"* We are reminded through God's living Word that we are entrusted with all that we have. All things were created by God and ultimately belong to Him.

Thank you for the many blessings we have received. You have given us the privilege of ownership for a season. May we be faithful with the possessions You have given us, Amen!

May 15: Day 135

THE GOD OF BIODIVERSITY

Psalm 29: 9-10 "The voice of the LORD makes the deer to calve, And strips the forests bare; The LORD sat as King at the flood; Yes the LORD sits as King forever."

The laws of nature and the interaction of all life is interdependent. In these verses, God is declared as the eternal king. As King, God rules over all the affairs of men and the beasts of the forest. He knows what is happening in all His creative realm. All creatures obey the instincts placed within them by their Creator God for the purpose of sustaining all life on this planet.

God created all the animals in the world on day 6 of creation week. Animals are necessary to sustain life in all its forms. God knows all the beasts of the field, the birds of the air and the insects on the ground. Each as a function to sustain life and to add beauty to God's creation. The animal kingdom is an amazing thing to behold, they sustain each other in the food chain. They provide food for man, companionship, and aid man in his work. We are all subject to His laws, and to His creation. Our God is the Creator and ruler of all living things. Genesis 1:25 "God made the beasts of the earth after their kind, and the cattle after their kind, and everything that creeps on the ground after its kind and God saw that it was good." All living things live in harmony with God's creation for our benefit and good, by His design.

Thank you Lord, for wonders of Your creation; for all Your wonderful creatures, great and small. Without the complexities of Your creation, Life would be unsustainable, Amen!

May 16: Day 136

GOD IS OUR ONLY TEACHER

Psalm 32:8 "I will instruct you and teach you in the way which you should go; I will counsel you with My eye upon you."

David submits to God's perfect instruction. God is pictured here as our teacher. It is God who grants wisdom and knowledge. God reveals His mysteries and wonders. Just as men today seeks to understand the mysteries of the universe. We are witness to the vastness of this creation as well as to its complexities. Richards and Gonzalez communicated in their book *The Privileged Planet,* we are in an ideal location for exploring the universe. David communicated the case that it is God's desire that we learn and that we gain knowledge and wisdom concerning the works of His creation. We are not left in the dark.

Science has exploded in recent years, as knowledge has increased. We understand more about the universe and life than ever before; yet man knows less about God. He is still ignorant of his purpose, denying God in ignorance. Ephesians 4:18 *"being darkened in their understanding. Excluded from the life of God because of the ignorance that is in them, because of the hardness of their heart;"* God has made Himself known, not only through the wonders of His creation, but through the revelation of His Word. Ecclesiastes 12:12 *"But beyond this, my son, be warned: the writing of many books is endless, and excessive devotion to books is wearying to the body."* Many books of science reveal to us many of God's wonders. The most important book however is the one that reveals God's love toward mankind.

Thank you Lord, that you are our teacher, making known your wonders, and the pathway to Life eternal, Amen!

May 17: Day 137

GOD SPOKE AND IT WAS SO

Psalm 33:6 **"By the word of the LORD the heavens were made, And by the breath of His mouth all their host,"**

Psalm 33:6 reflects upon the power of God's word to speak the universe into existence. The tools of science reveal to us a universe so vast, it challenges our understanding. Though the universe as we witness it is magnificent; the idea of this vast expanse being created from nothing, reveals a power beyond our comprehension. The amount of energy necessary to create even a small amount of matter would be staggering, the idea of the universe coming into existence by the power of God's word is incredible.

Psalm 33:9 repeats this theme of God speaking the world into existence. **"For He spoke, and it was done; He commanded, and it stood fast."** This world and all its beauty was made through the power of God's spoken word. The universe reflects God's power and glory, while the creation of our planet shows His love and kindness to us in providing a beautiful and habitable place to live that supports our existence; this planet is only a temporary home until our new home is complete. Hebrews 11:3 *"By faith we understand that the worlds were prepared by the word of God, so that what is seen was not made out of things which are visible."* God created the world we live in, and the universe we see from nothing.

Thank you Lord, for Your magnificent power, to create such a universe, and for providing a world to support our fragile lives, Amen!

May 18: Day 138

WE ARE GOD'S DESIGN

*Psalm 33:14-15 "From His dwelling place He looks out on all the inhabitants of the earth, **He who fashions the hearts of them all**, He who understands all their works."*

The all-Seeing Eye Nebula is illustrated above. God is able to follow the lives of every person on earth. The all-seeing eye of God illustrates His omniscience which keeps watch over all life. God knows our inter-working better than we know ourselves. Our God, the Creator is well acquainted with His designs. God is the designer of the human body, its anatomy, personality, sexuality and potential, including the talents, gifts and abilities given every person. We complement one another by God's design.

Civilization could not exist without the diversity of God's creative work. God knows us intimately, body, mind and soul. He knows our innermost thoughts. Psalm 94:*11 "The LORD knows the thoughts of man, that they are a mere breath."* We are completely under the hand of God who loves us and cares for us. We must not disappoint that love. Hebrews 4:2 *"For the world of God is living and active, sharper than any two-edged sword, piercing to the division of soul and of spirit, of joints and of marrow, and discerning the thoughts and intentions of the heart."* Our Creator God knows us, inside and out.

Thank you Lord, for loving us, for knowing us and for designing each of us with all the potential to be successful in this life, and giving us the hope for eternal life with You, Amen!

May 19: Day 139

LIFE IS SHORT

Psalm 39:5 **"Behold, You have made my days as handbreadths, And my lifetime as nothing in Your sight**; *Surely every man at his best is a mere breath."*

The shortness of man's life is amplified in contrast to our eternal God; we are but a breath in comparison. Life's shortness should challenge and spur us to diligence and service for each of our days which will soon come to its physical end. We must learn to use each day to honor and glorify our God. If we can lean to serve God in this short life, we have the hope of eternal life with God that will never end.

Our Creator God has given men a period of time on this earth in which to accomplish His purpose. In general, man's life span is between 70 and 80 years. Psalm 90:10 *"As for the days of our life, they contain seventy years, Or if due to strength, eighty years,"* We have a much greater purpose than just this life. Ecclesiastes reminds us that there is much more beyond. *"He has made everything appropriate in its time. He has also set eternity in their heart, yet so that man will not find out the work which God has done from the beginning even to the end."* God is eternal, but man has a very short span on this earth. James 4:13&14 *"Come now, you who say, "Today or tomorrow we will go into such and such a town and spend a year there and trade and make a profit"—yet you do not know what tomorrow will bring. What is your life? For you are a mist that appears for a little time and then vanishes."* Our life on this earth is very short, let us make the most of each day God has given us.

Thank you Lord, for the time we have been given to work, for the day is coming when we will have no more work to do on this earth.
Help us make the most of every day, Amen!

May 20: Day 140

GOD KNOWS OUR PATH

Psalm 40:5 "**Many, O LORD my God, are the wonders which You have done**,"

Psalm 40 acknowledges many of the works and wonders God has performed in our midst. Verse 2 "He set my feet upon a rock, making my footsteps firm." He provides the purpose, direction, and the hope for this life and eternity. Verse 3 "He put a new song in my mouth, a song of praise to our God; (Music). Verse 8 "Your Law is within my heart." Our conscience is a testimony to the truth of this statement. We are constantly challenged to follow a straight way; a way we often ignore.

God is continually active in our lives, directing and guiding our steps. Our Creator God sees the entire picture of our lives along with the history of the entire world. He is continuously active in guiding the affairs of man. Without God's direction, Man would walk hopelessly in darkness and chaos. We can see many of the wonders of God's creation today through our sciences. However, the big picture of history will not be recognized until the end. Psalm 119: 105 *"Your world is a lamp to my feet, And a light to my path."* The world we live in, and the lives we have been given are amazing to behold. Let us rejoice in all the wonders of God's magnificent creation.

Thank you Lord for Your wonders, we trust that You will guide and direct us according to Your purpose, Amen!

THE SONS OF KORAH

Psalm 42-49 "A chorus of praise to God."

These being of the priestly community lead Israel in worship. Many of the Psalms in Book two from Chapters 42 to 49 were written by those in charge of worship within the Temple and among the Jewish people. Many of these passages communicate God's power, ownership, and glory. He is a God worthy of our praise. Psalm 42:1 *"As the deer pants for the water"* God satisfies our thirst. Psalm 43: 1 *"God is our deliverer, He delivers us from our enemies."* Psalm 44: 4 & 5 *"God is our King . . . who will push back our adversaries;"* God knows our very thoughts *"For He knows the secrets of the heart."* God is our protector Psalm 46:1 *"God is our refuge and strength A very present help in trouble."* Psalm 47:2 & 8 God is absolute ruler of the earth. *"A great King over all the earth. God reigns over the nations,"*

God demonstrates His eternal Kingship over His people. He desires that men submit to Him and enjoy His presence for eternity. We are told about His eternal city. Psalm 48:1 *"Great is the LORD, and greatly to be praised, in the city of our God, His holy mountain Beautiful in elevation, the joy of the whole earth, Is Mount Zion in the far north, The city of the great King."* Psalm 48:8 *"In the city of the LORD of hosts, in the city of our God;' God will establish her forever."* God redeems man that he can live with Him forever. Psalm 49:7-9 *"No man can by any means redeem his brother Or give to God a ransom for him--- For the redemption of his soul is costly, And he should cease trying forever – That he should live on eternally, That he should not undergo decay."* Psalm 59:8 continues: *"But You, O LORD, laugh at them, You scoff at all the nations."* Psalm 96:9 *"worship the Lord in holy attire; Tremble before Him, all the earth."* Our Creator God is worthy to be praised for all He has done; His works permeate every area of our lives.

We have much to praise our God for all He has done for us, and will do for all those who seek Him, Amen!

May 22: Day 142

BEAUTIFUL SUN SETS

Psalm 50:1 "The Mighty One, God, the LORD. Has spoken, And summoned the earth from the rising of the sun to its setting."

We are living in a Theocracy (A system of government where God Himself is ruling directly). Whether we like it or not, God is ultimately in control of all the affairs of man. God is in control of all the universe; the movement of the sun, the moon, and the stars. God is in control of earth's movement through the solar system. All activities on earth along with all the movements of the planets are under God's complete control. Even though the sunrise and sunset are a direct result of earth's rotation, the rising and setting of the sun illustrates man's complete dependence upon God. We can neither control nor affect those conditions, but to watch in wonder the beauty of dawn and evenings colors.

The whole idea of movement or kinetic energy is universal. In addition to our solar system, our galaxy is rotating around a center, all galaxies are moving and expanding. Just as the cosmos is in constant motion, the very smallest elements are moving and active. All biological systems are in motion, our hearts are pumping blood, and our digestive systems are breaking down our food to provide nourishment to our bodies. Our God is in complete control of all physical movement. We must also stay active to remain healthy. Psalm 65:8 "*You make the dawn and sunset shout for joy.*" The portrait of God's magnificent creation is visible from day to day. However, God can and will intervene into the affairs of man based on the faith of the observer.

Thank you Lord, for the wonders of Your creation and the amazing movement surrounding us, Amen!

May 23: Day 143

GOD KNOWS HIS OWN

Psalm 50:10 "For every beast of the forest is Mine,
The cattle on a thousand hills."

The supreme ruler and landlord of the Earth is God. I know every bird of the mountains, and everything that moves in the field is Mine. Psalm 50:12 *"If I were hungry I would not tell you, For the world is Mine, and all it contains."* Each of these verses is testimony to God as the ultimate landlord and owner of our planet. He monitors not only the affairs of man with complete accuracy; He knows the activities of the animals and the birds of the air. He is not the absent landlord we see in many places in our neighborhoods. God keeps exact records and whereabouts of all of His creation.

God loves each of us with a perfect love, just as He loves and cares for His creation. He made this world for a reason; to bless us through His creation, and to reveal Himself to us, step by step. God has made Himself known to us through the wonders of His creation, and through the revelation of His Word. God alone is the ultimate owner and ruler of all things. What we possess, belongs to Him and is entrusted to us to use for our needs, and to help and bless the needs of others. I Corinthians 10:26 *"FOR THE EARTH IS THE LORD'S AND ALL IT CONTAINS."* Our Creator God is the ultimate owner and guardian of all life on this planet.

Thank you Lord, that you know all about us and, You are in complete control of your wondrous creation, all things belong to You, Amen!

May 24: Day 144

GOD IN US

*Psalm 51:10 "**Create in me a pure heart, O God**,*
and renew a steadfast spirit within me."

Creation is an ongoing reality for those who are seeking God. God is in the business of correcting men's failures. Even as King David failed, giving in to adultery, David's prayer of appeal was answered, and David's relationship with God restored. The consequences of his sin however continued to affect his family in the years that followed. God's scales must perfectly balance, as we may suffer consequences for our actions, while at the same time receiving God's absolute and complete pardon.

God is actively at work in the hearts and lives of all those who put their faith in Him. He is also working to draw man unto Him, for no man can come to God, unless the Spirit of God draws Him. John 6:44 *"No one can come to me unless the Father who sent me draws him. And I will raise him up on the last day."* Our Creator God is creating within the hearts of men, a holy priesthood that will follow Him into eternity. Philippians 1:6 *"For I am confident of this very thing, that He who began a good work in you will perfect it until the day of Christ Jesus."* God is continually at work within us conforming us to the image of His Son.

Thank you Lord, for drawing us to yourself, and granting us the privilege to become the sons, and daughters of God. Create within us a clean heart that we might be right with You, Amen!

May 25: Day 145

GOD'S UNCHANGING CHARACTER

Psalm 52:8 "I trust in the lovingkindness of God forever and ever."

Psalm 52 presents two attributes of God, giving us some comfort concerning the future. God's nature is one of love and kindness. He seeks no wrong but desires good for all men. James 1:17 *"Every good thing given and every perfect gift is from above coming down from the Father of lights, with whom there is no variation or shifting shadow."* Secondly, the nature of God's loving kindness is also unchanging. Isaiah 54:10 *"For the mountains may be removed and the hills may shake, but My loving kindness will not be removed from you."* Our God is unchangeable in His love and compassion for His people.

God's immutability guarantees that His character will never be any different. He is complete and needs no adjustments. God's kindness will continue on into eternity, a reality that will never end. We can put our confidence and trust in all of God's promises, God will never change His mind or His character. We can have full assurance before God, through His Son Jesus whose love and kindness will never vary. Hebrews 13:8 *"Jesus Christ is the same yesterday and today and forever."* We can put our trust in God, who is perfect in all things. His love and compassion for His people will never depart.

We give thanks to You oh God; Your love and compassion for all Your people will never change, Amen!

May 26: Day 146

DON'T BE A FOOL

Psalm 53:1 "The fool has said in his heart, 'There is no God."

Those who would deny God are labeled as fools according to this passage; this statement would reflect on those who would dismiss or ignore the signs regarding God's creative work. For many within Western culture, the concept of God is unfathomable. An infinite God is beyond imagination and well outside the scope of our limited reason. It is more convenient for many people to just dismiss God as a fairy tale and move on. The bigger problem with those who would dismiss God, is their unwillingness to take a closer look at the issues. Modern science is not the end of the discussion on origins; it is only the beginning.

The idea of something coming into existence from nothing (ex nihilo) is itself in conflict with the laws of science making the creative act miraculous. Can something come into existence from nothing, or is matter eternal? Secular science has no good answer to either question; it is unable to give us a First Cause. However, Romans 1:20 makes it clear: *". . . His eternal power and divine nature, have been clearly seen, being understood through what has been made. . ."* The wonders of God's creative power are evident throughout God's natural revelation (Creation). God also communicates about Himself through His written revelation found in the Bible. Romans 1:21 & 22 *"For even though they knew God, they did not honor Him as God or give thanks, but they became futile in their speculations, and their foolish heart was darkened. Professing to be wise, they became fools."* We must be diligent to examine God's Word in the Bible to learn the truth of God's creative power.

Thank you Lord for making Yourself known to mankind by the wonders of your Creation, and by Your written Word, Amen!

May 27: Day 147
GOD WILL JUDGE

Psalm 58:11 "Surely there is a reward for the righteous; surely there is a God who judges on earth!"

All men, even the wicked see the necessity for a structured and ordered reality. They see the need for purpose and accountability. If there is a God, and He created an orderly universe, there must be a system of rewards and judgments. This would be a sign, for why every culture has a system of checks and balances. We would deem it extremely unfair if someone was able to commit a crime and get away with it. We demand justice regarding those who hurt us in our culture. Why would God not be even more adamant in His judgments and rewards? He is perfectly holy, and just regarding His creative order. Everything must balance, all sins must be accounted for, even our wrongs; God will judge all men.

If modern man demands justice, even more so God, who is the one just Creator and Judge. We are reminded in Hebrew 9:27 *"And inasmuch as it is appointed for men to die once and after this comes judgment,"* God will judge the living and the dead. Although we don't experience immediate consequences for our sins (Thank you Lord). God will judge us all in the end. The Bible speaks of two judgments: The righteous before the Judgment seat of Christ (2 Corinthians 5:10), and the wicked before the great white throne (Revelation 20:11). God is perfect in His judgment, and since all men have sinned (Romans 3:23), all are condemned. God however revealed His remedy over 700 years before Christ. Isaiah 53:6 *"All of us like sheep have gone astray, Each of us has turned to his own way; But the LORD has caused the iniquity of us all to fall on Him."* Jesus was judged in our place, for our debt. John 3:19 *"This is the judgment, that the Light has come into the world, and men loved the darkness rather than the Light, for their deeds were evil."* Our Creator God will judge all men equitably according to His perfect standard.

Thank you Lord, for taking my judgment of sin upon yourself, and balancing the scales of justice, Amen!

May 28: Day 148

A PSALM OF PRAISE
FOR GOD'S POWER

*Psalm 62:11 "Once God has spoken; Twice I have heard this: **That power belongs to God.**"*

The Psalmist is presenting the reader with a perspective on God's ultimate power. Power is a relative term which usually indicated the ability or capacity to perform a task. The bigger the task, the more power necessary to bring it to pass. In the case of God, all power is at His disposal. He is by biblical definition, all powerful (Omnipotent). Luke 1:37 *"For nothing will be impossible with God."* The case for creation rests totally upon God's capacity to perform what for us would be impossible. The amount of power necessary for the creation of the universe is staggering. As a cause, God is presented as a sufficient cause for the universe we see. All other theories for the creation of matter, the universe, and life, fall far short of any rational explanation.

God rules by His power and through the Holy Spirit. We have access to God's power through His Holy Spirit which He gives to those who seek Him. Proverbs 1:23 *"Turn to my reproof, Behold, I will pour out my spirit on you; I will make my words known to you."* God's power is not limited to Creation; it is also the power by which He changes lives and enables all men to become a new creation, I Thessalonians 1:5 continues: *"For our gospel did not come to you in word only, but also in power and in the Holy Spirit and with full conviction; just as you know what kind of men we proved to be among you for your sake."* God's power is sufficient to create the universe in which we life, and to changes the hearts and lives of all those who seek Him.

Thank you Lord for Your power to create within us a new people fit for your Kingdom, Amen!

May 29: Day 149

OUR CREATOR AND SAVIOR

*Psalm 65:5 -7 "By awesome deeds You answer us in righteousness, O God of our salvation **Who establishes the mountains by His strength, Being girded with might**; Who stills the roaring of the seas, The roaring of their waves,"*

The Psalmist communicates numerous attributes of our Creator God. He is the force behind the ordered operation of our world. We do not fully understand or grasp the complexities that sustain us. All of nature, operates by God's order and design. The roaring of the seas and the waves are a result of gravitational forces from the moon and the sun. All of God's creation is balanced to make life possible on this earth. Most importantly, God is our salvation. He provides the way to enter into His presence.

We live in an extremely complex world; the most optimum part of the goldilocks zone (distance from the sun), suitability for life. The tilt of the earth is just right for seasons and moderation of temperature. Our Creator God is the author and designer of our world along with all its complexities. He also knows our condition, that we are but dust (Psalm 103:14), yet He cares about our righteousness and our salvation. Psalm 90:2 *"Before the mountains were born, Or You gave birth to the earth and the world, Even from everlasting to everlasting You are God."* Isaiah 45:21 *"and there is no other god besides Me, A righteous God and a Savior; there is none except Me."* Our God is our Creator, Redeemer, and Savior. He created our world, and everything in it. Our Creator God still rules His creation in righteousness and love.

Thank you Lord, for creating the world to sustain us. Thank you that You formed us in Your image, and redeemed us by your grace, Amen!

May 30: Day 150

GOD'S BEAUTIFUL CREATION

*Psalm 65:8 "They who dwell in the ends of the earth stand in awe of Your signs. **You make the dawn and the sunset shout for joy.**"*

The creator of the skies, the sun sets, and the dawn deserves our respect and worship for the beauty of His created order. Artists can only imitate the beauty of a sunset. The One who created these master displays shows us a small demonstration of His creativity. No two sunsets are the same, just as each dawn is unique in beauty. We can imitate, but never create the complexities of the world in which we live. God is the master artist who paints with natural beauty using the materials of His creation.

My mother always loved to walk to the edge of our community to witness the sunsets. She enjoyed the beauty and the colors each sunset displayed. It gave to her a sense of peace and a source of praise for her heavenly Father. Our God is marvelous in all His works. Science can only speculate and marvel at the wondrous complexities of the heavens, this world, and the life within it. Job 37:15-16 *"Do you know how God establishes them and makes the lightning of His cloud to shine? Do you know about the layers of the thick clouds, The wonders of one perfect in knowledge,"* Enjoy the sunsets, and all the wonders of God's creative power.

Thank you Lord, for the beauty of your creation, and for giving us life, that we may be able to enjoy it, Amen!

May 31: Day 151

GOD WATCHES OVER THE NATIONS

Psalm 66:7 "He rules by His might forever;
His eyes keep watch on the nations;"

Just as God is powerful in His creativity, He keeps a constant visual of all the events during the short history of this world. God is ever mindful of all that transpires among the nations. He never sleeps or slumbers, He keeps a constant watch on the nations with a final objective, to repair and restore man and His creation back to their prime condition. Only our Creator God can restore the damage brought on our planet by man's sin.

When we watch the news events of the day, we are constantly reminded of the evils in the world. It hard not to wonder where God is amid these daily calamities. Yet, the Bible is clear about God's continuing interaction with His Creation. Isaiah 40:15 reminds us: *"Behold, the nations are but a drop in the bucket."* He is far above this world, yet still, He cares about the affairs of man. God not only cares about the nations and their courses, He cares about each of us and the course of each life. Daniel 2:21 *"It is He who changes, the times and the epochs; He removes kings and establishes kings, He gives wisdom to wise men And knowledge to men of understanding."* Our God rules the nations, He alone raises up leaders and removes them.

Thank you Lord, for Your watchful care, over all the world, nothing happens outside your divine purpose, Amen!

June 1: Day 152

OUR LIVES ARE IN GOD'S HANDS

Psalm 66:8-9 "Bless God and sing His praises, for He holds our lives in His hands."

God is the ultimate gate keeper for every life form to have walked on the earth. Not only do we owe our existence to God's creative power, but our continuation in life depends upon His grace. We are under His constant protection for our lives which are bound to His continued provisions. We owe God our praises for His watchful care over us. There is no life outside the watchful hand of God.

God and God alone is the author of life. The majesty and complexity of life in all its form can be attributed only to the One whose infinite intelligence knows the workings of all life in all its forms. We give full credit and praise to the Lord for the marvels of life and thank Him for His continual sustaining power. As Psalm 139:14 states: "*I am fearfully and wonderfully made. . .*" We are all here by God's design; He made us for a purpose, that we would accomplish specific tasks for Him. Each day of life is a gift from God to be used to honor and serve Him. Psalm 118:24 "*This is the day which the LORD has made:* Let us rejoice and be glad in it." Give thanks and praise to our Creator God for our lives. He is our sustainer; He keeps us in the shelter of His hands until our life on this earth is complete.

Thank you Lord, for our lives, and for the privilege to serve You with the gifts and talents You gave us. Thank you for sustaining us and keeping us in Your merciful care, Amen!

June 2: Day 153

THE CHANGE OF SEASONS

Psalm 74: 16-17 "Yours is the day, Yours also is the night; **You have prepared the light and the sun***,* **You have established all the boundaries of the earth; You have made summer and winter***."*

The earth depends upon the light of the sun to maintain the cycles of the seasons along with our wellbeing. We have the blessed presence of the seasons, giving us variety in climate, unless we live in the tropics, even then seasons change, Rain and drought. We depend upon all God's provisions to keep healthy and alive.

The variation of the seasons is a gift from God. The uniqueness of the seasons gives a variety and color to the world we live in. The tilt of the earth at approximately 23° gives us the seasons as we see them. The northern and southern hemispheres enjoy the seasons at opposite ends of the year. All this by God's design. For those unfortunate enough to be living much closer to the equator where the seasons have little change, they may only experience wet and dry with little difference. How blessed we are to have such diversity in seasons. Genesis 1:14 *"Then God said, "Let there be lights in the expanse of the heavens to separate the day from the night, and let them be for signs and for seasons and for days and years;"* Our Creator God gave us the seasons to demonstrate the cycle of life in all its variety. All of creation works in harmony to give us these seasonal wonders.

Thank you Lord, for the beauty and diversity of the seasons. All of Your creation works together, giving us the beauty of seasonal change, Amen!

June 3: Day 154

A NEW ETERNAL WORLD

Psalm 78:69 "And He built His sanctuary like the heights, Like the earth which He has founded forever."

This physical earth will not last forever; both biblical and secular scholars agree. The time period for the destruction of our planet is somewhat different. For the ancients, God was preparing a New Heavens and a New Earth. For the modernist man, we can only look forward to a dark and dead universe. Unlike the first, the latter can never be proved or demonstrated. It is blind faith in a modern historical myth.

According to the biblical account, our current earth would seem to be a temporary habitat for humanity. Looking at our earth from this biblical viewpoint; our current planet is contaminated with sin. The promise given in the Psalms is of a new future earth, one without end. Only an eternal God would be able to make such a promise. 2 Peter 3:13 *"But according to His promise we are looking for new heavens and a new earth, in which righteousness dwells."* God's eternal sanctuary will be beyond anything we can imagine. We will one day experience the wonders of God's heavenly architectural designs.

Thank you LORD, for Your eternal attributes giving us the hope of a new heaven and earth. We look forward to seeing the New Jerusalem, and its many mansions. Most importantly, we long for eternal life with You, Amen!

June 4: Day 155

THE LORD CREATED THE NATIONS

*Psalm 86:9 "All nations **whom You have made** shall come and worship before You. O Lord. And they shall glorify Your name."*

God's creative work transcends the physical realities of matter, space, and time. God is the One who establishes the nations that inhabit the earth. By His will and pleasure, they exist. David makes the prediction that one day, all the nations of earth that remain will come before the throne of God to worship Him.

The many nations we have in the world today are a gift from God. The diversity of culture, language, and appearance makes each nation unique and interesting. The people learn to live and adapt to different weather, climate, and geography. They develop different clothing styles, communication patterns as well as different styles of worship. We all approach God from different perspectives. It was God's delight to create the nations, not only for their diversity, but to protect us from the negative effects of sin that would result from a single world empire. Job 12:23 *"He makes the nations great, then destroys them; He enlarges the nations then leads them away."* Our nation is a gift from God, let us give thanks for our country and the freedoms we have.

Thank you LORD, for Your wisdom and grace in giving us the nations along with all their different customs. Thank you for our country, we ask for Your continued blessing upon us, Amen!

June 5: Day 156

GOD IS THE TRUTH

Psalm 86:15 "But You, O Lord, are a God merciful and gracious, abundant in loving kindness and truth."

God's attributes of kindness, grace, and mercy should be a comfort as God affords man much more patience than we afford each other. The idea of purpose comes front and center regarding the one who possesses the ultimate reality. The concept of truth is flexible and extremely relative in modern culture. Some will even deny the existence of the commodity of truth altogether. According to David, God is the sole possessor of Truth. God knows not only the present, but the beginning and the end. All facets of History are already written within the mind of God; Truth is held firmly in His able hands.

Looking forward to Jesus' life as He testified before Pilot, "*I came to testify to the Truth.*" Absolutes are a reality and exist only because of God's absolute character. He is Truth, He has shown us His attributes of mercy, kindness and grace. By His grace, we can possess those same attributes. John 14:6 "*I am the Way, Truth, and the Life; no one comes to the Father but through Me.*" Truth is the acknowledgment of an ultimate reality that transcends our knowledge and understanding. Only our Creator could communicate that reality through His magnificent creation, and His written and living Word.

Thank you LORD, for showing us Your character of love, kindness, and truth that we may become like You, Amen!

June 6: Day 157

GOD CREATED THE POLES
NORTH & SOUTH

*Psalm 89:11 "The heavens are Yours, the Earth also is Yours; **The world and all it contains You have founded them.**"*

Maskil of Ethan the Ezrahite was the writer of this Psalm. This was written after the time of David by one who was most likely a worship leader in Judah before the fall. Maskil credits God for the origins of all that is in the world. As a praise leader, it was his job to praise and lead in the worship of God. Verse 12 solidifies God as creator: "*The north and the south, **You have created them**; Tabor and Hermon shout for joy at Your name.*" This passage gives God credit for the structure and organization of the earth, along with its poles, and position relative to the sun and planets. The earth, its tilt, its rotation, and place in the solar system uniquely define this planet as a place that is habitable.

God is credited for the creation of all we see in the world. Everything the eye beholds is created and given to us by God. For this reason, we are to be joyful and give thanks for all the wonders we see in the world. God is a masterful Creator who is the one responsible for all the details of this world. Mark 7:37a *"They were utterly astonished, saying, "He has done all things well;"* All creation belongs to God, He has entrusted us to care for this world in His name. Our Creator God designed our world to be inhabitable.

'Thank you LORD, for giving us such a wonderful and habitable world that we can live in and enjoy, Amen!

June 7: Day 158

OUR ETERNAL GOD

*Psalm 90:2 "**Before the mountains were born or You gave birth to the earth and the world**, Even from everlasting to everlasting You are God."*

God promises His people an eternal inheritance, a life without end. Only an eternal and infinite God would be able to make and keep such a promise. The Psalm writer continues this theme: Psalm 89:29 *"So I will establish his descendants forever And his throne as the days of heaven."* The eternal nature of God is examined and recognized. God is not limited by time and space.

Sometimes we may feel God is not listening or has delayed keeping His promises. We are bound to a finite existence on this world. However, God is not bound at all by time and space. Even though we may suffer in this existence, we have been given the promise of eternal life through God's Son Jesus who now sits on the throne. Our eternal God has provided for us the hope of eternal life, and a habitat suitable for that life. Romans 1:20 *"For since the creation of the world, His invisible attributes, His eternal power and divine nature, have been clearly seen, being understood through what has been made, so that they are without excuse."* Our world is the product of God's creative power, He existed from eternity past.

Thank you Lord, for the wonders of this earth, and for the promise of eternal life made possible through your Son Jesus, Amen!

June 8: Day 159

GOD ABOVE TIME

Psalm 89:4 "For a thousand years in Your sight Are like yesterday when it passes by Or as a watch in the night."

The concept of time has little consequence to the One having lived in eternity. An infinite God has no barriers, neither physical linear time, nor duration of time constrains God as His existence transcends all time. In addition, He is all powerful. He alone fulfills the definition of an all-powerful Creator. God is not only the Creator of this universe, He is the creator of time itself.

Our Creator God uses time for His story (history) to unfold in its proper order. *"To everything there is a season. A time for every purpose under heaven'* (Ecclesiastes 3:1*)*. Jesus, Himself, was constrained by time, Then Jesus said to them, *"My time has not yet come' John 7:6*. But time and future events should not trouble us. *"Therefore do not worry about tomorrow, for tomorrow will worry about its own things. Sufficient for the day is its own trouble. (*Matthew 6:34) He is the source of all life, and our purpose for living; in Him exists life, death, and eternity. God is above all His creation, He is above all the world, all the nations, and all rule. He places rulers, He endows men with gifts and skills. He alone sustains all peoples by His power and might. God will always be there with us. He was from the beginning, and will be in the end. 2 Peter 3:8 *"But do not let this one fact escape your notice, beloved, that with the Lord one day is like a thousand years, and a thousand years like one day."* Our eternal God is above time and space but is using it to bring all things to completion:

Thank you Lord, You have endowed men with life; You have given us the hope of eternal life. You are the Alpha and Omega, the beginning and the end, Amen!

June 9: Day 160

EVERLASTING GOD

*Psalm 90:2 "Before the mountains were born. **Or You gave birth to the earth and the world**, Even from everlasting to everlasting You are God."*

Where God was before the earth was created? He was from eternity past, He has not changed; He alone created our world. He elevated the mountains and created the seas with all their life. He existed in the past and will exist into eternity. He gave birth to our world with all its splendor and beauty. All life on the face of the earth with all its diversity was created and placed here for our good.

Our God is forever present; He will always be with us in our times of need. He will watch over us in all our difficulties and troubles. The name given to God describing His eternal attribute is El Olam, Everlasting God. We have the promise of eternal life because God is eternal. He gave man life; He redeemed man from his sins and restores man to a right standing before a perfect and Holy God. John 8:58 *"Jesus said to them, Truly truly, I say to you, before Abraham was born, I am."* Our Creator God has always existed, He is the first cause of our creation, He will always be there for us.

Thank you God, for your eternal nature, giving all those who seek you the privilege to enter into Your presence from this time forward into eternity, Amen!

June 10: Day 161

OUR WORLD IS THE CENTER OF A MOVING UNIVERSE

Psalm 93: "Indeed the world is firmly established, it will not be moved."

The earth is in a constant state of motion as is all of creation. This passage created a problem for the Medieval Church. For them, the earth must be the center of the physical universe based primarily upon this passage. The leaders accepted a Greek model (Ptolemy cosmology) for the universe that puts the earth as the center of Creation. This was a somewhat convenient solution to the problem of man's importance. Modern science seeks to demonstrate that man holds no special place in the world or the universe. The biblical documents answer that question.

The issue of man's importance before an infinite God begs the questions. Why would such a God be concerned with the affairs of man in any way? Psalm 8:4 *"What is man that You take thought of him, And the son of man that You care for him."* Yet, God entrusted this world to man. Even though the world is in constant motion, as is the entire universe around us; God is the creator of the entire universe. It displays His glory and power. He can choose whomever He wishes to serve Him. Man is important, not because of any location in the universe, He is important because God said so. We are created in His image with the capacity to do great service for Him. James 3:9 *"With it we bless our Lord and Father, and with it we curse men, who have been made in the likeness of God;"* This world is not static, but moving. We too need to be actively moving and serving our Creator God, who Himself is fixed and the center of our moving universe.

Thank you Lord for our world, You have revealed to us your power through your creation and through Your living Word. We are important to You regardless how the earth moves, Amen!

June 11: Day 162

THE GOD OF SENSES

Psalm 94:9 ***"He who planted the ear, does He not hear? He who formed the eye, does He not see?***

Perhaps two of the most complicated parts of our human anatomy are attributed to God's creative power. This verse reemphasizes God's infinitely higher capacity to hear our prayers as well as to see our suffering. God sees all our needs and our suffering. Genesis 16:13 recalls Hagar's suffering. *"Then she called the name of the LORD who spoke to her. 'You are a God who sees.'"* Our God knows our inner most needs even before we ask.

God is able to hear and see far beyond our abilities. Nonetheless, God has equipped us with the same ability to hear and see. God's creative power is a marvel to behold. The complexity of the eye staggers the imagination. There are literally dozens of subsystems supporting a functional eye. There are well over a 100 million light receptor cells able to receive and communicate information to the brain for processing. The ability of our brains to process all the data received from our eyes, and our hearing is even more amazing. To suggest these abilities are an accident is naive. Yet today, many scientists suggest just that. Only an infinite God, who knows our every need would also be powerful enough to create our most delicate senses. Proverbs 20:12 *"The hearing ear and the seeing eye, The LORD has made both of them."* God's ability to hear and see far surpasses that of Man. Our God is Omniscient, knowing all things, and lacking in nothing. He is well able to see us through our daily struggles.

Thank you Lord, that You see our every need; You hear our prayers. You alone are responsible for our sight, and our hearing, giving us the ability to process complex information. You continue to watch over us, Amen!

GOD MADE THE HEAVENS

*Psalm 96:5 "**But the LORD made the heavens.**"*

When we consider the creation of the heavens, we are looking at three separate regions; the immediate heavens in our skies above, the heavenly bodies consisting of stars and galaxies. Finally, the highest heaven as referenced by the Apostle Paul (2 Corinthians 12:2) to the third or highest heaven, the abode of God. This third heaven is recognized as outside of our time and space, a spiritual reality we cannot see. Our earthly heavens provide us our atmosphere that sustains our life. It provides us our air to breath, the rains for growing crops, protection from ultraviolet radiation, and beautiful sunrises and sunsets.

The second heaven consisting of the cosmos is a wonder to behold. The sheer number of stars and galaxies are innumerable. Just point a large telescope to any point in the sky, and the galaxy field would fill the lens, each galaxy holding billions of stars. Hebrews 11:12 compares this number to the number of sand particles on the earth: "*as many descendants as the stars of heaven in number, and innumerable as the sand which is by the seashore.*" According to some scientists, this is a number approximates 70 septillion or 70 followed by 21 zeros.

The highest heaven according to the Bible is beyond our imagination. God's dwelling place according to Paul's reference goes even beyond our observable universe. I Corinthians 2:4 "*Things which eye has not seen and ear has not heard, and which have not entered the heart of man, All that God has prepared for those who love Him.*" Our Creator God is the source of all reality, bringing with Him a future hope surpassing our understanding.

Thank you Lord for the grandeur of Your creation, but more so for the eternal hope of entering Your highest heaven, Amen!

June 13: Day 164

WE ARE GOD'S SHEEP

Psalm 100:3 "Know that the LORD Himself is God; **It is He who has made us, and not we ourselves.** *We are His people and the sheep of His pasture."*

Psalm 100 is a short Psalm of praise to almighty God. The author recognizes his complete dependence upon His Creator. This passage short circuits any idea that we are self-made men or women. We are a product of God's creative power. He not only created our physical bodies; According to Psalm 139:14, *"We are fearfully and wonderfully made."* God even knew us before we were born: Jeremiah 1:5 *"Before I formed you in the womb I knew you,"* God made us, and He knows every area of our lives, better than we know ourselves.

Every human being that walks the planet today was created by almighty God. He created every person for a specific reason. Even the wicked have a purpose (Proverbs 16:4). We are blessed in that we are known by God, created by God and given a specific purpose in life. Ephesians 1:4 *"just as He chose us in Him before the foundation of the world, that we would be holy and blameless before Him. In love."* God is our faithful shepherd, like the sheep, we must learn to follow Him.

Thank you Lord, for creating us, and giving us life, breath, and a purpose to live for; You formed us, and we are fearfully and wonderfully made, Amen!

June 14: Day 165

ENTROPY

*Psalm 102:25-26 "Of old **You founded the earth, And the heavens are the work of Your hands**. Even they will perish, but You endure; And all of them will wear out like a garment;"*

Psalm 102 introduces us to the concept of Entropy, moving from a state of order to disorder. This present Earth will not to last forever, but to run down after a period of time. Even through some passages suggest an earth that will last forever; Psalm 104:5 *"He established the earth upon its foundations, So that it will not totter forever and ever."* This earth, however, is not this present world but a future world.

We are told that this earth will eventually be replaced by a new heavens and a new earth. 2 Peter 3:13 *"But according to His promise we are looking for new heavens and a new earth, in which righteousness dwells."* The earth in which we now live is destined to destruction. All things are in the process of running down. Nothing in this current creation will last forever. Everything we own is running down and wearing out. Our current bodies are aging and will eventually die. We can however trust God to sustain us and bring us into His new creation. 2 Peter 2:10 *"But the day of the Lord will come like a thief, in which the heavens will pass away with a roar and the elements will be destroyed with intense heat, and the earth and its works will be burned up."* Everything on this earth will one day wear out and pass away, a new Earth will endure forever.

Thank you Lord, for the promise of a new heavens and a new earth that will not be affected by the forces of entropy, Amen!

June 15: Day 166

GOD'S UNCHANGING

Psalm 102:27 "But You are the same, And Your years will not come to an end."

If our God is perfect in all His attributes, He must be unchanging. There is no need for improvement with God. Unlike man, who strives to be more like our heavenly Father; man is in constant need of change. Romans 12:2 encourages man to conform to the image of Christ. "*And do not be conformed to this world, but be transformed by the renewing of your mind, so that you may prove what the will of God is, that which is good and acceptable and perfect.*" Man is expected to become more like God, in his attitude, behaviors, and conduct.

The task of becoming perfect is part of man's job description. Matthew 5:48 "*Therefore you are to be perfect, as your heavenly Father is perfect.*" At first glance, this goal is out of reach for anyone. We are still in the process of becoming as the Apostle Paul stated. Philippians 3:12 "*Not that I have already obtained it or have already become perfect, but I press on so that I may lay hold of that for which also I was laid hold of by Christ Jesus.*" It is our hope that one day we will be changed, to be like Christ. Only our Lord God is able to help us conform to His image, that we may be perfect in His sight by the power of His Holy Spirit. Hebrews 13:8 "*Jesus Christ is the same yesterday and today and forever.*" Malachi 3:6 "*For I the LORD do not change; therefore you, O sons of Jacob, are not consumed.*" Both the Old and New Testaments confirm; God does not change.

Thank you Lord, that you are unchanging, that You will always be there helping us conform to Your image, Amen!

June 16: Day 167

OUR EXPANDING UNIVERSE

*Psalm 104:4 "Covering Yourself with light as with a cloak, **Stretching out heaven like a tent curtain.**"*

God's creative ability is on display within this Psalm. The stretching of the heavens fits the apparent reality of the universe in which we live. As the universe expands, we see the redshift (indicating heavenly bodies are moving away from us) within the retreating stars. Though the idea of an expanding universe is expressed in terms of ancient understanding, using tents and cloaks to express the inexpressible. The truth of this reality is clearly presented.

The character and power of God are on display within this passage. Light is pure energy as we know it, God is described as Spirit. The omnipotence of God is characterized by light; the amount of energy necessary to move anything the speed of light is infinite. Only an infinite God would be able to stretch the heavens. The attributes of God are evident in His mighty works. His power is sufficient to create and order the heavens by His infinite wisdom. I John 1:5 *"This is the message we have heard from Him and announce to you, that God is light and in Him there is no darkness at all."* Science is continually confirming the wonders of God's created universe.

Thank You Lord for ordering the heavens and giving us the tools in science to discover many of your wonders, Amen!

June 17: Day 168

THE EARTH IS FIXED OR NOT

*Psalm 104:5 "**He established the earth upon its foundations,** So that it will not totter forever and ever."*

The passage expresses the unmasked acceptance of God as the Creator of the world. Though this world will pass away, the promise is given of a New Earth that will not. The idea of a fixed world is consistent throughout scripture. The idea of earth on a foundation is a different twist in our understanding of the Earth. Our world is suspended on nothing as we observe it. Job 26:7 "*He stretches out the north over empty space And hangs the earth on nothing.*" Job clarifies the physical realities of the Earth as we observe it suspended in space.

The fact that God established the earth bears witness to God's creative power. The idea of God placing the Earth on a foundation in light of Job's passage, points more to our planet being protected and secure. This world is a safe place to live in, in light of the many disasters that science predicts could happen to us. We have confidence that God is our protection and will keep this planet safe until the time of our departure is complete. Isaiah 28:16 "*Therefore thus says the Lord God, Behold I am laying in Zion a stone, a tested stone, A costly cornerstone for the foundation, firmly placed He who believes in it will not be disturbed.*" I Corinthians 3:11 expands this thought: "*For no man can lay a foundation other than the one which is laid, which is Jesus, Christ.*" The idea of a solid foundation goes well beyond a simple physical entity our earth, it transcends into a secure eternal reality.

Thank you Lord, for the security of your creation and for the promise of an eternal Earth that will never be moved, Amen!

June 18: Day 169

PLATE TECTONICS

*Psalm 104:8 "The mountains rose; the valleys sank down **To the place which You established for them**."*

This expresses a fairly accurate description of continental movement with resulting uplift of mountains and valley formation. The plate tectonics that created the mountain ranges fits well with the flood event as to how and why the earth could be covered as the highest mountains were most likely formed during and following the flood. This chronology does not follow the secular scientific version of events, but since no one living was present, we can only speculate on details of how that history unfolded. Another evidence that the mountains were once under water is demonstrated by the fact of marine life found in sedimentary rock at high elevations. This biblical description fits the events as well, much better than any speculative naturalistic old earth science theory.

We are privileged to live at a time when science is able to confirm and clarify Noah's flood. The flood event explains so much of the geology we see in the world today. We see sedimentary rock with fossil life laid down all over the world. We know that at one time the mountains were under water because of marine fossil life. Instead of millions of years, God performed these events in short order, using plate tectonics. The mountains were pushed up containing the fossil evidence, while the ocean trenches were deepened to contain the water. 2 Peter 2:5 *"and (God) did not spare the ancient, world, but preserved Noah, a preacher of righteousness, with seven others, when He brought a flood upon the world of the ungodly;"* The geography of our planet paints a clear picture of a universal flood.

Thank you Lord, that you preserved life, You have given us the rainbow as a reminder of the covenant given Noah, that You will never cause another universal flood, Amen!

June 19: Day 170

GOD OF THE HARVEST

*Psalm 104:14 "**He causes the grass to grow for the cattle**,*
And vegetation for the labor of man,
So that he may bring forth food from the earth,"

We can only plant, fertilize, and perhaps cultivate in hope that we will receive a crop. It is our Creator God that has the ultimate control over what grows and how much fruit we will receive. We have no control over the rains or what catastrophes will lay waste all our efforts. We are completely at the mercy of God regarding our livelihood. Verse 15 continues to express God's handiwork as he is responsible for the wine, the food, the trees and all that we need to build and live. God as creator knows His creation as he alone can provide the means to our livelihood.

We are blessed in that we are the product of a benevolent Creator who loves us and disciplines us according to our good. He knows our needs and provides accordingly. He sends the rains, He provided the water we find in the earth to irrigate when the rains are not in the forecast. God has given us wisdom as to how we can produce much food. Our God however is the ultimate provider. He alone provides us with the land, the sun providing photosynthesis, and the minerals for fertilizer. Matthew 5:45 *"so that you may be sons of your Father who is in heaven, for He causes His sun to rise on the evil and the good, and sends rain on the righteous and the unrighteous."* Our Creator God is the source for all our provisions.

Thank you Lord, for providing for all our needs according to Your great mercy, Amen!

June 20: Day 171

GOD'S UNIQUE SOLAR SYSTEM

*Psalm 104:19 "**He made the moon for the seasons**;*
The sun knows the place of its setting."

The structure of the Solar System plays a very significant role in protecting and preserving the Earth. All the bodies in our solar system play a function in our livelihood. The moon makes the seasons as well as stirring the tides that prevents stagnation and death in the oceans. The sun gives us the light of day as well as the photosynthesis for our crops. The outer planets absorb the major collisions of asteroids and comets. Such is the example of Shoemaker Levy 9 that struck Jupiter back in 1994. God has created for us a safe habitat for our survival.

All the heavenly bodies play a strategic role in the preservation of life on planet earth. God alone set up the movements of our solar system. He knows the movement of the planets and their purpose. Our planet Earth is placed in the most strategic location giving us sufficient heat and light to survive. All the movements of the sun and the moon provides us with a reference for time in days, weeks, months, and years. Jeremiah 31:35 *"Thus says the LORD, who gives the sun for light by day And the fixed order of the moon and the stars for light by night, What stirs up the sea so that its waves roar; The LORD of hosts is His name:"* All the heavenly bodies have a purpose, to protect life on the world, and to show His glory.

Thank you Lord, for the protection of our planet by the structure of our Solar System. We know that You are the ultimate protection of our habitat Earth, Amen!

June 21: Day 172

GOD PROVIDES
FOR ALL HIS CREATION

*Psalm 104:26 "There the ships move along, **And Leviathan, which
You have formed to sport in it.**"*

The question of who or what is Leviathan is still a matter of debate. In any event, it is a powerful sea creature of some sort. Extinct or not, again we can only speculate. God however is its Creator. Verse 27: "*They all wait for You To give them their food in due season.*" Verse 28 *You give to them, they gather it up; You open Your hand, they are satisfied with good.*" These verses clearly state that God provides for all life in its due season. God here is intimately connected to all His living creatures.

All of God's creation is dependent upon Him. His creations are interdependent upon each other; as all living things are connected and need each other for life. We raise livestock and many other species of animals for food. We depend upon insects to cross pollinate our crops for our produce. God has provided for all our needs through the vast assortment of living things we depend upon for our livelihood. Psalm 36:6 *"Your righteousness is like the mountains of God; Your judgments are like a great deep, O LORD, You preserve man and beast."* Our Creator God cares for all His creatures.

Thank you Lord, for the variety of life and for the provisions You have given to make life flourish throughout Your diverse creation, Amen!

June 22: Day 173

GOD ALONE GIVES LIFE

*Psalm 104:29-30 "You take away their spirit, they expire And return to their dust. **You send forth Your Spirit, they are created**; And You renew the face of the ground."*

God's Holy spirit is a direct influence on life and death. God is both the giver and terminator of life. He holds the keys to life in His hands, He gives and He takes away. Life is not an accident according to the Bible. God alone is Creator and the ultimate giver of all life. Man may be able to take a life, but he is not able to create it except by procreation; the mechanism of which comes from God. Man may possess all the building blocks of life, but without God's spirit, it is no more than organic matter.

The substance of life is a mystery indeed. Science is giving us a deeper understanding of life, and how it works, but the actual spark of life itself is still a mystery. Man cannot reproduce it, we can only study it, and seek to understand its mysteries. Upon death, the Bible tells us we return to God, the giver of life. Ecclesiastes 12:7 *"then the dust will return to the earth as it was, and the spirit will return to God who gave it."* Our lives are completely in His hands. Job 1:21 *"He said, Naked I came from my mother's womb, And naked I shall return there. The LORD gave and the LORD has taken away; Blessed by the name of the LORD."* God both gives, and takes away life, He is the arbiter of all life.

Thank you Lord for the precious gift of life you have given to each person. May we possess it with fear and trembling as we seek to honor You with each and every moment, Amen!

June 23: Day 174

GOD IS REVEALED THROUGH HIS CREATION

Psalm 105:5 "Remember His wonders which He has done, His marvels and the judgments uttered by His mouth,"

We are admonished to remember that God is the Creator. We are commanded not to forget the God of creation and His mighty works. The wonders of His creation become more marvelous as science reveals the extreme complexities of our world. The complex sequencing of the DNA protein; the finely tuned Laws that govern the universe and its design stagger the imagination. We live at a time in history where the mysteries of the universe are being peeled away, revealing even a greater mystery that defies our understanding. God is not yet finished revealing Himself to mankind.

God is continually revealing Himself to the world through the mysteries uncovered by science. Discoveries in DNA reveal complexity to rival or even exceed a functional city, with design, manufacturing, reproduction, transportation, and assembly. Our bodies are a marvel of design, able to heal themselves from many injuries and ailments. Many of the machines we use, and take for granted were a product of Intelligent Design such as the airplane wings, patterned after birds. The precise movement of time is driven by the motion of the heavenly bodies. We live in an extremely complex world full of design and wonder. Job 12: 7-8 *"But now ask the beasts and let them teach you; And the birds of the heavens, and let them tell you. Or speak to the earth, and let it teach you; and let the fish of the sea declare to you."* God has revealed His power and majesty through the many wonders of His creation.

Thank you Lord, for the marvels of Your magnificent Creation. We give you praise for the power and might You possess in creating us and the world we live in, Amen!

June 24: Day 175

REMEMBER TO ALWAYS
GIVE THANKS

Psalm 107:15 "Let them give thanks to the LORD for His lovingkindness,
And for His wonders to the sons of men*!"*

We are to be thankful for God's provisions. We are to remember God's works and to give thanks for the many provisions God has provided. The wonders of the heavens are a constant reminder to give thanks and praise to God for all He has done through His creative hand; even for providing all that sustains us from day to day.

We are called to be thankful for everything. We have been blessed with all the provisions necessary for life. God has provided a sustainable habitat, our earth; we have the means to produce food from the ground, and animals for food and sustenance. God has provided for our clothing and shelter. From the earth we have the resources to create medicines, raw materials to build great cities, and roads, for transportation for all the things we have need of. We have family for support and encouragement. For all those in the body of Christ we have His Church for prayer and support. Most important is the promise of eternal life through God's Son, communicated through the revelation of His Word. I Thessalonians 5:18 *"in everything give thanks; for this is God's will for you in Christ Jesus."* Give thanks to God for giving us His written word as a reminder of His lovingkindness toward us.

Thank you Lord, for the many blessings we continually receive from Your gracious hands, Amen!

June 25: Day 176

THE GOD OF NATURE

*Psalm 107:25 "**For He spoke and raised up a stormy wind**, Which lifted up the waves of the sea."*

A reminder not only is God the source of all creation, He is the One in charge of nature. Mother Nature, a term used to express God's creation, is at His command. God still speaks today through the power of His spoken word. According to this passage, God controls the events of nature for His purpose. He is in control over every aspect of this world, even as He rules over all the laws of nature. Since God is the creator of these Laws, it would be expected that He would also be the governor over nature for His ultimate purpose.

We are sometimes reminded during times of turbulent weather that God is ultimately in control of all aspects of our planet, even the weather. When windstorms affect our lives, or tornadoes destroy property; such events are called 'acts of God'. These are out of man's control, and reminders that God is the one who rules over our world. We are only passersby who are subject to the winds of God's ultimate provisions and grace.

God's ultimate control of the forces of nature is reaffirmed in Psalm 107:29. *"**He caused the storm to be still, So that the waves of the sea were hushed**."* God demonstrates His power over all the laws of nature for His purpose. The New Testament attributes this same power to Jesus. Approximately 1,000 years later, Jesus demonstrated the same control over the waves and the sea. Even though there are times of inclement weather; we must remember that all things work together for good. Matthew 8:27 *"The men were amazed, and said, "What kind of a man is this, that even the winds and the sea obey Him."* We can take courage that our Creator God is in full command of all the elements of nature.

Thank you Father, that You alone are in control of this world, keep us safe in the shelter of your mighty hand, Amen!

June 26: Day 177

I REMEMBER

*Psalm 111: 4 "**He has made His wonders to be remembered;**"*

The Canadian French have a great quote: "Je me Souviens" (I remember) As each generation passes its knowledge forward, God too presents a reminder to His people and later on to the entire world that He is the One responsible for the wonders of creation. We are the benefactors of His creative power. We must keep in mind that all we see is a product of God's design. The Intelligent Design inference is not about some unknown entity, it points clearly to the Creator Himself.

The Bible gives us several examples of our need to remember. Joshua 1:8 challenges us to meditate on His word continually that we may do all that He commands us. Joshua chapter 4 gives the account of The Children of Israel when they entered the Promised Land and were commanded to place pillars as a reminder to their children of what God did for them in bringing them out of the land of Egypt to their own land. The phylactery (a small box placed on the forehead) was another example given to the Jews to meditate and remember God's word and promises. Finally, we are challenged to put God's word in our hearts. Psalm 119:11 *"Your word I have treasured in my heart, That I may not sin against You."* We must remember the promises of God lest we forget and go our own way. Deuteronomy 8:18 *"But you shall remember the LORD your God, for it is He who is giving you power to make wealth, that He may confirm His covenant which He swore to your fathers, as it is this day"* Read and meditate on God's word daily, lest we forget.

We thank you Lord for all Your mighty deeds today and every day, Amen!

June 27: Day 178

GOD OF THE CHILDREN OF ISRAEL

*Psalm 111: 6 **"He has made known to His people the power of His works**, in giving them the heritage of the nations."*

The heritage of the Jewish people is the wealth and posterity of all nations. Down through the course of history, we are witnesses to the extraordinary achievements of the Jewish people. They have been successful in every era of history; this is one reason they have been so persecuted. This also explains why the nation of Israel was restored following the chaotic destruction of millions of Jews. Despite its tragic loses, Israel has become a successful economic power in the Middle East. Even though we have not witnessed the complete fulfillment of this promise in our time and age; it becomes an increasingly distinct possibility in the future as the Jewish race has accumulated an enormous economic base. In the midst of the wars and conflicts in the nation of Israel, the Jewish people are continuing to be successful, economically, technologically, and culturally.

We are the beneficiaries of the Jewish people and many of their accomplishments. They are this day and economic stronghold in the Middle East. All nations benefit from many of their accomplishments. Nearly a third of all Noble Prize winners are Jewish. Their heritage of diligence, hard work and devotion to their people has given them the ability to create and build in the midst of conflict and oppression. The greatest gift from the Jewish people is our Messiah, Jesus. It is His death on the cross that has won our freedom from the oppression of sin for everyone who accepts it. Genesis 22:18 *"In your seed all the nations of the earth shall be blessed. Because you have obeyed My voice."* God has given all who seek Him a Christian heritage that cannot be taken away.

Thank you Lord, for the blessings of the Jewish people, most important, is the gift of Your beloved Son Jesus, Amen!

June 28: Day 179

GOD OF JUSTICE

*Psalm 111:7 "**The works of His hands are truth and justice:** All His precepts are sure."*

The God of creation is not only powerful, but He is also just and true. His perfection translates into perfect justice. We do not see justice among men. We see violence and destruction along with injustices. We can know God for what He has said about Himself. We are witnesses to His power. We may disagree with His methods, but who are we to disagree. God will bring justice regardless of what men can do or think. He destroyed entire nations because of their evil societies. God is perfect in justice, all evil will be accounted for. If what He states is truth, everything promised to the Jews and to the nations will come to pass. A perfect Creator God will bring about perfect Justice.

God has placed within the heart of every man and woman a sense of justice. We all want Justice to be given when we or someone is the victim of a crime. C.S. Lewis expressed it as "a sense of oughtness" that God put inside of us. Our God is so exact in His justice, He is able account for every sin committed by Man. Proverbs 15:3 *"The eyes of the LORD are in every place, Watching the evil and the good."* God in His perfect justice not only keeps an exact account of all wrongs, He is also the one who satisfies the debt owed for all our injustices. His only Son, Jesus paid that debt on the cross. Deuteronomy 32:4 *"The Rock! His work is perfect, For all His ways are just; God of faithfulness and without injustice, Righteous and upright is He."* Our Creator God is able to right every wrong, right down to the last letter of the Law.

Thank you Lord, that you are the perfect arbiter of justice in our world, and for paying the debt we owed to You, Amen!

June 29: Day 180
ETERNAL COVENANTS

Psalm 111: 8 "They are upheld forever and ever; They are performed in truth and uprightness."

What God promised will come to pass. He will uphold His word for all time and all eternity. God's eternal attributes are on display. Verse 9b states *"He has ordained His covenant forever; Holy and awesome is His name."* God's Covenant will be fulfilled in time. For God, time is not a factor hindering Him from keeping His promises. His Covenant with the people of Israel will eventually be completely satisfied.

We are reminded in Deuteronomy 7:9 that God will keep His Covenant with mankind for many generations. *"Know therefore that the LORD your God, He is God, the faithful God, who keeps His covenant and His lovingkindness to a thousandth generation with those who love Him and keep His commandments;"* Since a new generation comes around about every 20 to 30 years; this earth has seen less than 400 generations. God is eternal, and He will be faithful to keep all His Covenants through all generations.

Jesus Christ is the fulfillment of many of these covenants. The Noahic Covenant, and the symbol of the rainbow reminding us, that God will never flood the entire earth again. The three most prominent Covenants are and will be fulfilled by God's son Jesus who is the fulfillment of the Abrahamic Covenant *"The seed of woman"*. The Davidic Covenant, promising that a descendant of David will always be on the Throne, and the most important; The New Covenant of the blood, expressed in our current communion, remembering the sacrifice of Jesus Christ on the cross. Isaiah 54:10 *"For the mountains may be removed and the hills may shake, But My lovingkindness will not be removed from you, And My covenant of peace will not be shaken Says the LORD who has compassion on you."* God is faithful to keep all His promises now and into eternity.

Thank you Lord, that you are eternal, and faithful to keep all your covenants with your people through all the ages of eternity, Amen!

June 30: Day 181

GOD IS ABLE TO SAVE

Psalm 115:3 "But our God is in the heavens;
He does whatever He pleases."

God is restricted by nothing except His own character. God cannot act in conflict with whom He is. His purposes will be accomplished despite men and their desires. God's existence is far above man, He is in the heavens; a realm man cannot reach. We are bound to the physical reality of this universe; we are privileged observers of God's power and grace. Men however has abused much of the grace given them.

Even though God has the power to do whatever He chooses; He is the creator of the universe. He is however limited in what He is willing to do. I Timothy 2:4 tells us that God desires the salvation of all men. Yet, it seems so few seek God, the narrow gate in Matthew 7:13 keeps many from entering. It would appear God is unable, or unwilling to save all men, even though Christ's crucifixion was sufficient to pay the debt for the entire world. God acted in history on behalf of all men to bring the way of salvation to all. It would appear, God is unwilling to force men to accept His offer of grace; rather He turned the decision of repentance back to man. May we learn to trust God with our earthly life and eternity, He is willing to save every man. Psalm 78:41-42 *"Again and again they tempted God, And pained the Holy One of Israel, They did not remember His power, The day when He redeemed them from the adversary,"* God is willing and able to save anyone who comes to Him.

Thank you Lord, that you are all powerful and able to do as You please by Your power, the same power that is able to save us, Amen!

July 1: Day 182

GOD OUR LANDLORD

*Psalm 115:16 "**The heavens are the heavens of the LORD, But the earth He has given to the sons of men.**"*

Earth is given to men as a possession. God has restricted His work out of respect to His promises. Earth is man's domain to use and prosper. It is God's desire that Man is a success. However, God is still the Landlord. We will one day be held accountable for what we do with the possessions we have been given. We are given a stewardship as we enter a tag-team relationship with our Creator.

God is all powerful, but He limited Himself in respect to our fallen world. When He gave Man the responsibility to rule over His earth, he relinquished some of His authority, having given it to Man. We then fell into sin, causing a curse to enter our world, leaving all creation in a state of decay. Roman 8:22 tells us: "*For we know that the whole creation groans and suffers the pains of childbirth together until now.*" God is now actively working to do the impossible, restoring Man into a right relationship with Him. Mark 10:27 "*Looking at them, Jesus said, With people it is impossible, but not with God; for all things are possible with God.*" We have been given a stewardship to care for this world, and to use all its resources for God's glory.

Thank you Lord, for our world and possessions You gave us to use. May we learn to honor You with all You have given us, Amen!

July 2: Day 183

ON TO ETERNITY

Psalm 115:18 "From this time forth and forever, Praise the LORD!"

Time is not a factor for God. He lives beyond the scope of time and space. Men are restricted in what they can know or understand. We are admonished to give praise to the Lord. The universe and all its wonders were designed in order to help us understand the power and grandeur of almighty God. It is all His creation that points to Him. Man cannot understand the power of God, except though His wondrous creation. Man will from this time forward and on to eternity praise the God of Creation. Man's existence had a beginning, just as His larger creation had a beginning. Man, however, is a creation, made in the image of God. All those who call upon God will have an existence that will continue on into eternity. Many promises are given man that he has a bright and glorious future extending into a spiritual reality forever.

In this life, we can get caught in the doldrums of routine and forget that we are headed for an eternity with our Creator. The cares of this life are a distraction from the realities of who we are in Christ. Eternity stands before us as we travel through this trouble laden life. But God has given us the hope of eternity and the pleasures of a life with Him forever. We must not lose focus as to why we are on this earth. We must come to know God's Son, to draw nearer to Him daily, and to help others find their way to Him; eternity is our destination. Colossians 3:2-3 *"Set your mind on the things above, not on the things that are on earth. For you have died and your life is hidden with Christ in God."* Let us give praise to our Creator God daily for the wonders of life, and the grandeur of His creation.

Thank you Lord, for the promise of eternal life through the sacrifice of your Son. May we learn to place our focus on the eternal realities before us, Amen!

July 3: Day 184
GOD'S CORNERSTONE

Psalm 118:22 "The stone which the builders rejected has become the chief corner stone."

The symbolism within this verse reverberates through recorded history. The God of the universe, responsible for all that we see is rejected and held in disrepute. The cornerstone of any structure is often considered the most important part of the building. Even as the creator is relegated to insignificance among men who knew no better than to reject the one responsible for all of God's creation, thereby rejecting the most important part, His Son. As the previous chapter indicated, God's completed work will one day be revealed.

Christ should be the cornerstone of our lives, as He has redeemed all those who have called upon Him to be saved. The Bible gives us many examples of who Christ is in relationship to what He has done for us. He is the Door to Life, the only way to God. He is the Bread of life, the nourishment that gives us eternal life. He is the Light of the World; He shows all mankind the way to God through His sacrificial death. We would do well to acknowledge Him as the Corner Stone of God's creation. We will one day realize the true importance of Jesus position as the most important part of God's creation. John 14:6 *"Jesus said to him, I am the way, and the truth, and the life: no one comes to the Father but through Me."* Let Jesus Christ become the corner stone in each of our lives.

Thank you Lord, You are our cornerstone, the truth, and the only door to our heavenly Father, Amen!

July 4: Day 185

GOD MADE US FOR A REASON

*Psalm 119:73 "**Your hands made me and fashioned me**; Give me understanding that I may learn Your commandments."*

God is personified (Your hands) as this reference points directly to the existence of man as part of God's creative plan. The prayer of the Psalmist is to understand our purpose in this life. We must first come to Know God and know His commandments. Along with Knowing God, we must learn to keep His commandments. We are designed for obedience, yet Man continually resists His call to enter into fellowship with God. Man often seeks his own way and his own understanding of reality. This will only result in futility.

We are continually challenged to seek God with all our hearts. We were created for a much higher calling than just the affairs of this life. We were created to enter a relationship with God, and to become ambassadors for His Son. II Corinthians 5:20 states: *"Therefore, we are ambassadors for Christ, as through God were making an appeal through us; we beg you on behalf of Christ, be reconciled to God."* Along with being a witness for God, we were created to serve a higher purpose. We must find that purpose and pursue it with all diligence. Psalm 100: 2-3 *"Serve the LORD with gladness; Come before Him with joyful singing. Know that the LORD Himself is God; **It is He who has made us,** and not we ourselves."* We must discover and learn the gifts and abilities God has given us to help in our witness and service to others.

Lord grant us understanding that we might learn to keep Your commandments. You created us that we might walk in obedience to Your Word, and to bear witness and serve others, Amen!

July 5: Day 186

OUR PLANET HAS A PURPOSE TO FULFILL

Psalm 119:90 "Your faithfulness continues throughout all generations; ***You established the earth, and it stands."***

What God has called into existence will stand as long as He desires. The Psalmist recognizes God's sovereignty over the earth. Psalm 119:91 continues to examine God's absolute power over His creation. *"They stand this day according to Your ordinances. For all things are Your servants."* Man is ultimately subject to God's absolute authority. We are not able to answer the difficult questions of life, why bad things happen to good people. We do know however that all things will result in ultimate good.

God's power is continually evident in the beauty and majesty of our world, along with the immense grandeur of the Universe. This world will not be destroyed or pass away until all God's work in the hearts of men is completed. This world, our Earth was put here for a reason, and nothing will happen to this planet until God's work is accomplished. God will establish both a physical and spiritual kingdom on earth in which He will sit on the throne. The angel of God spoke to Mary in Luke 1:31 *"And behold, you will conceive in your womb and bear a son, and you shall name Him Jesus. He will be great and will be called the son of the Most High; and the Lord God will give Him the throne of His father David."* This Kingdom will be established here on Earth and into eternity. Luke 1:33 *"and He will reign over the house of Jacob forever, and His kingdom will have no end."* This earth will remain until all God's work is completed. We have the promise, God will establish a New Earth that will never pass away.

Thank you Lord, for establishing our world. You are the guardian who preserves this world until Your work is completed, Amen!

July 6: Day 187

GOD'S TESTIMONIES
ARE TRUE

Psalm 119: 152 "Of old I have known from Your testimonies, ***That You*** *have founded them forever."*

The book of Psalms gives us another insightful look into God's creative power. These testimonies include His commandments and all the ordinances given to man that he may have a purpose filled life. God did not leave us without a standard to follow that would give us success. He alone is the author of Truth; the arbiter of right and wrong. He gave the direction and path that we must seek to follow in order to enter into a relationship with Him that will last forever.

If we are to be successful in life today, we must become aware of the standards and testimonies God has put before us in His Holy Word. When men would challenge us as to whose truth we live by, we must confess, we have no truth in ourselves. God is the only truth or standard we have. He is the Creator and Author of all truth, and the only pathway to God. We would do well to observe and listen to those standards or testimonies. I Peter 1:25 *"BUT THE WORD OF THE LORD ENDURES FOREVER." And this is the word which was preached to you."* We have a standard of how to live our lives, established and fixed forever; God's Holy Word is eternal.

Thank you Lord, for giving us a standard to live by that will never pass away, Amen!

July 7: Day 188

OUR GOD OUR KEEPER

Psalm 121:2 "My help comes from the LORD,
Who made heaven and earth."

The Bible is full of examples of God's willingness to come to the aid of His people. Verse two illustrates that He sustains us, keeping us from falling, Verse 3 *"He will not allow your foot to slip; He who keeps you will not slumber."* God is never asleep at the controls as He is always aware of the needs of His children. Verse 8 clarifies the name of God, not to be confused with any other. *"Our help is in the name of the LORD,* ***Who made heaven and earth****."* Our God, the creator of all things is not bound by the physics of this world. He is always there and aware of all that happens to us.

We can be confident in our God, who never sleeps, who always keeps watch over us and cares about us. He is willing and able to rescue us in times of need. God who made the heavens and the earth is powerful enough to see the entire world with all its troubles and woes. We can call upon Him at any time to help us through our difficult times. Psalm 121:8 *"The LORD will guard your going out and your coming in From this time forth and forever."* God is our constant companion, who watches over us day and night.

Thank you Lord, for always being there, even when we are unaware of the dangers, You still watch over us, Amen!

July 8: Day 189

COUNT YOUR BLESSINGS

Psalm 134:3 "May the LORD bless you from Zion,
He who made heaven and earth."

The book of Psalms reminds us: all blessings come from God; James 1:17 *"Every good thing given and every perfect gift is from above, coming down from the Father of lights, with whom there is no variation or shifting shadow."* Our God is not random, He is the God of Zion, Israel, the one and only God who made the heavens and the earth. This passage leaves no doubt as to where all our blessings come from.

If we were to sit down and actually count our many blessings, as the chorus goes: *"Count your many blessings, count them one by one."* We would have a list so long we would have an entire book and more. We take for granted so much of what we have; The air we breathe, gravity that keeps us from floating away, our pets for our joy, animals for food, plants and the trees, Most importantly, our family and friends. We have so many blessings from God, we could never make a complete list. Hebrews 6:7 *"For ground that drinks the rain which often falls on it and brings forth vegetation useful to those for whose sake it is also tilled, receives a blessing from God."* God's blessings are continuous, let us continue to give thanks to our Creator God for our daily blessings.

Thank you Father, for your many blessings. You alone are the author of this world and all the blessings we sometimes take for granted, Amen!

July 9: Day 190

GOD THROUGH ALL GENERATIONS

Psalm 135:13 "Your name, O LORD, is everlasting, Your remembrance, O LORD, through all generations."

God exists throughout all the generations life exists on earth. The Bible is a testament to God's continuous care of all those living on the planet. Our Creator God is not bound by time and space. He is always there and will always be there throughout the time this planet as we know it exists. God is also the author of time in that He created the planets and their motions (Genesis Chapter One). God existed before He created this world and all life, He will exist into eternity.

Since we Know a God who exists from eternity past, to eternity future, we are but a blip in the cosmos of time. In fact, the entire history of this world as well as this universe is a blip in comparison to the eternal existence of our Creator God. We are but grass that withers and dies, then we are gone; yet, God cares for us. I Peter 1:4 *"to obtain an inheritance which is imperishable and undefiled and will not fade away, reserved in heaven for you,"* God will always be there to see us through, and to give us an inheritance that will never fade away.

Thank you Father, that you are always there, and always will be. You are not dead, but alive, Amen!

July 10: Day 191

THE LOVING KINDNESS OF GOD IS ETERNAL

*Psalm 136:5-7 "**To Him who made the heavens with skill, To Him who spread out the earth above the waters, To Him who made the great lights.**"*

Many common themes are found in this scripture concerning God's powerful design in creation. His power to create is not limited. We continue with the reoccurring theme regarding God's creative works. Every verse ends with the same conclusion: "*For His lovingkindness is everlasting.*" His loving kindness is blended into His creative acts. Verse 4 "*To Him who alone does great wonders,*" The great lights include the sun, the moon and the stars. All of creation, our lives included reflect God's love and kindness toward us. We are the beneficiaries of His creative work.

Man was created to live and prosper on this earth, a habitat suitable for our existence. Just as we could not survive outside the atmosphere of this planet, so too, we cannot survive outside the grace and loving kindness of our heavenly Father. We are completely dependent upon His provisions provided to us through the resources of this world. I Chronicles 16:34 "*O give thanks to the LORD, for He is good; For His lovingkindness is everlasting.*" God is our great Provider, we are given everything we need to prosper and succeed in this life.

Thank you Father, for your loving kindness through all that You have created to sustain our lives. Most importantly, the grace You provided in Your Son Jesus, Amen!

July 11: Day 192

GOD CARES FOR HIS CREATION

Psalm 138:8b "Your lovingkindness, O LORD, is everlasting;
Do not forsake the works of Your hands."

God is not absent as some suppose, He cares intensely for all His creation. Even though corrupted by Man, and sin, God still cares about all His creation. He takes responsibility for His creation by restoring Man back into a right relationship with Him. The Psalmist seeks to remind God, though He needs no reminding that all His works carry a specific value. This is a prayer for God's continued support for His people and His creative work. God's creation is far too valuable to allow its demise. God's ultimate purposes will be accomplished, even if for the time being we cannot clearly see it.

We can be assured: God is not done with us yet. He is actively working at restoring Man along with all creation back into the pristine condition at creations beginning. Like the computer system that gets bogged down with corrupted programs and viruses; God is cleaning up and restoring man and all His creation to perfection again. Job 31:4 *"Does He not see my ways and number all my steps?"* God is not done with us yet; let's not lose hope.

Thank you Lord, that you have not given up on us, You still care for mankind and all Your created works, Amen!

July 12: Day 193

GOD INTIMATELY KNOWS HIS PEOPLE

Psalm 139:2 "You know when I sit down, and when I rise up; You understand my thoughts from afar. Such knowledge is too wonderful for me; It is too high, I cannot attain to it."

God knows us – He created us, He knows all about us. When we sit, and when we stand. He knows our every thought. Psalm 139:1 *"O Lord, You have searched me and known me."* We cannot obtain a full understanding of God, though God knows us fully. Just as Man is limited in his understanding, science is limited in its ability to fully explain the universe in which we live. We understand only in part, but not fully.

God knows His creation fully; He knows us intimately. We have a God who not only knows us, He understands and cares about our every need. He knows our struggles and seeks to help us through our darkest hours. Our Creator God knows us better than we know ourselves. For this reason, we must ultimately seek His presence and help. He has promised to help us in our time of need. Psalm 121:2 *"my help comes from the Lord;"* I Corinthians 13:12 *"For now we see in a mirror dimly, but then face to face; now I know in part, but then I will know fully just as I also have been fully known."* God is infinite in His knowledge; one day we will know Him in like manner.

Thank you Father God, that you know us completely, and care for our every need, Amen!

July 13: Day 194

GOD IS OMNIPRESENT

Psalm 139:8 "If I ascend to heaven, You are there; If I make my bed in Sheol, behold, You are there."

Psalm 139 Verses7-12 expands on the Character and nature of God's Omnipresence. He fills the universe and beyond, He fills all creation even to the heavens. It is hard to imagine how God can exist everywhere, Yet God gives us a hint if we examine the nature of light. I John 1:5 "*God is light, and in Him there is no darkness at all.*" Light exists in a state of subtle omnipresence. It is everywhere. We see the light from the furthest reaches of our universe. That light permeates our world every hour of every day. The light from the furthest stars, though not apparent, is still present. The sun, our closest star is overpowering in its light. Habakkuk 3:4 tells us God's "*radiance is like the sunlight,*" We can block the light with shades, but we depend upon the light of the sun for our livelihood. So too, we depend upon God who is always there, even when we don't see Him.

God's association as light can also represent His omnipotence. Light is a form of energy, and the amount of energy necessary for any object to travel the speed of light is infinite, a perfect description of God. Genesis 1 tells us God created the light on the first day of creation. God is both the creator, and essence of light. Just like the light, our God is ever present and always there, we don't always see or feel His presence, but the Bible promises that He is always with us, and sees our afflictions. God will always be there regardless of where we are. God's presence permeates the universe, showing Him to be outside of time and space.

Thank you Lord for your eternal presence that you are always there with us, Amen!

July 14: Day 195

FORMED IN HIS IMAGE

*Psalm 139:13 reads: "**For You formed my inward parts; You wove me in my mother's womb,**"*

Psalm 139:15 continues: "*My frame was not hidden from You, When I was made in secret. And skillfully wrought in the depths of the earth*;" Our God is the creator of all living things. He ordained the birthing process beginning with a single man. Then in the union between a man and woman, giving the power to pro-create. God created woman with the ability to carry a child to birth. God knows our inward parts and how they were put together. He not only knows all about our physical form in that we are a product of His design, but we are known by God in our innermost parts. Psalm 139:23 "*Search me, O God, and know my heart; Try me and know my anxious thoughts*;" God is the creator of our body, our minds, and our spirit.

We can hide nothing from our all-knowing creator God. He knows how we are put together, how we think, along with all the attitudes of our heart. He cares about His creation and most importantly, about man, His most valuable creation. We are of value to God, because we are created in His image and for His purpose. Colossians 3:9-10 "*Do not lie to one another, since you laid aside the old self with its evil practice, and have put on the new self who is being renewed to a true knowledge according to the image of the One who created him.*" We were created in God's image, and one day we will be like Him.

Thank you Lord, for creating us, that you know all about us and that you care about us, Amen!

July 15: Day 196

OUR DAYS ARE NUMBERED BEFORE WE WERE BORN

Psalm 139:16 "Your eyes have seen my unformed substance; And in Your book were all written The days that were ordained for me, When as yet there was not one of them."

Each one of us is given a certain number of days to live our life, and to accomplish all that God put before us. Our God created us to live on this world for a designated number of days. None of us are guaranteed tomorrow, but we are assured God will complete His work in us. Philippians 1:6 states: *"For I am confident of this very thing, that He who began a good work in you will perfect it until the day of Christ Jesus."* God is faithful to finish the work He started in our lives.

Since we have a specific number of days in our lifetime to work with, we need to be mindful of how we use those days. Paul tells us in Ephesians 5:16 *"Making the best use of the time, because the days are evil."* We must be wise stewards of each day given to us so as to be found faithful. Let us learn to appreciate and use each and every day constructively for God. Psalm 90:12 *"so teach us to number our days, that we may present to You a heart of wisdom."* Let us make each day count as we serve our God and others.

Thank you Lord, for today and may we be found faithful for each day you give us, Amen!

July 16: Day 197

REFLECTING ON GOD'S MIGHTY WORKS

*Psalm 143:5 "I remember the days of Old; I meditate on all Your doings; **I muse on the work of Your hands**."*

We are asked to give thought concerning God's creative works. They are meant to inspire mediation and reflection. Psalm 145:5 continues: "*On the glorious splendor of Your majesty And on Your wonderful works, I will meditate.*" The heavens are glorious in their splendor and size, man's smallness is amplified in contrast to the glories of the heavens, yet our Creator God is greater than these. Ancient man's perspective on creation pales in comparison to what we see and understand today. These verses are even more relevant than they were 3,000 years ago.

We are challenged today to give praise and honor to our Creator God. When we reflect upon the majesty of this world, and the grandeur we cannot help but be amazed. God's power and work however go well beyond His creative work. He is actively guiding and directing the affairs of man. He is conforming men and women to His image through the power of His Holy Spirit. Philippians 2:13 "*for it is God who is at work in you, both to will and to work for His good pleasure.*" As we meditate on God's works, we realize He is intimately connected to His creation both small and large. Psalm 77:11-12 "*I shall remember the deeds of the LORD; Surely I will remember Your wonders of old. I will meditate on all your work And muse on Your deeds.*" God will establish His ways in our hearts as we meditate on His word daily.

Thank you Lord, for all your works, but most of all the work You are performing in our lives, to make us more like You, Amen!

July 17: Day 198

GOD IS THE HELPER
OF THOSE IN NEED

*Psalm 146:5 ". . .whose hope is in the Lord His God, "**He who made heaven and earth**, The sea and all that is in them, Who keeps faith forever;"*

If God is powerful enough to have created heaven and earth, we should be able to depend upon His promises to be true." God is faithful to do all that He has promised; verse 7 continues: ". . . *who executes justice for the oppressed*." For all who are oppressed and distressed there is hope in the Lord God, the creator of the universe. A mighty God who is able to deliver the oppressed from the oppressor.

The Bible is full of examples of God's interaction and deliverance of the downtrodden and oppressed. Psalm 72:12 states: "*For he will deliver the needy when he cries for help, The afflicted also, and him who has no helper.*" God is the advocate of all those who are in distress; God will extend His saving grace to all who call upon Him. Romans 10:13 *"for Whoever will call on the name of the LORD will be saved."* God's arm is not so short as to save and help all those who call upon Him. God promised not only to help those in need, but to be a Father to the fatherless. Psalm 68:5 *"A father of the fatherless and a judge for the widow, Is God in His holy habitation."* Our Creator God is faithful to keep His promises.

Thank you Lord, the one who created the heavens and the earth. You continue to watch and care for your people. We thank you that You are forever faithful, Amen!

July 18: Day 199

GOD RESTORES SIGHT

*Psalm 146:8 "**The LORD opens the eyes of the blind**;*

For God to heal, He must understand the ailments. Only God who created the world and all life in it can truly heal. It is by the grace of God that man even discovers remedies found in God's creation. All the medicines we discover are only discoveries that have existed since the dawn of time. We are only now learning the healing effects of God's provisions found in nature. The God who heals, can also restore and preserve those He deems faithful for eternity.

Our Creator God is able to help not only physically, but also spiritually. Elisha's servant was unable to see the army of the Lord protecting Him until Elisha prayed to God. 2 Kings 6:17 "*Then Elisha prayed and said, O LORD, I pray, open his eyes that he may see. And the LORD opened the servants' eyes and he saw; and behold, the mountain was full of horses and Chariots of fire all around Elisha.*" God will open the spiritual eyes of anyone who calls upon Him. Mark 10:52 "*And Jesus said to him, Go your faith has made you well. Immediately he regained his sight and began following Him on the road.*" God alone gives sight, both physically and spiritually.

Thank you Lord, for opening our eyes to see and understand Your saving grace, Amen!

July 19: Day 200

GOD IS OMNISCIENT

Psalm 147:4 "God knows all the stars by name."

God's omniscience is revealed in this biblical cosmology. The God who created the universe is intimately connected with His creation. It would seem rather mundane to name stars that have little impact upon this earth and the affairs of mankind. But according to the Biblical text, God is connected to every aspect of His creation. His concern for the stars is a small indicator of his profound interest and desire to bring His entire creation back under His complete Lordship. God's knowledge of what the creation was before the Fall would seem to fuel an urgent desire to restore it to its former state. Much like the restoration of an infected computer system. God knows all His creation and is in the process of restoring it.

The number of stars in the universe is so large, it is hard to comprehend such a number, yet God knows each one by name; even more astounding, He created each one. Our God knows us completely, down to our inner most thoughts. Romans 8:27 *"and He who searches the hearts knows what the mind of the spirit is, because He intercedes for the saints according to the will of God."* God knows everything about us, where we are and what we are doing. God desires our fellowship and seeks us to enter a relationship with Him. How God can do this for every person on earth is truly astounding. Luke 12:6-7 *"Are not five sparrows sold for two cents? Yet not one of them is forgotten before God. Indeed, the very hairs of your head are all numbered, do not fear; you are more valuable than many sparrows."* God knows His creation, from the vast universe to the smallest living creature.

Thank you Lord that you know all your creation, including us, and that everything is under your control, Amen!

July 20: Day 201

POWER IN GOD'S WORD

*Psalm 148:1-6 "**For He commanded and they were created.**"*

The power of the word sometimes eludes us when we assume words are only audio. The impact of words however can be positive or negative in how they affect people. For God, His words carry meaning and immediate results. His creative words carried power well beyond our ability to grasp. We can only see the outcome in the case of creation. We have no means of deciphering the means by which God created, or how his commands resulted in the complexities of the universe or life; only that His words carried tremendous power. Romans 4:17b confirms this truth: "*. . . God, who gives life to the dead and calls into being that which does not exist.*"

Even the words of Jesus commanded obedience from the wind and the rains when Jesus spoke. Matthew 8:27 "*The men were amazed, and said, 'What kind of man is this, that even the winds and the sea obey Him?'*" When God speaks, things happen, His control over all creation is absolute. God's Word means something. His written or inspired Word is our guide to life and success, we would be wise to listen to it. Romans 10:17 "*So faith comes from hearing and hearing by the word of Christ.*" All of God's promises in His Word are trustworthy. I Thessalonians 1:5 "*for our gospel did not come to you in word only, but also in power and in the Holy Spirit and with full conviction; just as you know what kind of men we proved to be among you for your sake.*" The power of God's word was sufficient to create all things, including the promise of eternal life.

Thank you Lord, that you gave us your creation though the power of your word, and for giving us eternal life through the inspiration of your written Word, Amen!

July 21: Day 202

REJOICE IN OUR MAKER

*Psalm 149:2 "Let Israel be glad in his **Maker**"*

Our very existence should be a cause for Joy. The focus on Israel serves as a reminder to the Jewish people of their special place in God's creative order. Without their Maker God, they would have no special place in history. They would not be unique, and their culture and festivals would have no special meaning. Israel is blessed because it is from the seed of their father Abraham that God brought His Son Jesus into recorded history to redeem the world.

God is faithful in preserving the Jewish people through the course of history. Even in the midst of suffering and persecution, they were protected by God. All the Jewish festivals served to remind the Jewish people and even Christians today of the faithfulness of God. He will keep guard over His people to preserve and protect. We have great cause to be thankful and have joy for God's mighty works and His mercy toward all, both Jew and Gentile. Psalm 81: 1 *"Sing for joy to God our strength; Shout joyfully to the God of Jacob."* The faithfulness of our Creator God should bring us joy, gladness and praise.

Thank you Lord, for the celebrations both Jewish and Christian You have given us to remember Your faithfulness and protection. You created us, You sustain us, and You alone will bring us home, into Your presence, Amen!

PROVERBS

References to God as Creator from the wisest man to ever live. Solomon and the latter writers of Proverbs presents us with at least *seven* direct references to God's creative power.

July 22: Day 203

ALL WISDOM COMES FROM GOD

Proverbs 1:23 "Turn to my reproof, Behold, I will pour out my spirit on you; I will make my words known to you."

King Solomon, according to the biblical text is the wisest man ever to live. He was able to discern the intricacies of life in many diverse ways. Solomon gives us many specific texts regarding God's creative work. He gives credit to God along with some insights into His creative ability. Wisdom is an intricate part of that creative process. An all-knowing God alone would have the resources to assemble the complexities of the human body. In addition, an all-powerful God would be a necessary part of the universe we see today. A chance scenario can only operate with blind faith; the irony of this is completely opposite of the current accepted position of secular science.

The world we live in, and all the life it sustains, cannot be a product of blind random processes. In Proverbs 2:6 we read: "*For the LORD gives wisdom; From His mouth come knowledge and understanding.*" Solomon gives the origins of his wisdom to God alone. He is the One who proves and corrects our understanding if we will seek it. God will give us His Spirit and His word to help us understand the world we live in. 2 Peter 1:21 "*...no prophecy was ever made by an act of human will, but men moved by the Holy Spirit spoke from God.*" Our God reveals truth and corrects our wrongs.

Thank you Lord, for Your gentle corrective hand, for Your revelation of wisdom, available to everyone who seeks it, Amen!

July 23: Day 204

GOD'S WISDOM

Proverbs 3:19-20 **"The LORD by wisdom founded the earth, By understanding He established the heavens,** *and by His knowledge the depths were broken up and the skies drip with dew."*

The book of Proverbs brings us into clear view of wisdom's part in the creation of our world. Our world functions as it does because someone knew how to build it. The intricacies of the biosphere we live in transcends the minds of men. Both attempts to create a sustainable biosphere sealed off from the world failed (Biospheres I & II located in Arizona). Our world was perfectly oriented to support all life through its diverse complexity.

We have a living and natural biosphere, because someone knew how to build it. All the elements necessary to create our cities, to sustain our wellbeing were given us by our Maker. God gives us a moderate climate, the provisions of rain and sun to support us. God gives us more than enough diversity to sustain life on this fragile planet. God alone understands how complex this world is, Not only is the world created to sustain life, it is a habitat to an incredibly diverse array of life. All living things have a purpose in supporting each other; without this diversity of life, we could not exist. Genesis 1:31 *"God saw all that He had made, and behold, it was very good, And there was evening and there was morning the sixth day."* God's infinite wisdom was sufficient to create our universe and the wonderful diversity of life.

Thank you Lord, for the extremely complex universe, and habitat You created for our wellbeing, Amen!

July 24: Day 205

GOD GIVES GRACE

Proverbs 3:34 tells us: "Though He scoffs at the scoffers, **Yet He gives grace to the afflicted***."*

Our God is above His creation. God is able to grant grace and kindness to whomever He wishes. From this passage we learn that God takes special interest in those who have suffered the most. Both Old and New Testaments give us many examples of God showing kindness to those who have suffered the most. The story of Lazarus is just one example (Luke 16). In contrast, those who often have privilege, or the most affluent, are the ones who scoff. Wealth often distracts one from being dependent upon God and His grace. Riches give a false sense of security and self-dependence. We don't realize, we all are still in need of God. Revelation 3:17 *"Because you say, 'I am rich, and have become wealthy, and have need of nothing.' And you do not know that you are wretched and miserable and poor and blind and naked,"*

Everyone on this planet depends upon God's grace to survive. Even those with the most possessions have the same need for grace and forgiveness. We cannot save ourselves; as a result, many who have the good things in life, resist God's extended grace. Knowledge brings the same barrier, the most educated often believe they can figure out the grand scheme of the universe and life. Even through God has granted us the foundations for science and truth, many seek to interpret our reality to fit their beliefs, outside the knowledge of God. Hebrews 4:16 *"Therefore let us draw near with confidence to the throne of grace, so that we may receive mercy and find grace to help in time of need."* God's grace will extend to all who honestly seek Him.

Thank you Lord for caring about the most needy and for extending Your saving grace to all mankind, both rich and poor, Amen!

July 25: Day 206

GOD SEES ALL OUR WAYS

Proverbs 5:21 "For the ways of a man are before the eyes of the LORD, And He watches all his paths."

Our God sees everything, and He is intimately connected to His creation (a consistent theme). The omnipotence of God is revealed concerning His people, and His creation. He knows us completely. He sees all our actions, and all things are considered. Our God who cares about us is not interested in our destruction, but rather our redemption. John 3:17 *"For God did not send the Son into the world to judge the world, but that the world might be saved through Him."* God knows us, He also knows our needs, and our greatest need is to know Him.

Our God who knows all things, and sees all things desires that we seek Him. Because God sees our needs, He has opened up a way for all men who seek Him, to bring every need before Him in prayer. Matthew 7:7 *"Ask, and it will be given to you; seek, and you will find; knock, and it will be opened to you."* Our God who knows everything about us is willing to forgive us of all our wrongs. Proverbs 15:3 *"The eyes of the LORD are in every place, Watching the evil and the good."* Let's not disappoint the One who sees, yet seeks our greatest good.

Thank you Lord that you know our innermost needs, and that You have made a way to restore us to a right relationship with You, Amen!

July 26: Day 207

GOD'S WISDOM CREATED

Proverbs 8: 23 explains: "Before His works of old. From everlasting I was established, From the beginning, from the earliest times of the earth."

Proverbs 8 gives us some insights into God's creative power. Wisdom was at the very heart of God's creative character, enabling Him to accomplish all His creative works. Wisdom was an integral part of God's ability to design with great complexity, diversity, and detail. Wisdom was always a part of God's creative design abilities. Verse 24 continues, when there was nothing, there was Wisdom, with God accompanying the creative process. The term 'Wisdom' in the Hebrew is defined by the word '*Hokmah* המקוה' meaning both a knowledgeable and skilled worker. Our God is a wise Master builder who knows His craft, creating an incredibly complex universe.

We do not build something without first designing what we want it to look like. We need some knowledge of how it is supposed to work, and what it is to accomplish. In God's case, He was not only building a world, but a universe. The universe, it seems was designed to reveal His power; while the world was designed to support a vast diversity of life. While all these are extremely complex, their ultimate design was to create an environment suitable for mankind to thrive. Colossians 2:2-3 *"that their hearts may be encouraged, having been knit together in love, and attaining to all the wealth that comes from the full assurance of understanding, resulting in a true knowledge of God's mystery, that is, Christ Himself, in whom are hidden all the treasures of wisdom and knowledge."* Our Creator God is the source of all wisdom and knowledge.

Thank you Lord, that you are our wise master building, You do all things well. Grant us the tools of knowledge and wisdom that we may serve one another, Amen!

July 27: Day 208

GOD'S DESIGN IS INTELLIGENT

*Proverbs 8:27-29 : "**when He stablished the heavens, I was there, When He inscribed a circle on the face of the deep, When He made firm the skies above, When the springs of the deep became fixed, When He set for the sea its boundary so that the water would not transgress His command.**"*

Wisdom was the essential element of God's creative process. Proverbs 8:27-29 relates the following events to Wisdom. All the elemental structures that hold our world and our universe together, were a product of God's creative power. The order or fine tuning we see in the universe and all life, is a direct result of God's wisdom and creative power. The Father worked together with His Son in this marvelous act of creation.

As we examine the vastness of the universe, and the extreme complexities of life with all its interdependent diversity, we can better appreciate God's creative power. He is indeed above all things, sustaining and preserving our world for an ultimate purpose. Our world is masterfully designed, it sustains us, it provides for all our needs, and it gives us a beautiful platform from which we can examine and explore the universe. God has gifted man with the ability to explore, develop and build society of intricate complexity because we inhabit a very beautiful creation. Hebrews 1:2 *"in these last days has spoken to us in His Son, whom He appointed heir of all things, through whom also He made the world."*

Thank you Lord, You have created such a beautiful world, with all its complexities working perfectly together, Amen!

July 28: Day 209

MASTER WORKMAN

Proverbs 8:29-31 "**When He marked out the foundations of the earth;** *Then I was beside Him, as a master workman; And I was daily His delight, Rejoicing always before Him, Rejoicing in the world, His earth, And having my delight in the sons of men.*"

We continue to examine Wisdom and its role in the creation of the world. Proverbs 8:29-31 displays the close working relationship between Wisdom and God. Wisdom was more than a tool, but a foreman or work manager who oversaw the process and evaluated the quality of the work. The results being good from His response being delighted; similar to the scene in Genesis 1 where God declared His work 'good'.

The relationship between Wisdom and the person of Jesus Christ becomes more apparent when we examine this text. John 1:3 emphasizes this relationship between Jesus and His Father in the creation of the world "*All things came into being through Him*". Jesus is here working alongside His Father giving insight and instructions, as He is forming the world and His master work, the creation of Man. We are the essential part of God's master plan of creation. The idea that Jesus was a carpenter and a builder of physical structures is implied in Mark 6:3 "*Is not this the carpenter, the son of Mary, and brother of James and Joses and Judas and Simon?*" Jesus' role as a Master builder takes on many forms both Spiritual and Physical. John 14:3 "*If I go and prepare a place for you. I will come again and receive you to Myself, that where I am there you may be also.*" Jesus is indeed the Master builder.

Thank you Jesus, for your part in the creation of the world, and for the promise of a new creation to come, Amen!

July 29: Day 210

GOD OUR MAKER CARES ABOUT THE POOR

*Proverbs 14:31 "He who oppresses the poor taunts his **Maker**, But he who is gracious to the needy honors Him."*

Our Creator God is a God of compassion who cares about the needs of the poor and downtrodden. God will defend those who are oppressed. He cares for each or us, but those who have the greater needs, God expects us to reach out and meet those needs. Those who make life more difficult for the lowly will be in conflict with their Maker.

May we seek opportunity to reach out with compassion to those with greater needs. Even when each of us is at a low point in our lives, God will raise up others to bring meals, or assist us in a task, or simply to pray for us. God will prompt us to reach out to meet the needs of others because He cares for all of us. God desires a special blessing upon those who have the deepest needs. Mark 14:7 *"For you always have the poor with you, and whenever you wish you can do good to them; but you do not always have Me."* We must show compassion to those in need around us that we may honor our Creator God.

Thank you Lord, for caring about all Your creatures high and low, and for sending brothers and sisters in Christ to help in times of need. May we honor You by supporting missions both home and overseas, Amen!

July 30: Day 211

GOD THE GREAT ORCHESTRATOR

*Proverbs 21:1 "the king's heart is like channels of water in the hand of the LORD; **He turns it wherever He wishes**."*

A common theme is being repeated regarding God's ability to lead and guide leaders according to His ultimate purpose. Though man cannot see the overall picture, only tiny glimpses of the picture. Man is not privy to the bigger image; we have too short a life span. We can see glimpses of the big picture from the biblical documents, only because God revealed it to us. According to this passage, God is totally sovereign; He can do what He wants consistent with His character, while extending to mankind a measure of freewill. How He can do all this is a mystery, but we can be assured, God is in control.

God is in control of each of our lives. He is guiding and instructing each of us according to His ultimate purpose. Psalm 37:23 shows Gods intimate involvement in the lives of people. "*The steps of a man are established by the LORD.*" He alone sees the big picture of humanity, and He is the One who directs and orchestrates all people and events. As Philippians 1:6 states God begins a work and will perfect His work in our lives. *Ephesians 1:11 "also we have obtained an inheritance, having been predestined according to His purpose who works all things after the counsel of His will,"* God will orchestrate our lives as we surrender to Him daily.

Thank you Lord, that You are in control of our lives, seeking our ultimate good, Amen!

July 31: Day 212

SEEING AND HEARING

*Proverbs 20:12 "The hearing ear and the seeing eye, **the LORD has made both of them.**"*

Two of the most complex systems in our body are the ear, and the eye. Proverbs 20:12 affirms who is responsible for the complexities of our body. An interesting contrast is made between this biblical text and a quote from Charles Darwin. "To suppose that the **eye** with all its inimitable contrivances for adjusting the focus to different distances, for admitting different amounts of light, and for the correction of spherical and chromatic aberration, could have been **formed** by natural selection, **seems**, I confess, **absurd** in the highest degree. . ." The complexity of the eyes is staggering to say the least. Literally billions of connections are required to make eyesight possible. The ear is equally complex when we consider all the processing data connected to our brains and the sound receptors required to make the ear operative is a marvel.

We have a God who does all things well. He is our Creator and He alone understands how our bodies are made. To give chance scenarios credit for such complex systems, like what Darwin said is completely absurd. Yet here we are, in a society that accepts the impossible. *Mark 7:37 "They were utterly astonished, saying, He has done all things well; He makes even the deaf to hear and the mute to speak."* All our senses are a marvel of God's creative power.

Thank you Lord, for the many wonders of our physical bodies. Psalm 139:14 sums it up: "I will give thanks to You for I am fearfully and wonderfully made; Wonderful are Your works. And my soul knows it very well." Amen!

August 1: Day 213

GOD CREATED THE RICH & THE POOR

*Proverbs 22:2 "The rich and the poor have a common bond, **The LORD is the maker of them all.**"*

We learn God created everyone for a purpose. Each of us is gifted with different skills, abilities and aptitudes. The rich are given the ability to help the poor. Leviticus 19 tells the farmers to leave a portion of their fields to help the poor. Jesus commands us to meet the needs of the poor: Mark 14:7 *"For you always have the poor with you, and whenever you wish you can do good to them."* All things have a purpose, even in the contrast between the rich and the poor.

We may ask, why did God create so many poor people? It would seem as if God wanted people to suffer; yet all the scriptures clarify God's special compassion for the poor and the needy. Psalm 12:5 *"Because of the devastation of the afflicted, because of the groaning of the needy, Now I will arise, says the LORD; I will set him in the safety for which he longs."* We all have a role to play in this world; we all have an obligation to reach out to others in need. Proverbs 30:8-9 *"Keep deception and lies far from me, Give me neither poverty nor riches; Feed me with the food that is my portion, That I not be full and deny You and say, who is the LORD? Or That I not be in want and steal, And profane the name of my God."* May we be found faithful in whatever circumstances we are found.

Thank you Lord, for creating each of us, and giving us the task of serving one another. As God enables, may we be faithful in helping others in greater need, Amen!

August 2: Day 214

GOD'S UNSEARCHABLE CREATION

Proverbs 25:3 "As the heavens for height and the earth for depth, so the heart of kings is unsearchable."

There is an interesting truth in science, for every question that is answered, two or more questions arise. There always seems to be another black box to open in our search for understanding the mysteries of God's creation. Proverbs 25:3 gives us such an insight, even though this passage refers to kings, it translates to the unsearchable nature of man and his ways; and ultimately to God. Since God's ways are unsearchable, we may well need an eternity to search out the mysteries and wonders of our Creator God.

We are gifted with a brain capacity far in excess of what we use in this life. This reality begs the question, how could evolution create such capacity in the human brain? The obvious response to this, it did not. Our Creator God gave man the capacity to perform great deeds, even though we use so little of what God has given us. Even we do not understand all our thoughts and ways. God however knows our every thought and motive. Jeremiah 17:10 *"I, the LORD, search the heart, I test, the mind, Even to give to each man according to his ways, According to the result of his deeds."* Even though man's ways are unsearchable to us, God knows. Isaiah 55:8-9 *"For My thoughts are not your thoughts, Neither are your ways My ways, declares the LORD, For as the heavens are higher than the earth, So are My ways higher than your ways And My thoughts your thoughts."* I Corinthians 13:12 reminds us that one day, we will see all things clearly.

Thank you Lord, that you know your creation, you know us and created us with the capacity to do great things by Your strength, Amen!

August 3: Day 215

ALL KNOWLEDGE AND WISDOM

Proverbs 24:3-4 **"By wisdom a house is built and by understanding it is established, by knowledge the rooms are filled with all precious and pleasant riches."**

Even though this passage is speaking about the wise builder who builds his life in an orderly way through wisdom and knowledge; such insights in understanding come from God. He is the storehouse of wisdom, knowledge, and understanding. He has given us a guidebook in the Bible to instruct anyone willing to examine how to live a successful life. Proverbs 28:29 reemphasizes this same reality: "*God is the source of all wisdom and council."* We would do well to listen.

Proverbs is a valuable book for instruction on how to live effectively for God. Solomon, the writer of Proverbs supposedly the wisest man who ever lived was granted wisdom by God. God speaking to Solomon I Kings 3:12b "*Behold, I have given you a wise and discerning heart, so that there has been no one like you before you, nor shall one like you arise after you."* God offers this knowledge and wisdom to us if we will seek and obey Him. Proverbs 2:6-7 "*For the LORD gives wisdom; From His mouth come knowledge and understanding, He stores up sound wisdom for the upright; He is a shield to those who walk in integrity,"* God is the source of all knowledge and wisdom, we need only ask and pray.

Thank you Lord, for the precious gifts of knowledge and wisdom, available through Your Spirit and Your Word, Amen!

August 4: Day 216

GOD THE SON

Proverbs 30:4 **"Who has established all the ends of the earth?** *What is His name or His son's name? Surely you know!*

Proverbs 30 gives us a contrast from Solomon to a man named Agur. It is suggested by some, that Agur is Solomon. The contrast comes from Agur's perspective; he sees himself as *"more stupid than any man"* (verse 2). He continues to denigrate himself as being without understanding, wisdom, or knowledge. Yet he goes on to express profound insights into God's creative power. Agur's demonstration of humility suggests that wisdom and understanding are inversely proportional to the extent we are willing to humble ourselves before God. In verse 3, he confesses his lack of knowledge concerning God's Holy One. This awareness would have come from Psalm 16:10b: *"Neither will You allow Your Holy One to undergo decay."* The men of this generation had only glimpses of God's plan.

Proverbs 30:4 demonstrates a desire to know and understand who this Great Holy One and Creator is. *"who has ascended into heaven and descended? Who has gathered the wind in His fists? Who has wrapped the waters in His garment?"* Only the Creator could do such might acts. Matthew 13:16-17 *"But blessed are your eyes, because they see; and your ears, because they hear. For truly I say to you that many prophets and righteous men desired to see what you see, and did not see it, and to hear what you hear, and did not hear it."* The case for our God as the mighty Creator along with His Holy One, is clearly presented.

Thank you Lord, that You have revealed Yourself to us. We know the Holy One of God and the name of His Son, Jesus, Amen!

ECCLESIASTES

God through Solomon gives sound advice. God has made everything at the right time for a purpose. God has placed eternity in the hearts of men as we realize our greater purpose.

August 5: Day 217

ONLY BY GOD'S HAND

*Ecclesiastes 2:24 "There is nothing better for a man than to sit and drink and tell himself that his labor is good, This also I have seen that it is from **the hand of God**."*

Ecclesiastes is the second book written by Solomon. He often takes a bleak look at life in its repetitive cycles. *"Nothing new under the sun."* If this statement is true, there must have been planes, cars, and computers in the distant past. We can only speculate, but the cycle of life seems to be repetitive. Nothing happens by chance; a bid of Idealistic thought is presented in this short phrase. God is behind everything that happens, a grand design behind the scenes. Without God, nothing happens, just as in creation, from nothing, nothing comes. We can only assume something, if we were not witnesses. All the events of history to this day are by the hand of God. If this passage is correct, even the bad things work toward a proper conclusion.

Ecclesiastes gives us a heads-on view of the futility of life. This seems to be more apparent even in today's culture. We have so much, yet we are unfulfilled. None of the labor saving devices we have created can fill the empty areas of our lives. When all is said and done, we are encouraged to fear God for all will be brought to account. John 15:5 *"I am the vine, you are the branches; he who abides in Me and I in him, he bears much fruit, for apart from Me you can do nothing."* All work is good if done for the glory of God.

Thank you Lord, for the gift of life; your guiding hand is always with us directing our paths. You alone keep and protect us to the end or our days, Amen!

August 6: Day 218

AN ETERNAL PERSPECTIVE

Ecclesiastes 3:11 "**God has made everything appropriate in its time. He has also set eternity in their heart**, *yet so that man will not find out the work which God has done from the beginning even to the end.*

This passage gives us a direct reference to God's creative nature from the wisest man that ever lived. As the old adage goes, there is a time and a place; God sets the time and the place. Everything in history has a purpose to fulfill. The passage continues: "*He set eternity within the hearts of men.*" He gives us the eternal perspective on life, the one who designed man is the one who has a much higher purpose than what is apparent today. Eternity extends man's influence far beyond our limited understanding. We have eternal value that goes well beyond this life. As God is the creator of all life, all life is valuable and precious.

God designed everything for a purpose in our present day lives. Along with Solomon, we too are witnesses to the futility of life, with all its ups and downs. There can be much joy, yet along with it much sorrow in this life. We lose loved ones, we still have accidents, and people get sick. It is important to remember, God has given us a much higher purpose than just this life. We have an eternity to look forward to. Revelation 21:4 reminds us: "*. . . and He will wipe away every tear from their eyes and there will no longer be any death; there will no longer be any mourning, or crying, or pain; the first things have passed away.*" We have a future hope that will last for eternity.

Thank you Lord, for the good and the bad. You have given us Your Spirit and a hope that will never be extinguished for eternity, Amen!

August 7: Day 219

THE BATTLE FOR LIFE

Ecclesiastes 8:8b "No man has . . . authority over the day of death; and there is no discharge in the time of war, and evil will deliver those who practice it."

Just as man has no power over the wind, so too man has no say in the day of his death. Each person who lives and who has lived on this earth is ultimately in the hands of God. God has established the day of our death. Even those who would commit suicide will be accountable before God at the judgment. Can man hasten the end of a war? We are all in a conflict with evil in this world; every person must overcome it and win the battle. Just as God challenged Cain to overcome the evil before him. Genesis 4:7a *"And if you do well, will not your countenance be lifted up?"* God is actively challenging His people to overcome the evil and wickedness in the world; not to let evil overcome us.

God has allowed each person to enter the battle of life. We all must overcome the evil and the wickedness in the world. There is no discharge of this battle until our life is complete; and that day is in God's hand. God however has given us insights and the equipment to win that battle. Now it is up to each of us to appropriate these tools; God's spirit is available to us along with His written word to guide us in this earthly battle. I Timothy 6:12 *"Fight the good fight of faith; take hold of the eternal life to which you were called, and you made the good confession in the presence of many witnesses."* We all must fight the battle of life to win, for the glory of God.

Thank you Lord, for the victory. Help us to fight the good fight that we might be victorious over sin in our lives, and to help others see their way to victory with us, Amen!

August 8: Day 220

WE KNOW SO LITTLE

*Ecclesiastes 11:5 ""Just as you do not know the path of the wind and how bones are formed in the womb of the pregnant woman, so you do not know the activity of **God who makes all things.**"*

As much as man has learned through the exercise of science, we are still but scratching the surface of all there is to know. With each answered question we gain from our research, more questions arise. As we unlock the mysteries of life, this reality becomes even more complex. God is the absolute creator of all that exists; He alone understands the complexities of life, and how our bodies are formed. As man is able to unlock many of the mysteries of life, the manufacturing processes of cell division and the insane complexities of the components that build and create our bodies, we can only marvel at the majestic precision of God's creation. Our God's creation is a wonder to behold.

Our bodies and our world is so much more complex than we can realize. We take for granted the wonders of God's creation, for we can only comprehend so deep. Much of our science must speculate that which goes well beyond our ability to grasp. Job 38 is filled with examples of God reminding Job, his friends, and us of the limits of our understanding. Job 38:36 *"Who has put wisdom in the innermost being Or given understanding to the mind?"* The mysteries of this world will take an eternity to uncover.

Thank you Lord, for the wonders of your creation, for our world and everything in it. You alone understand the complex workings of Your creation. May the discoveries of science point more clearly to You as the Creator, Amen!

August 9: Day 221

REMEMBER YOUR CREATOR

*Ecclesiastes 12:1 "Remember also **your Creator** in the days of your youth. Before the evil days come and the years draw near when you will say, 'I have no delight in them."*

This passage is a reminder of the shortness of life. We have but a few years on this planet, we must make the most of it for our Creator God. Accepting God's grace and forgiveness at an early age grants us a special measure of peace and security as the days of our life come to a close. Life become more difficult as we age; this verse suggests that there may be little delight in those years as it is much more difficult to live. However, knowing our Creator God gives us a special hope for a future eternity with Him. Knowing God as our creator gives the believer the expectation of a new life and a new body, one that will function beyond what we can imagine for all eternity.

No one wants to live their lives alone in a nursing home, apart from their family and friends. God has put within each of us the expectation for eternity. We know we have but a few years, having a future hope removes much of the fear and worry of leaving our family and friends. We know we will have a reunion with them again. Matthew 8:11 reminds us: "*Many will come from east and west, and sit down with Abraham, Isaac, and Jacob in the kingdom of heaven.*" We can avoid many of the pitfalls of life by coming to faith at a young age.

Thank you Lord, for creating us; for giving us a future hope, and of a full life with you in heaven, Amen!

August 10: Day 222

CREATOR OF MAN'S SPIRIT

*Ecclesiastes 12:7 "then the dust will return to the earth as it was, and the spirit will return **to God who gave it**."*

At the end of life, all things return to their place, and the spirit of man returns to God. The creator of life will require of man the spirit from which his life was derived. We are not able to exist outside the confines of God's sustaining grace. We are all destined to that eternal reunion with our Creator. Our spirit inside us is a gift and vessel from God; we could not exist without it. Our spirit upon death returns to God, who is the giver and sustainer of all life.

We are reminded that God grants us a period of time to live and to strive on this Earth. God has equipped each of us with a spirit of life, and a measure of His grace to do specific tasks. Some are equipped with more talents or gifts than others. The important thing is not how much we do, but what we can accomplish with the measure of grace given us. Our spirit is a gift from God, allowing us to commune with God while on this earth. In the end, our spirit will return to the One who created us. Even Jesus' spirit was returned to God: Luke 23:46 *"And Jesus, crying out with a loud voice, said, 'Father, Into Your hands I commit My Spirit.' Having said this, He breathed His last."* In much the same way as Jesus, once our lives are complete, our spirit will return to the One who created us.

Thank you Lord, for the gift of life you have given us. We shall return to the One who created us, with the hope of our spirit which You possess, to be reunited with a new resurrected body, Amen!

August 11: Day 223

GOD'S SPOT LIGHT

Ecclesiastes 12:14 "For God shall bring every work into judgment with every secret thing, whether it be good, or whether it be evil"

There is nothing hidden in light of God's judgment. We have no place to hide. We are always in sight of God's vision. We have but one life to live as the saying goes; we must make the most of it. Though God sees all our deeds, good and bad; He is not a harsh judge. Our Creator God created each of us for specific tasks. He is in fact our biggest (no exaggeration) supporter. He is for us, not against us. He has given all of us gifts with the expectation that we use them to serve Him.

We have a huge opportunity in the world to serve God. What we do with those opportunities will have eternal consequences. God not only sees what we do, He knows our thoughts and the motives of our hearts. Psalm 139:1 *"O Lord, You have searched me and known me."* God not only knows our innermost thoughts, He is in constant communication with us through our conscience, His Spirit, and through His Word. He provided all the resources we need to be successful in life. Proverbs 5:21 *"For the ways of a man are before the eyes of the LORD, And He watches all his paths."* God desires that we overcome the evil of this world, and learn to honor God and serve others.

Thank you Lord, that You are not a negligent landlord. You care deeply for Your children, enabling each of us to overcome and succeed in this life, Amen!

SONG OF SOLOMON

King Solomon: God is the creator of **Perfect love. He is the designer and creator of romantic love. He is the creator of the woman's body. He created sex** to be enjoyed and to guarantee the continuation of the species.

August 12: Day 224

AUTHOR OF LOVE

*Song of Solomon 7:1 "How beautiful are your feet in sandals, O prince's daughter! The curves of your hips are like jewels, **The work of the hands of an artist**."*

Our Creator God designed woman for man as much more than a help mate. The entire process of love is by design; men and women were made as a complimentary unit. This parallels God's love for mankind, both man and woman. Without the unity of the man and woman, all human life would soon cease. The deep intensity of the love relationship assures the continuation of our species. Procreation depends upon a man and a woman coming together into a unity of commitment and purpose.

The entire concept of sexual arousal communicates an intimate or romantic relationship between a man and a woman. This aspect of love is called Eros love; this is the deepest form of love drawing people of the opposite sex into a very close relationship. God created woman to compliment man, to become one flesh with him. By God's design, men and women were created to enjoy one another and to complement each other. Genesis 6:2 *"That the sons of God saw that the daughters of men were beautiful; and they took wives for themselves whomever they chose."* The beautiful relationship between a man and a woman is by God's design.

Thank you Lord, for the beauty of romantic love. You are the designer and creator of our physical bodies and our minds. May we honor and serve you with all You have given us, Amen!

August 13: Day 225

WOMAN'S BEAUTY IS FROM GOD

Song of Solomon 7:1 "How beautiful are your feet in sandals, O prince's daughter! The curves of your hips are like Jewels, **The work of the hands of an artist.***"*

The remaining verses continue to illustrate the intricacies of God's creative work in the design of the woman's body. It is regarded as a work of art by a designer and creator. The woman's form is made to be enjoyed by the opposite sex, and vice versa. God's designs are perfect.

Our culture it seems has taken the process of pro-creation and turned it into a recreational toy. We have lost the value, the beauty, the dignity, and closeness of this part of God's creation. We have deviated from the purpose of man's desire for his wife to establish a tight secure environment to raise a family. A man's love and enjoyment of his wife creates such a climate of harmony. Genesis 2:24 *"For this reason a man shall leave his father and mother and be joined to his wife; and they shall become one flesh."* God created man and woman to complement one another.

Thank you Father, for the joy and pleasure of the sexual relationship. Help us to appreciate the uniqueness that each person brings to that relationship, Amen!

ISAIAH

A future hope for God's people, Israel. No book other than Genesis and Psalms carries more references to God as creator than Isaiah. Nearly two dozen references give God the glory for His creative works.

August 14: Day 226

GOD GATHERS HIS PEOPLE

Isaiah 11:12 "And (God) will assemble the banished ones of Israel, And will gather the dispersed of Judah From the four corners of the earth."

The reference to earth again suggests a physical corner either of a flat surface or the corner of a cube. This is used by skeptics to indicate a naïve understanding of the planet and the universe. For ancient man, this notes a shallow understanding of the physical universe. In this case however, the term does not denote a physical reference. To use it as such is to miss not only the context but the etymology of the word. In the Hebrew, the word four corners designates . . . a separation, much as the context indicates. God is now in the process of gathering because He in earlier days scattered the Jewish people to the far corners (Places) of the earth. Deuteronomy 28:64 "*Moreover, the Lord will scatter you among all peoples, from one end of the earth to the other end of the earth; and there you shall serve other gods, wood and stone, which you or your fathers have not known.*"

The far more important aspect of this verse demonstrates God's faithfulness in returning His people to the land promised to their father Abraham. God, the author of history has given us a clear example of His power over all history. The Jewish people were indeed scattered to every country on earth (the four corners of the earth). We are witnesses to the return of the Jewish state of **Israel** in 1948. Ezekiel makes the same claim as Isaiah in chapter 37 verse 21 "*Say to them, Thus says the Lord GOD, Behold, I will take the sons of Israel from among the nations where they have gone, and I will gather them from every side and bring them into their own land;*" Our history demonstrates the validity of God's faithfulness to His people Israel.

Thank you Lord for the return of the Jewish people to the land of Palestine. You alone are faithful, knowing the beginning from the end, Amen!

August 15: Day 227

ALL WILL KNOW GOD IS CREATOR

*Isaiah 17:7 "In that day man will have regard for his **Maker**."*

In a future date, God will be recognized as Creator without exception. This is in reference to a future time where man recognizes God as Creator and Lord of His own universe. There will be no question as to how the universe began. All people will know God is the force, the first cause and the One responsible for all things that exist. Men will no longer be able to fabricate or rationalize how something can come into existence from nothing. All creation will give due praise to God as Creator.

Today we often use the phrase, "Be prepared to meet your Maker." We can often toss around terms without thinking of the ultimate reality behind those terms. We will all one day stand before our Maker God. God has given each person a number of days to live on this planet, after which we will all be judged. Hebrews 9:27 *"And inasmuch as it is appointed for men to die once and after this comes judgment."* This is a purposeful life, let us make the most of it.

Thank you Lord, that our lives are not an accident. We all have purpose driven lives, may we be found faithful to the tasks you have given us, Amen!

August 16: Day 228

GOD PLANNED HIS CREATION FROM AGES PAST

*Isaiah 22:11 "But you did not depend on Him who made it, Nor did you take into consideration **Him who planned it long ago**. God's plans are ancient,*

Isaiah 25:1 "***For You have worked wonders, Plans formed long ago,*** *with perfect faithfulness.*" These passages give us an insight into God's preparation for His creation. Our universe along with our planet and the billions of lives in it are not an accident. God planned this far in advance of His creation. We are the result of God's careful preparation and planning. None of the events of history are any surprise to our Creator God. He knew man would fail, having prepared a plan to restore Man into a right relationship with his Creator.

The biblical account contains the works of God from Genesis to Revelation. God is still actively working to perfect His creation. Those who would deny miracles are most likely the same who deny God as the creator. The wonders of creation carry little or no effect on many who prefer to trust nature as the sole creative force. The whole of creation is not an accident. Miracles are but a drop in the bucket for the God of Creation. According to this passage, God planned the reality we see today long before Genesis One. Miracles and wonders continue today if we are willing to look for them. Life is a miracle from God who knew us before we were conceived. Psalm 139:16 "*Your eyes have seen my unformed substance; And in Your book were all written The days that were ordained for me, when as yet there was not one of them.*"

Thank you Lord, that no part of Your creation is an accident. All things happen for a purpose that You planned from ages past, Amen!

August 17: Day 229

GOD IS THE FOUNDATION

Isaiah 26:4 "Trust in the LORD forever, For in God the LORD we have an everlasting rock."

Trust and faith are key elements to bridging the gap between seeing God or seeing only the world. God is a rock, only to those who are willing to trust Him. God will reveal Himself to all who earnestly want to know and understand the realities of life. A rock is solid and steadfast. We can rest upon a rock without fear of being shaken off. God is a staple of hope amidst a dark and shaky world. The world offers only a dark and bleak future. No hope for eternity, and no hope for a future life. Only death and destruction, await those who place their trust in this world only.

Our Creator God is Himself the foundation of this world. He provided the bases for life, purpose, and hope. We know who we are, where we came from, and where we are going. We are given specific purpose and rationale for life that goes well beyond just speculation. We have a hope that goes even beyond this life, into eternity. Secular science is not able to make any ultimate claims to purpose and meaning in this life. Psalm 18:3 *"the LORD is my rock and my fortress and my deliverer, My God, my rock into whom I take refuge; My shield and the horn of my salvation my stronghold."* We have a solid rock in God, giving us a purposeful life and a hopeful future without end.

Thank you Lord that we can put our trust in You, not only for this life, but for eternity, Amen!

August 18: Day 230

THE UNSEEN GOD

Isaiah 26:11 "O Lord, Your hand is lifted up yet they do not see it."

The works of God are not blind to man, they are obvious. However, our understanding of their complexity is only beginning to be tapped. Even with the majesty of creation, man does not see God. God can only be seen by those who willingly want to find Him. The works of God become more clearly relevant as one is honestly seeking to find Him.

As magnificent and grand is the universe we behold, the extreme complexities of life, along with the orderly operation of nature, man still has difficulties seeing the handiwork of God. Yet, in God's grand design, God will reveal Himself only to those who honestly want to find Him. King Solomon brings this point home: Proverbs 8:17 *"I love those who love me; And those who diligently seek me will find me."* God is always willing to reveal Himself to those who honestly seek to know Him.

Thank you Lord that you humbled yourself to such an extent that You became and man, to show God's great love for His creation, Amen!

August 19: Day 231

GOD WILL JUDGE HIS CREATION

Isaiah 27:1 "the Lord will punish Leviathan the fleeing serpent, With His fierce and great and mighty sword, Even Leviathan the twisted serpent; And He will kill the dragon who lives in the sea."

All of God's creation is under the shadow of God's incoming judgment. He is the Creator of all life, giving sustenance to every living thing. Leviathan is considered one of the greatest of God's creation; even this great beast is not immune to God's eventual justice. God will eventually restore all of creation to its pre-fall condition. Romans 8:22 *"For we know that the whole creation groans and suffers the pains of childbirth together until now."* All things will be restored and set right in the day of our Lord.

We all must stand before God, who will examine each of our lives according to how we have lived. Nothing is immune to God's ultimate justice. God will bring all things to their proper conclusion. Psalm 96:13 *"Before the LORD, for He is coming, For He is coming to judge the earth, He will judge the world in righteousness And the peoples in His faithfulness."* For the believer, God's judgment will be based upon the perfect righteousness of His Son Jesus.

Thank you Lord, for caring about every creature and every part of Your creation. We can put our trust in You to restore all things, Amen!

August 20: Day 232

GOD'S EXAMPLE OF JUSTICE

*Isaiah 27:11 "Therefore **their Maker** will not have compassion on them and **their Creator** will not be gracious to them."*

The context of this passage is pointing to the Jewish people who were not faithful to God's commands. God had given them ample warning this would happen if the people failed to repent. They spurned the warnings and continued on with their disobedience. God is reminding the people and the readers of this passage that God is their Maker and Creator; He will hold His people accountable for their sins.

All men live under the condition of God's standard. We are given a guide to life (The Bible), and the verdict, if we fail to live a perfect life. However, no one is able to life a perfect life. We all live under the consequences of our own sins; none of us are immune. God Himself provided the solution for our own disobedience. He paid our debt on the cross by living the perfect life, and dying in our place. God demonstrated His faithfulness to His Word by following through on the consequences of Israel's failures. I Corinthians 10:11 *"Now these things happened to them as an example, and they were written for our instruction, upon whom the ends of the ages have come."* God has provide us with many object lessons to help us navigate this life.

Thank you Lord, for the warnings regarding our sins, and how we are to live. You have given us clear examples of what will happen if we fail to follow your instructions, Amen!

August 21: Day 233

THE LORD OPENS AND CLOSES EYES

Isaiah 29:10 "For the LORD has poured over you a spirit of deep sleep, He has shut your eyes, the prophets;"

The nation of Israel of the northern tribes were being conquered by the Assyrians. Two centuries earlier God allowed the nation to be divided to preserve the tribe of Judah from the corruption that was taking place in the northern tribes. We see the division within nations even today as people continue to have conflicts with one another. Our Creator God is the ultimate arbitrator of the nations. Job 12:23 is a reminder, God is in control. *"He makes the nations great, then destroys them; He enlarges the nations, then leads them away."* God closes the door on those who continually reject Him. As Israel moved farther away from God, they became dull in hearing and understanding of God's warnings. God allowed that falling away as the people became disinterested in obeying Him.

We too must pay attention to our responsibilities before God. He granted to us life, that we might be a blessing to those around us. Our failure to draw near to God daily can result in our hearts being dulled and our eyes being shut. God will only shut the eyes of those who have already hardened their hearts toward Him. Romans 11:8 *"God gave them a spirit of stupor, Eyes to see not and ears to hear not,"* The greatest danger in continually rejecting God, is that God will eventually reject us.

Thank you Lord that you love us, and continually seek after us that we would not fall away. Keep us in the shelter of Your protective care, Amen!

August 22: Day 234

GOD PROVIDED A CORNERSTONE

Isaiah 28:16 "Behold I am laying in Zion a stone, a tested stone, A costly corner stone for the foundation, firmly placed, He who believes in it will not be disturbed."

Isaiah repeats the theme of the cornerstone; it is the most important part of a structure. It provides for the location, the orientation, and the direction of the building. It gives the time, the place and the name of the structure. We know that God is our foundation; He gave us life and established a purpose for our existence. He alone is our cause for being, giving us an ultimate goal for life. We are to seek Him and to find what that purpose is for which He created us.

The most import cornerstone of our lives is the person of Jesus Christ. He is the most important part of the structure. He is our Creator, Sustainer, and Redeemer. He is the One who restores us into a right relationship with God. He is our cornerstone, as He is the most important part of our lives. He is creating within us a new creation; as we conform to His image, becoming like Him. The apostle Paul clarifies in Ephesians 2:20-22 *"Christ Jesus Himself being the corner stone, in whom the whole building being fitted together is growing into a holy temple in the Lord, in whom you also are being built together into a dwelling of God in the Spirit."*

Thank you Lord, for making us part of Your kingdom and Your body. May You become the most important part of our lives, that we may serve you more effectively, Amen!

August 23: Day 235

THE LORD IS THE CREATOR OF LAWS

Isaiah 33:22 "For the LORD is our judge, The LORD is our lawgiver, The LORD is our king; He will save us—"

God gave man a standard by which to live and be successful in life. Man was designed for a purpose, to honor and serve God. God desires our success in this life; to use the talents and skills He bestowed on every person to contribute to the welfare of all mankind. God sets a standard to guide us in life (rules to live by). Much of our success depends upon how well we follow His instructions. Many of the Levitical Laws were meant to protect the Jewish people from eating bad foods. All foods were meant for our good but some foods carried health risks to the people at that time.

Moral laws, such as the 10 commandments were designed as a guidepost on how to live and please God. Our willingness to keep and obey God's moral laws provided a pathway to success, prosperity and a closer relationship with God. Our faithfulness in keeping His laws will result in a closer walk with God and a more satisfying life. The New Testament boils these moral laws down to two; Luke 10:27 *"You shall love the Lord your God with all your heart, and with all your soul, and with all your strength, and with all your mind; and your neighbor as yourself."* In the end, all men will stand before God in judgment; a sobering reality for all people. We are reminded in Hebrews 10:31 *"it is a terrifying thing to fall into the hands of the living God."* Knowing we will someday stand before our Lawgiver, Judge, and King, we should do all we can do to follow His standard and to honor and please Him in this life.

Thank you Lord, for providing us with a standard for life and how to be successful in serving You and others. Help us be faithful in our responsibility to be obedient to Your Law, Amen!

August 24: Day 236

SOLAR ANOMALIES

Isaiah 38:8 "Behold, I will cause the shadow on the stairway, which has gone down with the sun on the stairway of Ahaz, to go back ten steps. "

So the sun's shadow went back ten steps on the stairway on which it had gone down. This reference rivals or even exceeds the stopping of the sun during the battles of Joshua. Wouldn't such an event create enormous chaos on the entire planet? One would think; but consider the power of the One who created the universe. Would such a task even be difficult? For us, that would be impossible; but for almighty God, a drop in the bucket. Would not God be able to slow the rotation of the earth over a period of say half an hour, would such an effect even be noticeable? However, the power of God transcends our feeble ability to understand; just ask Job.

Our Creator God is able to do beyond what we understand. He challenges us to seek Him in any and all circumstances. Philippians 4:6 "Be anxious for nothing, but in everything by prayer and supplication with thanksgiving let your requests be made known to God." Our God is not limited by physical circumstance. By God's power, He is able to go infinitely beyond our understanding. "Ephesians 3:20 *Now to Him who is able to do far more abundantly beyond all that we ask or think, according to the power that works within us."* There is no limit to what God can do in us if we trust Him.

Thank you Lord for the freedom to enter into Your presence and make our requests known; even though You know our requests before we ask, Amen!

OUR GOD IS IN THE DETAILS

Isaiah 40:12 "who has measured the waters in the hollow of His hand. And marked off the heavens by the span, And calculated the dust of the earth by the measure."

This entire chapter concerns the creative work of our Creator. God in this case seems to carry a very exacting balance. Our entire universe is sitting on this amazing balance. Science has discovered over the past 60 to 70 years that our universe is extremely fine-tuned. He alone understands the working of the universe and the intricacies of His creation. The idea of a balance shines a bright light on the Anthropic Principle and its fine tuning of the universe for life. Without God's insight into the finer workings of His creation, we would not experience the habitat which now supports us.

It has taken science literally hundreds or thousands of years to figure out how complex our universe is. Any variations of our cosmic fine-tuning would render this universe completely uninhabitable. Our planet earth is situated in just the right location from the sun (called the goldilocks zone); the tilt of the planet and its rotation are just right to enable life. God has given us a diverse animal kingdom and plant population to sustain our lives. He provided the raw materials to build, construct, and to power the systems that sustains our society today. Without God's exacting details fine-tuned into our world and universe, we would not be here. Job gives us a reminder: Job 38:4 *"Where were you when I laid the foundation of the earth? Tell Me, if you have understanding."* If science has taught us anything over the past 500 years, we have only scratched the surface in our understanding.

We give thanks and praise to You our God for the many wonders of Your Creation. You alone sustain our very lives along with the world we live in, Amen!

August 26: Day 238

GOD SITS ABOVE THE EARTH

Isaiah 40:22 "It is He who sits above the circle of the earth, and its inhabitants are like grasshoppers, Who stretches out the heavens like a curtain And spreads them out like a tent to dwell in. "

The personification of God is a common theme in scripture as we read of God sitting above the circle of the earth. God however is omnipresent in His existence; He is everywhere. The idea communicates God as one who is above the earth watching the affairs of man. We are but grasshoppers before Him, even less than an insect, when compared to the infinite God of Creation. Even our planet Earth is insignificant compared with God. The extreme contrast between God and man becomes even starker when we consider the idea of God spreading out the heavens. For our God to be able to move stars and galaxies at will, reveals a God of enormous power.

Even with the great contrast between God and man; Man is of great value to God. We are created in the image of God with a purpose to fulfill. James 3:9b *". . . people made in the likeness of God."* Our God watches over His creation because we have an assigned purpose to complete. Ephesian 2:10 *"We are His workmanship created in Christ Jesus for Good works . . . "* As great as God is above His creation, He still cares about us, giving us both a purpose and a hope.

Our Creator God is far above the heavens. You Lord are worthy of praise and thanks for giving us a purpose, a hope for the future, and eternity with You, Amen!

August 27: Day 239

OUR GOD DOES NOT REST

*Isaiah 40: 28 "Do you not know? Have you not heard? The Everlasting God, the LORD, **the Creator of the ends of the earth** does not become weary or tired. His understanding is inscrutable."*

Fatigue is a curse to anyone who wants to get things done; we however are not able to continue beyond a certain point. We become weary and need rest; God needs no rest. Our Creator God is able to continue working on our behalf indefinitely. He is our eternal, everlasting God who does not tire, or wear out; He operates 24/7. Our God is continually guiding, encouraging, strengthening, and watching over His creation. We are limited, but He is not. He knows our weaknesses and shortcomings. He knows we are but dust, but He still loves and cares for His creation.

We can take confidence in the fact that God is able to connect with His creation at any time, or any place. We can bring all our requests before Him for He does not sleep or slumber. Our God is so great, and far beyond our ability to comprehend or understand. He knows us, our struggles, and our hearts. He is operating at a level infinitely above our ability to understand. Romans 11:33 *"Oh, the depth, of the riches both of the wisdom and knowledge of God! How unsearchable are His judgments and unfathomable His ways!"* Even the energizer bunny cannot keep up with our God. As the song writer put it "Our God is an Awesome God."

Thank you Lord, that You are in control of our lives. We give praise to You O God who endures through all generations, all time, and all eternity. You will always be there for us. You alone know the beginning from the end, Amen!

August 28: Day 240

GOD GIVES STRENGTH

Isaiah 40: 29-31 "He gives strength to the weary, . . . Yet those who wait for the LORD will gain new strength."

Our sufficiency to accomplish anything depends upon God's enabling. We were designed by God to work in harmony or in tandem with Him. We are co-workers with Him to advance His kingdom on earth. In one sense, we are apprentices to His kingdom work. God does not need us to do His work, but He chose us to work alongside Him, that we may learn to love and trust Him.

God also desires for us to wait upon Him. Psalm 37:9 *"But those who wait for the LORD, they will inherit the land."* God knows the perfect time, and the perfect place for us to speak, or to be quiet, to serve or simply listen. We are vessels in the hands of the Master Potter. Jeremiah 18:4 *"But the vessel that he was making of clay was spoiled in the hand of the potter; so he remade it into another vessel, as it pleased the potter to make."* We must seek God, and learn to follow Him, He will direct our paths. John 15:5 *"I am the vine, you are the branches; he who abides in Me and I in him, he bears much fruit, for apart from Me you can do nothing."* We need the direction and strength from God in order to do His work; we cannot operate or accomplish Kingdom work in our strength alone.

Thank you Lord, for strengthening us and equipping us to do the work You assigned us. May we learn to serve according to Your time and place, Amen!

THE GOD WHO STRETCHES OUT THE HEAVENS AND PEOPLE

*Isaiah 42:5 "**Thus says God the LORD, who created the heavens and stretched them out,** Who spread out the earth and its offspring, Who gives breath to the people on it and spirit to those who walk in it."*

Our Creator God is still operating in our universe. It would appear our universe is still expanding at a rapid rate. The Big Bang Theory suggests the initial universe expanded quickly; some scientists believe at faster than the speed of light. As a result of these findings, some within cosmology are abandoning the Big Bang Theory. Our Creator God is still active within our universe. Our Bibles are not out of date as some would suggest.

God spread out the human race by confusing language causing people groups to separate across the planet. Our planet is now populated by 7 plus billion people. According to Genesis 10 all races have a common origin coming out of Shinar located in current day Iraq. The mound of the tower of Babylon is with us today. All human life has its origin from God who breathed life into man. John 6:63a *"It is the Spirit who gives life;"* God continues to sustain the life of all men while He continues to control the movements of the heavens.

We praise You Lord, for Your power and majesty. You alone are the Creator of the universe and all life on this planet, Amen!

August 30: Day 242

GOD CREATED THE JEWISH NATION

*Isaiah 43:1 "But now thus says the LORD, **your Creator O Jacob, and He who formed you,** O Israel, Do not fear, for I have redeemed you, I have called you by name; you are Mine!"*

History gives us a remarkable event in the establishment of the nation of Israel in 1948. Most nations of antiquity have fallen off the map of history. We remember them no more. Such nations as Moab, Edom, the Philistines, and the empires of Assyria, and Babylon have fallen out of existence. Israel is special; in this passage God makes clear, He is the One who created the nations of Judah and Israel. Even though God scattered the Jewish people among the nations where they still live; He gathered them back into their own land as a new, reestablished nation.

What makes Israel unique to other nations of antiquity that have survived, such as Greece and Egypt? Israel as a reborn nation retained its culture, it language, and its religious faith. They are the same people as those of antiquity. They worship God in the same way, with the same traditions. God indeed redeemed the nation. Isaiah 43:14 "*Thus says the LORD your Redeemer, the Holy One of Israel.*" God restored His people to the land, totally intact, a testimony to God's eternal faithfulness.

Our God is Faithful to His chosen people, just as He is faithful to all who call upon the name of the Lord. Thank you Lord, for your faithfulness to us in giving us the example of the restoration of Israel, Amen!

August 31: Day 243

ALL THINGS ARE CREATED FOR HIS GLORY

*Isaiah 43:7 "Everyone who is called by My name, **And whom I have created for My glory, Whom I have formed, even whom I have made.**"*

We are God's creation, created in God's image, having extreme value. Our value as human beings becomes more substantial as we enter into an eternal relationship with God. Our purpose is highlighted by the over whelming joy in giving praise and glory to God and God's eternal Son Jesus who paid our very costly debt on the cross. We also have been given a new name, a name signifying our relationship with Christ; that being Christian. Acts 11:26b *"the disciples were first called Christians in Antioch."* We have a new identity and purpose in Christ.

The Church is the earthly institution housing the body of Christ in the World. As Christians, we are to glorify God in how we live, serve others, and die. We are to manifest God's presence in the world by our conduct so as to encourage and win others to Christ. II Corinthians 5 explains this calling upon the Christian Church like being an ambassador to another country. 2 Corinthians 5:20 *"Therefore, we are ambassadors for Christ, as through God were making an appeal through us; we beg you on behalf of Christ, to be reconciled to God."* All mankind is created and formed by God into the image of God. The final goal for all people is to be transformed into the spiritual image of God both in attitude and conduct.

Thank you Lord, for creating us in Your image. May we transform our bodies and mind with Your help into conformity with Your will, Amen!

September 1: Day 244

GOD IS KING OF ISRAEL

*Isaiah 43:15 "I am the LORD, your Holy One, **The Creator of Israel, your King.**"*

In the early years of Israel, God was King of Israel, as no man sat upon the throne of Israel. This form of government is known as a theocracy, where God Himself is King and rules according to His perfect law. We often hear this term thrown around today when our government gives any recognition to religion, regardless how mundane. Current secular society has no stomach for God to be in charge of any part of our lives. Most countries are either democratic, or socialist in structure, some are monarchs having a king or queen, while a few are dictatorships. The latter having total reign over the operation of the government. If that dictatorship is benevolent, the people will probably prosper. If however that dictator is self-serving or malevolent, the people will suffer.

Most dictatorships are likely to be of the malevolent type. Man is a sinner by nature, as absolute power corrupts. If there is no accountability to power, money seems to disappear while foreign bank accounts prosper. Our creator God however owns the cattle on a thousand hills. Psalm 50:12b *"The world is mine, and all it contains."* He doesn't need our money. He is the absolute benevolent dictator who cares about His creation down to every detail. We can trust Him to take care of us. God was King of Israel for a few hundred years but was rejected by His people in favor of a human king. We must also decide who is king of our lives, God or us.

Thank you Lord, that You will someday be the absolute King of our hearts and lives. Even now You alone are the Creator King of our world, and the entire universe, Amen!

September 2: Day 245

GOD FORMED ISRAEL FOR HIS PRAISE

*Isaiah 43:21 "**The people whom I formed for Myself**
Will declare My praise."*

We all are a people formed by almighty God. Not one of us can claim we formed ourselves, or were formed in a test tube, or by accident. We were all created by Him, and for Him; He has a purpose for every one of our lives. We were created to fulfill a specific role in the world. We are not our own possession to do as we please. This may come as a shock for some people as we often become accustomed to doing what we want. We still must obey laws, we cannot cross other people who may have offended us. Jail is still a real thing if we decide to do whatever we want.

We are bound by laws to treat other people with some respect. The 10 commandments were given to curb our malevolent behaviors. Our purpose is to Know God and to learn what pleases Him. God has granted His creation the opportunity to live forever with Him, if we learn to honor and serve Him. When we come to realize how great our creator God is, and what He did to rescue us from our sins, we have a cause to worship and praise Him. Our God takes great pleasure in our sincere worship. Psalm 22:3 *"Yet You are holy, O You who are enthroned upon the praises of Israel."* May we learn to Praise our heavenly Father from the heart.

We give You Praise heavenly Father for the wonders of Your creation. We acknowledge You, Lord and King of all creation. We give You praise for the precious gift of salvation, Amen!

September 3: Day 246

GOD OUR CONSTANT PROTECTOR

Isaiah 44:6 Promise "I will also hold you by the hand and watch over you."

Our Creator God is not an absent landlord. He cares deeply for His creation and all creatures big and small. Psalm 51:11 *"I know every bird of the mountains, and everything that moves in the field is Mine."* How God can keep track of every moving thing is a mystery. Yet, an infinite God is not limited in knowledge as are His people. We know only in part, but God knows all things, including all His creation.

Our God watches over His people just as a father watches over his children. We are concerned about their safety just as God seeks to protect us from danger, including our own foolishness. II Samuel 22:3 *"My God, my rock, in whom I take refuge, My shield and the horn of my salvation, my stronghold and my refuge; My savior, You save me from violence."* We are reminded to remain in the arms of the Almighty; we remain safe within the confines of His presence. Even when we fail to remain close to God, He gives us His promises to protect us. Psalm 23:4 *"Even though I walk through the valley of the shadow of death, I fear no evil, for You are with me; Your rod and Your staff, they comfort me."* God is our continual protection in this life and into eternity.

Thank you Father, that You are constantly with us; holding our hands through the trials and victories of life. We praise and thank you for watching over us, Amen!

September 4: Day 247

WE ARE GOD'S SERVANTS

*Isaiah 44: 21 **I have formed you, you are My servant,** O Israel, you will not be forgotten by Me."*

All people are servants to God by the simple reality of being the product of His creative power. We owe our very existence to God. Our habitat, this planet Earth is our home and provides shelter from the vacuum of space and sustaining life. We would not continue to exist without these provisions. God is both our creator and sustainer, enabling us to continue to live on this planet. Israel was God's servant providing the environment to bring His Son into the world through the Jewish culture and the linage of King David.

Our role as parents is much like God, we bring our children in to the world through pro-creation. This is the mechanism God instilled between a man and woman to create and form new life. We nourish and protect our children until they are able to take care of themselves. We provide shelter to them from the elements; give them clothing to wear until they decide they don't like our choices anymore. Like our parents, we often forget how much God has done for us. We are truly indebted to Him for our very existence. Romans 2:4 "Or do you think lightly of the riches of His kindness and tolerance and patience, not knowing that the kindness of God leads you to repentance?" Like the nation of Israel, God desires that we serve Him with a joyful heart for all He has done for us.

Thank you Lord, for creating us in Your likeness. We give you praise and thanks for all You have done on our behalf. May we be faithful stewards of all You have given us, Amen!

September 5: Day 248

GOD OUR MAKER AND REDEEMER

Isaiah 44:24 "Thus says the LORD, your Redeemer, and the one who formed you from the womb, **I, the LORD am the maker of all things**, *Stretching out the heavens by Myself, And spreading out the earth all alone."*

This passage is packed full of God's interactive work in the world. Other adjectives would include: Causing, Making, Turning, and Confirming. God is constantly at work among those who seek and love Him. Even those who do not seek, He will work through the circumstances to bring about His perfect objective. Looking backwards through God's interaction, we see His redemptive work, being called your Redeemer. We fell away from His protective presence but God found a way to restore us without breaking His own standard of perfection.

Our God formed us in the womb, and knew us before we were born. Jeremiah 1:5a *"Before I formed you in the womb I knew you,"* Our God knows how we were made and what makes us tick. He is our Creator, who loves and cares for His creation. He alone is the creator of all that exists; He is the one causal agent responsible for the universe, and all that is in it. Jeremiah 51:15 *"It is He who made the earth by His power, Who established the world by His wisdom, And by His understanding He stretched out the heavens."* God is the author of our universe, all life, and the One who restores those who seek Him.

Lord, you alone are the creator of the universe. Thank you for giving us life, for placing us on Your Earth for a purpose to fulfill. You redeemed us that we could spend eternity with You, Amen!

September 6: Day 249

DON'T ARGUE WITH GOD

*Isaiah 45:9 "Woe to the one who quarrels **with his Maker** – "*

We may all have argued with God from time to time, because we don't understand what He is doing. We only have a small picture of God's overall creative plan. We know things in part, but the big picture is mostly fuzzy. I Corinthians 13:12 *"For now we see in a mirror dimly, but then face to face; now I know in part, but then I will know fully just as I also have been fully known."* In the end, we have the promise that we will see clearly. Before then, we must put our trust in Him, who alone knows the beginning from the end. He is aware of all the circumstances in our lives that we do not see until later, or in some cases we may never see.

We would not be alone if we have quarrels with our Maker God. God desires our interaction with issues concerning our lives. He tells us to bring everything before Him in prayer. Rather than arguing with God, we need to bring every request before Him. I Peter 5:6-7 *"Therefore humble yourselves under the mighty hand of God, that He may exalt you at the proper time, casting all your anxiety on Him, because He cares for you."* We may argue our case before the Lord, but ultimately we must trust Him for the results.

Thank you Lord, for hearing my requests. May I learn to trust You for the results, even if they don't turn out the way I would like; knowing in the end Your way is much better than my way, Amen!

September 7: Day 250

THE HOLY ONE IS THE MAKER OF ISRAEL

Isaiah 45:11 "Thus says the LORD, the Holy One of Israel, ***and his Maker:"***

Who is the Holy One of Israel? A distinction often referring to the person of Jesus Christ, part of God's person. Psalm 16:10 gives us another hint into who this individual is "For You will not abandon my soul to Sheol; Neither will You allow Your Holy One to undergo decay." This is a reference to the person of Jesus Christ not being held bondage to death. His resurrection from the grave gives us evidence of His power over death, and the promised hope that we will someday rise. The Holy One of Israel is also a reference to Him as creator of the nation from which He came. The nation of Israel is the culture from which Jesus came and lived His life on this planet.

The person and nature of God is revealed in many ways through God's revelation in the Bible. We learn that God is the creator of the universe, the earth, and the nation of Israel along with the culture in which Jesus Christ was raised. He is the Holy One of Israel that came into the world to redeem all mankind. The nation of Israel and the primary people of that nation are the Jews; a people, culture, religion, and language that remains with us to this day. All other cultures eventually die away, while the Jewish culture and people of the book remain with us as an example of God's continuing faithfulness to His original covenants. Isaiah 41:20 "That they may see and recognize, And consider and gain insight as well, That the hand of the LORD had done this, And the Holy One of Israel has created it." God's Holy One is both He who creates and sustains the nation of Israel.

Thank you Lord for Your nation, and Your people, the Jews. Thank you for all the wonders of Your creation, including the trials of the Jewish people, given to us as an example that we can learn about You, Amen!

September 8: Day 251

GOD KNOWS THE BEGINNING FROM THE END

*Isaiah 46:10 "Declaring the end from the beginning And from ancient times things which have not been done, Saying **My purpose will be established**, And I will accomplish all My good pleasure."*

God existed before His creation. Isaiah 48:12 *"Listen to Me, O Jacob, even Israel whom I called; I am He, I am the first, I am also the last."* The eternal nature of God is indicated by God's presence at the beginning and at the end of His creation. He will continue to exist beyond this earth and universe. Our Creator God is immortal and eternal; He is not a movie character, He exists beyond our reality, yet He is the integral part of our world, holding it together, interacting with its characters (us). We are part of that reality event known as history and life.

Our God however is in complete control of the plot and direction of our Historical event which is our reality. Not only does He know the beginning from the end, He interacts with each of us in real time. He (our God) cares about us as He desires our interaction with Him through the events of our life. Psalm 56:8 *"You have taken account of my wanderings; Put my tears in Your bottle. Are they not in Your book?"* God already has the written story completed, we, the actors are simply carrying it out to its conclusion.

Lord, You alone know the beginning and the end. You also know the end of my story. I thank and praise You for including me in your plot. May my life reflect Your glory and presence to the end, Amen!

September 9: Day 252

OUR INFINITE GOD

Isaiah 46:1 ***"Surely my hand found the earth, And My right hand spread out the heavens;*** *when I call to them, they stand together."*

Even though many passages demonstrating God creative power may seem somewhat repetitive. All scriptures are in agreement, God is the Creator. There is no question as to who is responsible for the creation of the earth according to the Bible. The scientific concept of a creator is hard to contemplate. He, our God is so far beyond us, it is laughable to imagine; we can't wrap our brains around it. The amount of power necessary to create the earth is unimaginable, let alone the expanding universe.

The scriptures make it clear, our God is infinite in power, knowledge, presence, and transcendence. He is far above our ability to comprehend. *2* Chronicles 2:6a *"But who is able to build a house for Him, for the heavens and the highest heavens cannot contain Him?"* Our Creator God is not limited, He has no boundaries. We can only be in awe of His power, the only sufficient power able to create the universe we see.

Thank you Lord, that You are able to create with such infinite detail and grandeur that we cannot begin to understand or imagine the breadth of Your power, Amen!

September 10: Day 253

GOD CREATES DARKNESS AND LIGHT

*Isaiah 50:3 "**I clothe the heavens** with blackness And make sackcloth their covering."*

If there is so much light in the heavens, why is space black? Blackness and sackcloth could be viewed as judgment and the curse. Genesis One tells us that God created the darkness and formed the light (Isaiah 45:7). Genesis 1:3-4 states: *"then God said, 'Let there be light'; and there was light. God saw that the light was good; and God separated light from the darkness."* Without darkness, we would not understand the contrast between light. We would be limited in our understanding of creative reality. Light requires a source; without a source of light the space is void and dark. When in proximity to the sun, light is overwhelming. Sackcloth is often the symbol for repentance. The repentant heart will see light in the midst of the darkness.

What is light? Photons, particles, waves, science is still seeking a definitive answer. One clue is found in Isaiah 45:7 *"The One forming light and creating darkness, Causing well-being and creating calamity."* Light is an object of creation, darkness is not, it is an opposing effect of the absence of light. I John 1:5 gives us another hint: *"God is Light, and in Him there is no darkness at all."* Our God is not only the creator of light, He is the essence of light having no darkness or evil. The darkness flees from His presence; so too will no evil or injustice stand before Him.

Thank you Lord, for removing our sin, and clothing us in Your righteousness, that we can enter into Your presence without fear, Amen!

September 11: Day 254

EVERYTHING HAS A PURPOSE

Isaiah 45:12 **"It is I who made the earth, and created man upon it. I stretched out the heavens with My hands and I ordained all their host.**

A theme permeating scriptures attributes to God the creation of the earth. God's **crea**tive purpose is revealed for the earth; a habitat for all mankind. Man is created to live on the earth, and the earth is created for man. We are not an accident as a result of blind chance. The universe and the universal constants that control the conditions of our universe are so precisely fine-tuned as to render chance an impossibility. This universe was so designed to make life possible for man to exist on earth. Chance carries no weight as an explanation for our being here on earth.

According to the Bible, God placed Man on earth for a purpose; to demonstrate His power, His glory, and His love for all mankind. We are the beneficiaries of His creative hand. Our prime purpose for being on this planet, is to learn about God, His love and compassion for mankind. He revealed Himself to us through His written word, the Bible. He revealed His power and majesty through His creation. Our ultimate purpose points to a future hope of an eternal existence with Him. "*Isaiah* 45: 17 *"Israel has been saved by the LORD With an everlasting salvation; You will not be put to shame or humiliated To all eternity."* This ultimate purpose goes far beyond what we can fully understand now.

Thank you Lord for the life giving conditions You created on this planet for us. You alone created the conditions of the universe, showing us Your magnificent power and precision, Amen!

September 12: Day 255

THE EARTH CREATED FOR MAN

*Isaiah 45:18 "For thus says the LORD, **who created the heavens** (He is the God who formed the earth and made it. **He established it and did not create it a waste place, but formed it to be inhabited**)."*

The idea or concept of our earth being made to be inhabited is called the anthropic principle. All things that work together to make this planet livable for mankind suggests the inevitable result of our being here. It gives no real rationale for our existence, only chance conclusions. However, for those who acknowledge God, the logical conclusion is the one Isaiah states in this passage. Our Creator God established this planet for a purpose. Our physical bodies depend upon the right atmospheric conditions to breath. Our atmosphere and magnetic fields protect us from harmful solar rays. Our distance from the sun is just right to give us warmth and light to live without burning up, or freezing to death. Such conditions are perfect for our lives and the lives of the animal kingdom to exist.

God is the one who created this planet to be inhabited. We are here for a reason; we are in the process of learning what that reason is, but it is still being revealed. I John 3:2 *"Beloved, now we are children of God, and it has not appeared as yet what we will be."* As inhabitants of this planet, we are here for a purpose, to enter into a relationship with God, to grow in our knowledge of Him, and to win and serve others. What we will ultimately become, is yet to be revealed in time.

Thank you Lord for creating such a wonderful planet to inhabit. The beauty of Your creation is a marvel to behold. The complexity of the bio-system of life is a testimony to Your creative power, Amen!

September 13: Day 256

GOD CLOTHED THE HEAVENS

Isaiah 46:13 **"Surely my hand founded the earth, And My right hand spread out the heavens; when I call to them, they stand together."**

Cosmology is the observation of God's universe from within. We can observe God's handiwork through our telescopes. The current scientific view is that of an expanding universe, consistent with this biblical view. God is actively involved with His creation as we observe it today. The vast distances are a testimony to God's immense power and of His omnipresence. We are witnesses to a universe of amazing beauty, size, and complexity.

Today we observe a majestic and complex universe full of surprises. The variety of stars, planets; even those planets outside our solar system vary in size and appearance. Our Creator God is in complete control of His creation; the many mysteries of our cosmos confound secular cosmologists. Isaiah 51:13 reminds us: "*that you have forgotten* **the LORD your Maker, Who stretched out the heavens And laid the foundations of the earth**," The extreme power of God is made plain by the things He created. Our Creator God made the universe with all its complexity and vastness to demonstrate a small portion of His great power.

Thank you Lord, for stretching out the heavens. For showing a display of your omnipotence. You are the creator of the universe as well as the One who knows the innermost parts of our hearts, Amen!

September 14: Day 257

GOD OUR REDEEMER

Isaiah 50:2 "Is My hand so short that it cannot ransom? Or have I no power to deliver? **Behold, I dry up the sea with my rebuke, I make the rivers a wilderness;"**

Our Creator God is also our redeemer. God not only controls all the forces of nature; He is able to redeem His people. God's power is not limited by nature, a reminder to the nation that God is well able to redeem them and to rescue them from any trial. He delivered them from the hand of Assyria and those who would destroy the nation. God is reminding His people (Israel) that He is well able to deliver them.

God's power is able to rescue even today everyone who calls upon Him. God's power is sufficient to rescue His people from whatever calamity would fall upon them. What is even greater, God will redeem His people from their own sins. We all need to learn of God's sufficient power to save. God has rescued us through the work of His Son Jesus on the cross. John 3:17 *"For God did not send the Son into the world to judge the world, but that the world might be saved through Him."* The LORD is all powerful, and able to rescue and redeem His people.

Thank you Lord, for redeeming us and restoring us to a right relationship with You. You alone are able to bring us into Your presence, Amen!.

September 15: Day 258

THE LORD GIVES SPEECH

Isaiah 51:16 ***"I have put My words in your mouth and have covered you with the shadow of My hand to establish the heavens, to found the earth, and to say to Zion, You are My people."***

The prophet Isaiah encourages us to use our speech for God's purposes. The ability to talk is a gift from God. The ability to communicate through speech and words is a unique gift from God. We may need to learn the language, but simple communication is only one aspect to speech. It is most important, that our speech is an encouragement to others. We must practice our speech with a purpose, to help sustain others in need. Isaiah 55:4 "The Lord God has given me the tongue of disciples, That I may know how to sustain the weary one with a word."

All speech has a purpose, according to this passage, speech is to accomplish a higher purpose. Isaiah 55:11 "So shall My word be which goes forth from My mouth; It shall not return to Me empty, Without accomplishing what I desire, And without succeeding in the matter for which I sent it." We all must learn to use our speech wisely, to not only encourage, but to communicate the good news of God's redemption. Proverbs 15:23 "A man has joy in an apt answer, And how delightful is a timely word!" Our speech is not only the ability to make sounds, it carries the even more complex ability to comprehend and communicate for the purpose of uplifting people. God is our provider, not only in the material things that makes life possible, He provides man with a text book for life, and the ability to communicate through word and speech.

Thank the LORD for the gift of speech and the ability to communicate with others. May we learn to be wise in all our speech, Amen!

September 16: Day 259

A NEW CREATION AND NEW LIFE

Isaiah 65:17 **"For behold, I create new heavens and a new earth**; *And the former things shall not be remembered or come to mind."*

Not only is God the creator of our current universe, He has plans for an upgrade that carries with it infinite spiritual depth. We cannot comprehend such a reality in light of the vastness of our own universe, but a God who is as powerful as the Bible indicates would have no problem constructing an infinite cosmos to reflect His power and majesty. All those who call upon the God will be witnesses to these events, and partakers of this ultimate reality.

The transition from the physical realities to the spiritual reality is not limited to a future event. It is a reality that is taking place in the present as each person who confesses Jesus Christ is in the process of transformation into a new person. II Corinthians 5:17 *"therefore if anyone is in Christ he is a new creature; the old things passed away; behold new things have come."* Anyone who calls upon God in faith will begin this transformation. Romans 10:13 *"for Whoever will call on the name of the LORD will be saved."* All who call upon God and seek His face will be witnesses to the new heavens and the new earth.

Thank you Lord for the promise of a new creation and the gift of new life we have been given in Your Son Jesus. May Your light shine though us that we might win others, Amen!

GOD CREATED JERUSALEM FOR REJOICING

*Isaiah 65:18 "But be glad and rejoice **forever in what I create; For behold, I create Jerusalem for rejoicing** And her people for gladness."*

God is compassionate toward His holy city Jerusalem. He cares about His people in the great city of The King (Jesus). The great city of Jerusalem is the object of God's concern. He desires that we will always rejoice in it. We have a future hope in that great city, and we are commanded to pray for its peace and prosperity. Psalm 122:6 *"Pray for the peace of Jerusalem; May they prosper who love you."* The focus of God's love and grace are fixed on Jerusalem.

The center of God's active involvement in our world is found in Israel and its capital city Jerusalem. It is in this city that God performed His greatest work; our redemption on the cross. It is in this city that the good news of the gospel went forth into all the world. We are blessed through the works completed by our Lord and Savior Jesus Christ in this city. Revelation 21:10 *"And he carried me away in the Spirit to a great and high mountain, and showed me the holy city, Jerusalem, coming down out of heaven from God."* We have glimpses of what this city will be, a place beyond description.

Thank you Lord for Your great city and for the future rejoicing it will bring to us in eternity. We give You praise for the future hope that we will rejoice together within its walls, Amen!

September 18: Day 261

GOD IS THE CREATOR OF EVERYTHING

*Isaiah 66:2 "**For My hand Made all these things, thus all these things came into being**." Declares the LORD."*

God's greatness is far beyond our ability to comprehend. This passage is highlighting a reality of the awesomeness and power of God. The preceding passage gives us an image of God's majesty; this picture gives us a glimpse into the incomprehensible nature of God. Isaiah 66:1 states: "*Thus says the LORD, Heaven is My throne and the earth is My footstool.*" The planet in which we reside is no more than a footstool to its creator; if even that. God is responsible for everything we see. All things came into being by the infinite power and knowledge of God.

The greatness of God's power becomes even more profound when we look at the advances of science today. The James-Web Telescope can peer back even farther into the cosmos of the distant past. We can see clear images of very distant galaxies showing amazing details. These images only serve to amplify the power and grandeur of almighty God. The complexities of life, and the precision necessary for the universe to exist in such a state as to make our lives possible is amazing. We look back at Job, as God explained some of His creation: Job 38:31 "*Can you bind the chains of the Pleiades, Or loose the cords of Orion?*" Without God's revelation in His Word, we would have no clue!

Thank you Lord, for showing us, if only glimpses of the exceeding grandeur of Your magnificent creation, Amen!

September 19: Day 262

ALL THINGS WILL BE MADE NEW

*Isaiah 66:22 **"For just as the new heavens and the new earth, Which I make will endure before Me,** 'declares the LORD."*

We give thanks for the wonders of God's creation. The heavens are marvelous in their size and grandeur. The more our sciences explore the complexities of our current world and the universe in which we live, the more complex and profound it becomes. We understand so much more than the ancients who wrote the scriptures, yet they tell us there are new worlds coming. God is preparing new heavens and a new earth; a reality beyond what we can imagine. To contrast what that reality will be like in light of the complexities and vastness of the one in which we now live is truly mind boggling.

We have a God with powers to create from nothing vast worlds. We are given the hope of entering into this new reality. The New Jerusalem will be placed on this marvelous new earth. We will experience a new heaven with no destruction or decay. Revelations 21:1 *"then I saw a new heaven and a new earth; for the first heaven and the first earth passed away, and there is no longer any sea."* The size and beauty of this new reality will be beyond anything we can imagine.

We give thanks and praise to You God, for the hope of eternal life in a new spiritual world and reality which will never pass away, Amen!

Jeremiah

Jeremiah reveals a small portion of God's creative and sustaining power in reference to His sustaining and protecting the Jewish people. God not only created us through the process of pro creation, He knew us before we were born. Jeremiah affirms God's creative role nearly a dozen times throughout the book.

September 20: Day 263

GOD KNEW US BEFORE CREATION

*Jeremiah 1:4 "**Before I formed you in the womb I knew you**, And before you were born I consecrated you: I have appointed you a prophet to the nations."*

For Jeremiah, God was his Creator, his purpose and direction in life was to serve God. He was known by God, and his life was to serve a specific mission. If Jeremiah was known, every person ever born was also known by God. If God was able to name the multitude of stars in the universe, it is a much less difficult task to know the entire population of earth from the beginning to the end. Even those who never lived to see the light of earth would also be known by God.

We have a God who is intimately connected to His people and all creation. He has a plan for our lives, and for every person who has lived on the face of the earth. Even the wicked serve God for a specific purpose: Proverbs 16:4 *"The LORD has made everything for its own purpose; Even the wicked for the day of evil."* We are known by God, and even those who reject Him serve a purpose. We can have confidence in God's ordering of each and every person who seeks Him. "Jeremiah 29:11 *"For I know the plans that I have for you, declares the LORD, plans for welfare and not for calamity to give you a future and a hope."* Even before the foundations of the earth, God knew us and equipped us for a specific work.

Thank you Lord for bringing us into this world and giving us life. You created us for a purpose, may we be faithful as was Jeremiah to do the work You've given each of us, Amen!

September 21: Day 264

GOD CREATED BY HIS WISDOM & UNDERSTANDING

Jeremiah 10:12 **"It is He who made the earth by His power, who established the world by His wisdom; And by His understanding He has stretched out the heavens.***"*

According to Jeremiah, our planet is here only because of God's creative power. God has the power to create, and the wisdom to construct all its delicately balanced systems that makes life possible. God endowed this world with its beauty, resources, and variety of life enabling man to survive. The Bible continually reminds us this world is not an accident, it is far too finely tuned for that. God is an extremely intelligent agent capable of designing the complexities of this world and the vast universe we are able to observe.

Jeremiah adds an astounding idea in addition to God's creative power regarding the Earth. A theme repeated in scripture is the stretching out of the heavens, a scientifically verified reality, totally unknown to ancient man who would have no understanding of this concept. The heavens are indeed expanding as the galaxies are moving farther apart. Our God orchestrated the heavens with its beauty and vastness. Jeremiah 5:16b **"For the Maker of all is He,***"* God, by His wisdom and power, created the world, our universe and all that exists.

Thank the Lord that we have such an astounding record of Your creative power. The earth in its diversity of life; the heavens in their grandeur declare Your glory, Amen!

September 22: Day 265

GOD IS CREATOR OF THE FORCES OF NATURE

Jeremiah 10:13 "And He causes the clouds to ascend from the end of the earth; **He makes lightning for the rain and brings out the wind from His storehouses.***"*

God is in complete control of the weather. Since He is the creator of the world, He must also be in control of the weather patterns. We are recipients of His blessing as the rains make our crops possible. Even destructive weather has a larger purpose. Why God is accused of evil is another question, but even the troubles weather brings may have a greater purpose for good. Matthew 5:45 *"He makes the sun rise on the evil and the just."* All good things come from God.

God alone is in control of the world; He directs the weather according to His purpose. Jeremiah 14:22 *"Are there any among the idols of the nations who give rain? Or can the heavens grant showers? Is it not You, O LORD our God? Therefore we hope in You, for You are the one who has done all these things."* God also allows drought, sometimes for the purpose of challenging our faith and to understand, rain is a blessing from God. Our timely rains are a gift from God given to both the good and the wicked. Matthew 5:45b *(God)* *". . . sends rain on the righteous and the unrighteous."* Our Creator God is the author of the hydrologic cycle as well as all the forces of nature.

Thank you Lord, for the rains giving us food, for the winds turning our windmills, and the lightening as reminders of Your great power, Amen!

September 23: Day 266

GOD MADE THE EARTH AND ALL LIFE ON IT

*Jeremiah 27:5 "**I have made the earth, the men and the beasts which are on the face of the earth by My great power and by My outstretched arm**, and I will give it to the one who is pleasing in My sight."*

This passage emphasizes God's creation of the entire biosphere consisting of our planet earth and all living creatures within it. God made the Earth for a purpose; to bless man who is pleasing to Him. Life would be difficult if it wasn't for the great variety of animals in the animal kingdom. Even our plant food needs the pollination made possible by the small honeybee. All plants and animals on the planet are in a symbiont relationship with each other.

The extreme complexity of life can only be explained by our powerful Creator. The diversity of life gives us animals for food, to do work, to give companionship, and for the diversity of life, both plants and animals, necessary for all life to continue. We depend upon all God's creatures for our livelihood. Psalm 50:10-12 *"For every beast of the forest is Mine, The cattle on a thousand hills, I know every bird of the mountains, And everything that moves in the field is Mine."* Our Creator God is the great conductor orchestrating the amazing complexities of life. Jeremiah 33:2 confirms God's creative power: *"thus says **the LORD who made the earth**, the LORD who formed it to establish it, the LORD is His name,"* All reality comes from the mighty hand of God.

Thank the Lord for our habitable planet earth, for His great provision in the diversity of life among the animal kingdom, and the variety of plants for pollination, food, medicines, and the beauty they bring, Amen!

September 24: Day 267

GOD PUTS HIS LAWS WITHIN US

Jeremiah 31:33: **"I will put My law within them and on their heart** *I will write it; and I will be their God, and they shall be My people."*

God is in the process of creating a new people after His image. All who are called into a relationship with Him will someday be conformed into His likeness and image. We were initially created in the image of God, having body, spirit, and soul. We were created for a purpose, to live with Him for all eternity. Man however fell into sin and was separated from God. We fell from grace and out of fellowship with God. As a result of our fall, God needed to intervene on our behalf to restore that damaged relationship and bring us back into harmony with our Creator.

The New Testament clarifies that process as conforming to the image of Christ. Romans 8:29 *"For whom He foreknew, He also predestined to be conformed to the image of His Son,"* God's law is already written in the hearts of all people. Our conscience is a guide convicting us of sin and confirming good. Many have killed their conscience by continual disobedience. God is continually at work pursuing His people. Ultimately God fills us with His Spirit establishing His law within our hearts to guide and direct His people to keep His statutes. John 3:34 *"For He whom God has sent speaks the words of God; for He gives the spirit without measure."* Through His Spirit we can know God's will and purpose intuitively. His law will then be written on our hearts.

Thank you Lord, for giving us Your Spirit to guide us according to Your will and purpose, Amen!

September 25: Day 268

GOD'S POWER IS SUFFICIENT TO CREATE THE HEAVENS

*Jeremiah 32:17 "**Ah Lord God! Behold**, You **have made the heavens and the earth by Your great power and by Your outstretched arm!** Nothing is too difficult for You."*

God is our one and only sufficient cause for the reality of our universe, and our world. The amount of energy necessary to create even a small amount of matter would be enormous. To destroy even a small amount of matter in a nuclear explosion reveals the power of the atom. God however was sufficient in power to create the entire universe, a staggering amount of power. Only an omnipotent power would be able to create the enormous universe we see today.

A sufficient cause has always been a dilemma for current science. How do we get something from nothing? The laws of thermodynamics would conflict with the idea of a spontaneous creation. From nothing, nothing comes. Yet we are asked to accept such a reality. The only person who was present at creation was God, who preserved for man a testimony of His creative works. The same theme is repeated in Jeremiah 51:15 *"It is He who made the earth by His power, who established the world by His wisdom, And by His understanding He stretched out the heavens."* An infinite all powerful God gives us the only sufficient cause for complexities of our world and the vastness of the universe.

Thank you Lord, for our existence, without Your creative power, we would not be here. You have done all things well in the creation of our world. You have demonstrated Your power in the immensity of the universe, Amen!

September 26: Day 269

GOD MULTIPLIES AND PRESERVES HIS PEOPLE

Jeremiah 33:22 "As the host of heaven cannot be counted and the sand of the sea cannot be measured, so I will multiply the descendants of David My servant and the Levites who minister to Me.' "

The prophet Jeremiah repeats what King David declared in His Psalms centuries earlier. The heavens are vast. For ancient man to declare the heavens uncountable is not as profound a statement as it would be in the 21st century. With the Hubble Telescope, James Web, and other deep space devices, we have learned the number of stars to be exactly as this verse indicates, uncountable. Even the number of galaxies is nearly uncountable, each containing billions of stars. Though we could possibly count the numbers of Jews and Christians today, the number going into eternity could well be uncountable; we don't really know.

Jeremiah 33:25-26 continues to establish the promise of God's protective hand on the Jewish people. *"thus says the LORD, If My covenant for day and night stand not, and the fixed patterns of heaven and earth I have not established, then I would reject the descendants of Jacob and David My servant, not taking from his descendants rulers over descendants of Abraham, Isaac and Jacob. But I will restore their fortunes and will have mercy on them."* God's promises concerning the Jewish people continue to bear witness to the truth. God is able to protect all those who seek Him and are called according to His purpose.

Thank you Lord, that You have numbered the sands of the sea as well as knowing the hearts of every person who has ever lived. You have multiplied and preserved Your people by Your great power, Amen!

September 27: Day 270

GOD IS GREATER THAN ZEUS OR THOR

Jeremiah 51:16 "And he causes the clouds to ascend from the end of the earth; **He makes lightning for the rain."**

Fictional characters seem to garner more attention in the movies today than our Creator God. Greek mythology holds that Zeus somehow throws lightning bolts. Thor on the other hand creates lightning and thunder with his hammer. These diversions however pale in comparison in power to the one true God, who through the power of His word controls all the elements of nature. God alone provides the rains for our crops, the sun for photosynthesis, and the minerals necessary for plant life to grow. He alone created and holds all the information and details for life on this planet.

The factual nature of lightning creating rain is documented scientifically. Ancient man again would not be able to verify such a relationship between lightning and rain. A New York Times article from August 7, 2012 states: ". . . *Lightning often precedes rain.*" When ice crystals form in the upper atmosphere, they will have a negative charge. Water droplets form with a positive charge; when these charges are great enough, we have lightning. God's Word is consistent with what science has discovered to be true. God's Word is greater than science, since scientists are consistently trying to discover and understand what God created.

Thank you Lord, for the wonders of Your creation, You alone know all the workings of creation as You are the Creator and Architect of lightening, rain, and thunder, Amen!

September 28: Day 271

OUR MAKER KEEPS HIS PROMISES

*Jeremiah 51:19 "The portion of Jacob is not like these; **for the Maker of all is He**, And of the tribe of His inheritance; The LORD of hosts is His name."*

God speaks of the foolishness of mankind and contrasts this with His compassion for the tribe of Judah. God promised His people the Jews whom He chose to fulfill a roll, to bring the savior into the world to redeem all mankind. Our creator God is actively preserving the Jewish people for the purpose of demonstrating His faithfulness to His word. We have the nation of Israel with us today due in part to God's promises to return His people to the land of their inheritance.

The fulfillment of this great promise, the preservation of the Jewish nation gives greater substance to the promises of salvation made available through God's Son to all mankind; to all who are willing to accept it. We can have confidence that all God's promises can be trusted to be fulfilled in their proper time.

1 Thessalonians 5:23-24 *"Now may the God of peace himself sanctify you completely, and may your whole spirit and soul and body be kept blameless at the coming of our Lord Jesus Christ. He who calls you is faithful; he will surely do it."* God our Maker is also our great promise keeper, He alone can be trusted.

Thank you Lord, that all Your promises are true. You are faithful to bring about all Your promises to Your people, Amen!

Lamentations

Jeremiah's Lamentations gives no direct reference to God as creator, He is credited with His ongoing presence in directing the lives of men and of nations. God is definitely sovereign. God is continually at work moving within the hearts of men. Just as Jeremiah learned that he could not remain silent. Even though the leaders of Judah rejected his message. It was still his responsibility to speak out God's warning.

September 29: Day 272

WE ALL HAVE AN APPOINTMENT WITH GOD

Lamentations 1:15 "The LORD has rejected all my strong men In my midst; He has called an appointed time against me. . ."

Jeremiah contrasts the difference between man and God. God's reign does not end but extends from generation to generation on to eternity; this is not the case for men whose rule may extend upwards to 50 to 60 years and they die. Their power is given then from above and is temporary. There is no real power among men, they are given a stewardship of which they must make an accounting. Lamentations 5:19 *"You, O LORD, rule forever; Your throne is from generation to generation."* Our Creator God is eternal and He must be treated as Holy.

We all have an appointed time when we will meet God. We have a specific number of days to our credit. We will according to the biblical text give an exact accounting of our entire life. God is exacting in His appropriation of time for every human being. In the same way, God created a universe for a specific purpose, to provide a habitat for His creation Man. We are each appointed a number of days, after which we will be judged or graded. Hebrews 2:27 *"And inasmuch as it is appointed for men to die once and after this comes judgment,"* We all have an appointed day to come before our Maker.

Thank you Lord, for giving us life and days on this earth. May we be faithful to the tasks given us so that we may come before your throne unashamed, Amen!

Ezekiel

The preservation of His people. Ezekiel reminded the Jewish people in exile to settle in with their new home in Babylon for the short term. God has not abandoned His promises to the Jews.

September 30: Day 273

GOD CREATED THE NILE
AND ALL RIVERS

Ezekiel 29:3 "***My Nile is mine, and I myself have made it***." *God created the Nile along with the whole earth.*

We learn some of the specifics concerning God's creative power. God is specifically credited with the creation of the Nile River. This, the largest river in the world, and is a result of God's creative power. All rivers on the planet have their origins from God. God created the terrain and the elevations of the land that allows rivers to flow. God is the one who makes gravity work to cycle water into the oceans. The Nile River was the life blood for the Egyptian in early antiquity. They needed the Nile for their food, for drinking water, for navigation; it became the center for their way of life. Even Jesus spent time in Egypt and was most likely familiar with the Nile, and the ways of life for the Egyptian people.

In today's world, rivers are still an intricate part of our way of life. We use rivers for irrigation, transportation of commodities, recreation, and hydroelectric power. Rivers are responsible to recycling water through evaporation, rains, and snow. The hydrologic cycle of water movement is clearly spelled out in Isaiah 55:10 *"For as the rain and the snow come down from heaven, And do not return there without watering the earth And making it bear and sprout, And furnishing seed to the sower and bread to the eater;"* the Nile River as with all bodies of water are sustaining life on this planet, without which we would soon die. Rivers are an integral part of God's many provisions for our continued existence in this world.

Thank you Lord, for water, and its sustaining capabilities for our livelihood. You have ordered our world in such a precise way to filter and clean our water for its continued use. You have created all things well, Amen!

Daniel

God's miraculous preservation of those in captivity. God rules over the Realm of mankind. God gives Daniel a foretaste of the future. God is regarded as the one in control of all elements of life and nature.

October 1: Day 274

GOD KNOWS OUR DREAMS AND ESTABLISHES KINGS

*Daniel 2:21 "It is **He who changes the times and the epochs**; He removes kings and establishes kings: He gives wisdom to wise men, And knowledge to men of understanding."*

All knowledge, even the dreams of men are known by God. Daniel and his friends were confronted with a problem by King Nebuchadnezzar. He demanded that the wise men tell him the dream and give the interpretation. Whether he forgot his dream, or just didn't trust the wise men to give him the correct interpretation is unclear. It was Daniel who rescued them by consulting with God about the contents of the dream along with its interpretation. In this case, God demonstrates His total knowledge and understanding of man, including his thoughts and dreams.

Even to this day, God knows the hearts of all men. God can even use dreams to communicate His will to men. God intervenes in the life of Joseph the husband of Mary to alter his plans to divorce her. Matthew 1:20 *"an angel of the Lord appeared to him in a dream, saying, 'Joseph, son of David do not be afraid to take Mary as your wife; for the Child who has been conceived in her is of the Holy Spirit."* Dreams can often be used by God, to change people's lives. Daniel expresses his thanks to God for intervening and saving his life. Daniel 2:23 *"To You, O God of my fathers, I give thanks and praise, For You have given me wisdom and power; Even now You have made known to me what we requested of You For You have made known to us the king's matter."* God knows our plans, our innermost thoughts and our dreams.

Thank you Lord that you are ultimately in control of the affairs of all men. You alone know the hearts, thoughts, and dreams of men. You alone rise up and take down kings, rulers, and princes, Amen!

October 2: Day 275

ONLY GOD GRANTS POWER TO MEN TO RULE

Daniel 5:11-12: The Highest God: this reference acknowledges man's tendency to worship lesser images. **God alone is above the entire earth.** *"Most High God is ruler over the realm of mankind and that He sets over it whomever He wishes."*

All rulers of this age are granted power for a limited amount of time for God's purposes. There is no such thing as real power, it is only an illusion. Even the riches granted men are given as a temporary blessing or curse, depending on one's relationship with God. God alone holds real power, power sufficient to create and sustain the continuation of earth, and the universe is firmly in God's hands.

Even though God is the One in power and ultimate control of earth, and the affairs of man; He has temporarily granted man a portion of power for the purpose of teaching us submission to authority, to teach those in power how to use that power for the ultimate good. The hierarchy of authority is a critical part of an orderly society. Levels of authority exist throughout society in the form of Government, military, religious, and social family units. The purpose of these hierarchal structures is to bring order to all of society, without which we would be in chaos. Concerning the centurions who came before Jesus, Matthew 8:9 gives us a clear representation of such an authority structure. *"For I also am a man under authority with soldiers under me; and I say to this one, 'Go!' and he goes, and to another, 'Come!' and he comes, and to my slave, 'Do this!' and he does it."* God is the supreme authority, and gives authority to whom He wishes.

Thank you Lord, for the hierarchy of structure and authority making an orderly society possible. We would not be able to function freely without conflict if not for Your ultimate benevolent authority, Amen!

October 3: Day 276

OUR LIVES ARE PROLONGED BY HIS POWER

*Daniel 5:23 "**But the God in whose hands are your life-breath and your ways,** you have not glorified."*

Man is completely dependent upon God's continuing grace. Man's very breath rests upon God's provision to sustain life; this was in reference to the Chaldeans drinking from the vessels taken from the temple in Jerusalem during the reign of Nebuchadnezzar, a reminder to those who used objects without knowledge of their nature. These were instruments for worshiping God, not to be used superficially at a party. Like Uzzah who died touching the Ark improperly, so too the Chaldeans died not just for lack of knowledge but for willful disrespect; God will not be disrespected.

We live today because of God's sustaining power. Our lives depend upon His provisions for air, with the right balance of oxygen to carbon dioxide, while the body is delicately designed to transfer oxygen to all vital organs. Life systems are extremely complex, requiring many things to operate succinctly in harmony. Our life and breath are gifts from God. Acts 25:17b ". . . *He Himself gives to all people life and breath and all things;*" We are the beneficiaries of God's continual provision of grace.

Thank you Lord, for the gift of life. For the conditions making life possible on earth. All things work together to give us life, Amen!

October 4: Day 277

GOD RESTRAINS THE BEASTS AND CONTROLS THE ELEMENTS

*Daniel 6:26-27 "For He is the living God and enduring forever, And His kingdom is one which will not be destroyed, And His dominion will be forever. **He delivers and rescues and performs signs and wonders In the heaven and on earth** Who has also delivered Daniel from the power of the lions."*

The statement given by king Darius demonstrates the respect gained as a result of Daniel's survival of the lion's den without harm. Following Daniel's release, his accusers were thus cast into the same den, being devoured immediately. The lion's frustration at their inability to feast on Daniel obviously took it out on Daniel's enemies. God is in control of all nature. Even the beasts submit to His will. God takes special care of those who honor Him as Daniel did. God's kingdom can never be destroyed, no matter what men try to do in opposition to God's purposes.

Even as the animals are under God's domain and control. God is also in control of the elements of nature. In Daniel 3:25 we read that Shadrach, Meshach, and Abednego. *"He* (King Nebuchadnezzar*) said; 'Look!' I see four men loosed and walking about in the midst of the fire without harm, and the appearance of the fourth is like a son of the gods!"* Daniel's friends were willing to be thrown into a fiery furnace rather than deny God. God demonstrated His complete control over the normal actions of a lion, and the unprecedented outcome of 3 men walking out of a fiery furnace unharmed. It should be of no surprise that our Creator God is able to control the events of His creation.

Thank you Lord, for the example of extraordinary men, willing to face death rather than deny You. May we be so bold in our faith to stand faithful in this world even at the risk of death, knowing that You will save, either by overcoming the elements, or by bringing us safely into Your presence through death, Amen!

Minor Prophets

Each of the Minor Prophets, consisting of 12 men, carries a specific reference to God's creative ability. Even though the latter prophets rarely focus on God as creator, His power, and creative attributes are clearly visible. Just like the number 12 indicates God's divine Power to create. He is "God over Creation." Each of the prophets carried a specific message to the people of Israel and Judah. They were being warned of impending judgment unless they repented. Even in the midst of their rebellion, God was still faithful in His promises as they would be carried forward into the future.

Hosea

Hosea reminds the reader, we were created by God for a reason, don't forget it. God will restore His people to Himself.

October 5: Day 278

DON'T FORGET HIM
WHO CREATED YOU

*Hosea 8:14 "For Israel has forgotten **his Maker** and built palaces; And Judah has multiplied fortified cities,"*

The divided nation of Israel fell to the Assyrians during the lifetime of Hosea around 722 BC. The reason given was their rejection of almighty God. The entire nation drifted away from God during the nearly two centuries of separation from Judah where the temple worship was located. They sought to worship God in their own lands, in their own way. They forgot about the Law of God and moved steadily away from putting God at the center of their worship, setting up idols. While many within the lands of Israel moved to Judah when the nations split (2 Chronicles 34:9). The northern kingdom's first king Jeroboam moved the people of the northern tribes away from God.

Since the nature of God does not change, He is the same Yesterday, Today, and Forever; we must not forget we were created in His image to honor and serve Him. We must not forget the price our Messiah, Jesus, paid on the cross to restore us back into a right relationship with Him. God is seeking an intimate relationship with His people today. Hosea 2:19: *"I will betroth you to Me forever."* Man's relationship with God is compared to that of a man and wife and their marriage commitment. God desires a close relationship with man to last forever. We must never take that relationship for granted or forget the blessing available to us if we will earnestly seek Him.

Thank you Father, for reminding us of Your great love. May we never forget the price You paid to redeem us to Yourself, Amen!

Joel

There is no specific mention of God as creator. However, God still controls the movement of the sun, moon, and stars. He will pour out His spirit on mankind, being our faithful provider. He will intervene into the affairs of His people, restoring them back to Him.

October 6: Day 279

GOD'S CONTINUAL PROVISIONS & JUDGMENTS

Joel 2:23 "For He has given you the early rain for your vindication And He has poured down for you the rain, The early and latter rain as before."

God's eternal promises are again affirmed by Joel. Joel reminds the people that God provided for your wellbeing by giving you timely rains for their crops. God is in control of the elements as He sees fit, to bless, or discipline the people. For the Jewish people, rain was an indication of God's blessings. But for those opposed to God's people, He makes a prediction of future judgment on the nations. God is well aware of all the events concerning history of nations as well as individual needs.

The **Creator of the nations**, is also the judge over all the nations. Joel 3:12: *"Let the nations be around And come up to the valley of Jehoshaphat, For there I will sit to judge All the surrounding nations."* The nations surrounding Judah were often the same nations hostile to the Jewish people. It is these people that would be judged either through the circumstances of history, or at some future event. The nations who were hostile to Israel and Judah, no longer exist. Historical events displaced those nations. This warning applies to the nations today who would oppose the nation of Israel. God's warnings are still valid, and His judgments will eventually come in time.

Thank you Lord, that you care about us by providing what we need to live. We pray for Your people, the Jews, and the nation of Israel, for their continued protection and salvation, Amen!

October 7: Day 280

GOD ENABLES THROUGH HIS SPIRIT

*Joel 2:29 "I will pour out My Spirit in those days. **I will display wonders in the sky and on the earth**,"*

God intends to do a future work that will require the power and influence of His Spirit. The wonders being displayed in the sky by the James Web Telescope show in part the majestic magnitude of the universe as seen through the marvel of modern technology. Even wonders discovered on the earth through advances in technology demonstrate the unquenched desire of man to know and understand God's creation. It is God's intention for man to discover the wonders of His creation. Proverbs 25:2 *"It is the glory of God to conceal a matter, But the glory of kings is to search out a matter."* What is discovered by man, is not a creation of man; we may forget the surrounding advances of science and technology are a result of man's unquenchable thirst to discover. Man is only the discoverer and not the creator. God alone creates, all the materials, the physical laws, and the necessary resources to discover God's wonders.

God instills His spirit in man, granting the skills and ability within people for accomplishing great works. A review of Exodus 35:31 demonstrate the necessity of God's Spirit in man: *"and He has filled him, with the Spirit of God, in wisdom, in understanding and in knowledge and in all craftsmanship;"* All that is necessary for advancements in our knowledge is already provided by God's creative work and the presence of His Spirit. God's Spirit is the most important part of learning about God. It is His Spirit that draws men to Himself as well as enabling men to discover great things.

Thank you Lord, for the gift of Your Holy Spirit helping us to serve You and mankind. Without Your spirit guiding, encouraging, and directing toward you, we would be at a loss, Amen!

Amos

Amos paints a more descriptive picture of God's creative power over the forces of nature. God is responsible for forming the mountains; He is the creator of stars and their constellations.

October 8: Day 281

GOD'S CREATIVE POWER TAKES MANY FORMS

*Amos 4:13 "For behold, **He who forms mountains and creates the wind** And declares to man what are His thoughts, **He who makes dawn into darkness** And treads on the high places of the earth, The LORD God of hosts is His name."*

For those who have climbed a mountain, know of its immensity, yet even a mountain is but a drop in the bucket compared to the complexities of the universe. Our Creator God has infinite power to create; this condition is not possible through any other natural process. Only our God is sufficient in power and knowledge to create the balanced beauty of our complex world.

God is the One who created all the components of our wonderful creation. The wind, the rains, all the scientific wonders that we explore and understand. God knows our very thoughts as we contemplate His majesty. Without God's orderly and constructive creation, science could not begin to work, let alone understand any of its complexities. God as creator made the universe to be understood. Yet, the more we explore, the more complex it becomes. Genesis 1:28 "*God blessed them; and God said to them, Be fruitful and multiply, and fill the earth, and subdue it; and rule over the fish of the sea, and over the birds of the sky and over every living thing that moves on the earth.*" God formed our complex and orderly world to be understood, at least in part.

Thank you Lord, for giving us a window into understanding some of Your creative power, Amen!

October 9: Day 282

THE CONSTELLATIONS
ARE HIS HANDIWORK

*Amos 5:8-9 "**He who made the Pleiades and Orion** And changes deep darkness into morning, Who also darkens day into night, Who calls for the waters of the sea And pours them out on the surface of the earth, The LORD is His name, It is He who flashes forth with destruction upon the strong."*

God created the constellations to be seen and understood. Genesis 1:14 explains their purpose: *"And God said, Let there be lights in the firmament of the heaven to divide the day from the night; and let them be for signs, and for seasons, and for days, and years;"* God is the one who ordered our days, our seasons and our calendars. He provided the day and night sequencing making our routine of life possible. He paints the skies with deep blue and our night skies in black. He orchestrates the colors of heavens through the power of His Word.

God assembled not only the heavens but poured out upon the earth all the waters of the sea. He separates the water from the land, giving habitat for many varied forms of life. Our God who created the universe is not confined to our Earth. Amos continues to explain the grandeur of God by placing His abode in the heavens. *Amos 9:6 "**The One who builds His upper chambers in the heavens** And has founded His vaulted dome over the earth, He who calls for the waters of the sea And pours them out on the face of the earth, The LORD is His name."* From the placement of the stars and constellations in sky, to the precision of the hydraulic cycle, God is in control of His creation.

Thank you Lord, for the beauty of Your creation. You formed the constellations, Your abode is in the heavens; You designed all things well, Amen!

Obadiah

We are given no direct reference to God as creator in this short book of one chapter. God however is clearly in control of the nations, as He warns them of eventual judgment.

October 10: Day 283

GOD IS CREATOR AND JUDGE OF THE NATIONS

Obadiah verse 4 "Though you build high like the eagle, Though you set your nest among the stars, From there I will bring you down," declares the LORD."

God's omnipresence is on display as He warns the people of Edom there is no place they can hide. God knows all the deeds of the nations as He prepares to set judgment upon the nation of Edom. In Obadiah verse15, we are given the standard by which God will judge Edom as well as the nations. *"For the day of the LORD draws near on all the nations. As you have done, it will be done to you. Your dealings will return on your own head."* Every nation is ultimately accountable to God for the treatment of all people good and bad; there is no escaping that reality.

The verdict was already given concerning the nation of Edom. Obadiah confirms in verse 18. *"So that there will be no survivor of the house of Esau."* (Edom). Even the wise men are not excluded from this judgment. Obadiah verse 8*: "Will I not on that day, 'declares the LORD,' destroy wise men from Edom."* A warning to the kings of the earth not to persecute Israel (Jews); the consequences of such behaviors will be their destruction. This warning applies even to the nations who oppose Israel today. No nation on earth is immune to God's ultimate justice. *Amos 3:2 "Therefore I will punish you for all your iniquities."* All people are accountable before God, there is no place we can hide from His presence.

Thank you Lord, that You are a just and perfect Judge who knows all things. We give you praise for the pardon You granted us through Your Son, Amen!

Jonah

Jonah makes a clear reference to God as the creator. God created all peoples for a purpose, and desires all men to be saved. God is quite able to rescue someone out of the belly of a whale or large fish.

October 11: Day 284

THE WITNESS RETURNED FROM THE DEAD

*Jonah: 1:9 "He said to them, 'I am a Hebrew, and I fear **the LORD God of heaven who made the sea and the dry land.**"*

Jonah is one of the least accepted books in the Bible. The idea of a man being swallowed by a fish, then being thrown out alive is a bit much for some to accept. History however has a way of restoring confidence in the biblical account; another such event took place some years past, giving credibility to Jonah's experience. As Jonah was fleeing from God's command to go to an evil nation, he is intercepted by God. In this case, Jonah's fear was misplaced, if he truly feared God, he would have gone to Nineveh the first time.

Jonah demonstrates the compassion God has for the nations. Jonah 4:2 *"I knew that You are a gracious and compassionate God, slow to anger and abundant in lovingkindness, and one who relents concerning calamity."* The same God who created the land and the sea, seeks to reach out to the nations. Assyria was one of the most wicked nations on earth at the time. Jonah did not want the nation of Assyria to repent because of their wickedness. Jonah 3:5 *"Then the people of Nineveh believed in God; and they called a fast and put on sackcloth from the greatest to the least of them."* God is seeking all men to come to repentance. It is God: 2 Timothy 2:4 *"who desire all men to be saved and to come to the knowledge of the truth."* It would seem that God is more concerned with the needs of the lost than many believers.

Thank you Lord, that You love all people. You sacrificed Your Son in our behalf because of Your great love. May we, be more compassionate for the lost, and seek to reach out to others with the good news of Your mercy and grace, Amen!

Micah

God reveals Himself to the people as He reigns over Israel. He gives us the power through His Spirit to do His work.

October 12: Day 285

GOD GIVES US THE POWER TO DO HIS WORK

*Micah 3:8 "**I am filled with power --With the Spirit of the LORD** -- And with justice and courage to make known to Jacob his rebellious act, Even to Israel his sin."*

God instills more than just talents and skills; He grants specific individuals the power and courage to become faithful witnesses in difficult situations. Micah relates how, through God's creative power enables him to speak. As a prophet of God, he does not speak on his own account, the message comes from God. It is His power that communicates and establishes His purpose. God is continually in the process of guiding and directing His people.

We are called as witnesses to the power and mercy of God in an increasingly secular culture today. God has promised to equip those who seek Him to be witnesses to the power of God to save His people from their sins. Everyone who calls upon the name of the Lord is called to be an evangelist in some way. God promises to equip us for this task according to His grace. As we draw near to God, He equips us for the task, giving us the strength and the words. Luke 12:12 *"for **the Holy Spirit will teach you** in that very hour what you ought to say"* As we draw near to God, we will know His purposes and He will equip us to be witnesses of His grace and mercy to a dying world in need of a Savior.

Thank you Lord, for the privilege of being a witnesses for You. You have filled us with Your Spirit to do the work of an evangelist. May we be faithful in that task to serve and encourage others by Your power and spirit, Amen!

Nahum

God demonstrates His remarkable power. Even though God's creative power is not mentioned, His power to control and guide His creation is clearly revealed.

October 13: Day 286

GOD'S INFINITE POWER

Nahum 1:3 "The LORD is slow to anger and great in power."

Numerous passages throughout the Bible portray God as possessing power. God is the ultimate possessor of power in the universe. He is the Creator and the only one with sufficient power to create the universe we see. The amount of energy (power) necessary from the creation of matter as it exists in the universe is unfathomable. Even the slightest conversion of energy to matter would require huge amounts of power and energy. The God of the Bible is continually presented as the One with sufficient power necessary for the creation of all things.

Nahum illustrates how God can do great works requiring power and control. Nahum 1:*4 "He rebukes the sea and makes it dry,"* in much the same way His Son (Jesus) was able to rebuke the winds and the waves. He dries up all the rivers. The power of God's Word in His rebuke can effect massive change. God is in charge of the forces of nature. God can do what He pleases within the context of His ultimate will. Nahum continues this theme in verse 5 *"Mountains quake because of Him and the hills dissolve: Indeed the earth is upheaved by His presence, the world and all the inhabitants in it."* His presence can result in geological upheavals.

A comforting thought concerning God's power is His goodness. God is in complete control and seeks the good of man, not evil. Nahum 1:7 *"The LORD is good, A stronghold in the day of trouble, And He knows those who take refuge in Him."* God's knowledge is complete, He knows the status of the entire world. He is continually seeking the good of all those who seek to serve Him.

Thank you Lord, that You are our stronghold. It is by Your power and strength our universe exists and that we have life and purpose. You alone are the possessor of all power, Amen!

Habakkuk

Our eternal God, He is the creator of time. God can even use evil to accomplish His purposes.

October 14: Day 287

GOD IS THE CREATOR OF TIME

Habakkuk 1:12 "Are You not from everlasting, O LORD."

The Bible makes a clear case, God has no time constraints, He existed before time as we know it. The biblical account gives us a description of God that transcends not only time, He existed from eternity past. For time to exist, One must be above and beyond the confines of time and all recorded history. This typifies our Creator God; He is not bound by time constraints but is able to exist beyond its grasp. Time comes into existence at the same moment of creation.

God has a splendor that transcends our reality. Habakkuk 3:3 "*His splendor covers the heavens.*" If the heavens refer to the universe, this places God above all creation. It gives modern man proof of His infinite creative power. He must then be much greater than the universe we can only see in part. In the same way, we can only see God in part. We are only able to get a small glimpse of His Glory, only that which He has revealed to us in His Word (Special revelation) and His creation (Natural revelation). This Word was revealed through a people (Jews) over a course of 2,000 years. We are privy to some details through His Word. God's splendor is still above our grasp but will be revealed in time.

Another common theme revolves around God's eternal ways. Habakkuk 3: 6 "*His ways are everlasting.*" No end to His existence. God stands above and beyond His creation. He is the answer to problem of existence; why is there something rather than nothing? There is much more to existence than what is currently observable. We have the hope, that one day we will see all things clearly.

Thank you Lord, for revealing to us a portion of You power and glory. You alone are eternal, because of Your eternal existence, we have the hope of eternal life, Amen!

Zephaniah

No direct mention is made of God's creative power; God however is shown to be perfect and without fail. God will judge Judah for its wickedness. God will save a remnant of the sons of Judah. God will rule over and judge the nations on earth with perfect justice.

October 15: Day 288

GOD RULES HIS CREATION WITHOUT FAIL

Zephaniah 3:5 "He does not fail."

God stands in complete contrast to the frailties of man. Though man will fail many times over, God will never fail in His words, promises or warnings. We must take heed concerning the words of God. They will not fail. Time is not the determining factor. Since God is slow to anger and slow in His judgments, man becomes callous and careless regarding God's judgments. All that God says, will eventually come to pass.

The entire book of Zephaniah is a warning to the nations surrounding Israel of their impending judgment. Zephaniah 3:8 *"Therefore wait for Me,' declares the LORD, For the day when I rise up as a witness. Indeed, My decision is to gather nations, To assemble kingdoms, To pour out on them My indignation, All My burning anger; For all the earth will be devoured by the fire of My zeal."* The One responsible for the nations, is also He who will judge and destroy. We are all accountable to God for how we live and what we do with the lives God has given us. God who is perfect, and does not fail, is like the accountant who balances the books to the penny; so too God will be exacting in His judgments; He will not fail.

We trust You Lord, to make all things right in Your time. All accounts will be balanced, and all things will be made right, Amen!

Haggai

God places His Spirit in men to accomplish His work. He who shakes the heavens, He is one and same with Him who created the heavens.

October 16: Day 289

GOD'S SPIRIT WORKS IN US

*Haggai 1:14 "**So the LORD stirred up the spirit of Zerubbabel** the son of Shealtiel, governor of Judah, and the spirit of Joshua the son of Jehozadad, the high priest, and the spirit of all the remnant of the people; and they came and worked on the house of the LORD of hosts, their God,"*

In the Old Testament, God accomplishes His purposes by placing His Spirit upon key individuals. It is questionable whether the second temple would have been built had God not intervened within the hearts of key individuals. Nations rise and fall, but those who would return, are often converted to the religious systems of the nations who conquered them.

Haggai looks into the future as God indicates His ultimate plan to shake the heavens and the earth. Haggai: 2:6 *"I am going to shake the heavens and the earth, the sea also and the dry land."* Verse 7 continues with the same theme. *"I will shake all the nations; and they will come with the wealth of all nations, and I will fill this house with glory, says the LORD of hosts."* The primary emphasis is upon God's actions to instill within man the desires to move and act according to God's purposes. In the ultimate sense, man is not very highly motivated toward spiritual acts of worship or service. God intervenes to bring about a higher purpose.

Thank you Lord, for stirring the hearts of those men so long ago. May You continue to stir our hearts to follow You with passion driven by a sincere faith, Amen!

Zechariah

God creates the storm clouds, He formed the heavens, and He puts His Spirit within man. God will restore His people to the land. Our God would be pierced for our transgressions.

October 17: Day 290
GOD RESTORES THE LAND TO HIS PEOPLE

Zechariah 3:9 "I will remove the iniquity of the land in one day."

Zechariah is the longest of the Minor Prophets. It was during this period that Jews were returning to their homeland in Palestine. Zechariah's primary mission was to challenge those who returned to complete the reconstruction of the temple. Zechariah also made many prophetic statements regarding the coming of the Messiah. Zechariah makes a clear statement regarding God as the Creator in Chapter 12:1. Zechariah makes many statements concerning God's plan to remove all sin, and to restore the people to a right relationship with their God. From this we can surmise God has a redemptive plan for mankind and is intimately connected with His people (The Jews and the Church) for the completion of that plan.

Zechariah 1:17 *"My cities will again overflow with prosperity, and the LORD will again comfort Zion and again choose Jerusalem."* The promise to restore Jerusalem was being fulfilled during the time of Zechariah. God's promise to restore Jerusalem was filled again in 1947 after the rise of the Zionist movement. May 15, 1948, witnessed the return of Palestine as a Jewish state, for the first time since before Roman rule.

Only God can remove sins and wrongs in that it is against God that we are held accountable; the God whose books must balance perfectly. Sin and iniquity give man no out before God. God is an exacting Judge. Just as our universe is perfectly balanced to support life; the Anthropic Principle is not an accident that made life possible. Precision is a vital part of the existence of man and the presence of sin is in direct conflict with a holy and perfect God. How God removed iniquity in one day was a story yet to be understood from the perspective of Zechariah's day. We understand it as Christ's sacrifice on the cross.

We thank you Lord for removing our sins from Your books in one day: through the shedding of Your Son's blood on the cross for our sins, Amen!

October 18: Day 291

GOD MAKES THE STORM CLOUDS

Zechariah 10:1 "Ask rain from the LORD at the time of the spring rain— **The LORD who makes the storm clouds; And He will give them** **showers of rain**, *vegetation in the field to each man."*

God as Creator will bring storms into our lives from time to time. Ecclesiastes 8:8a *"No man has authority over the wind. . ."* Only God. When weather causes great destruction, as in the form of a tornado, it is regarded as an 'Act of God." Though God allows such acts for a purpose in our fallen and broken world, God will allow only that which will ultimately result in Glory to Him. The New Testament gives us a direct example of this. Matthew 8:27 *"The men were amazed, and said, 'What kind of a man is this that even the winds and the sea obey Him?"* This passage would strongly suggest that Christ is God, He had complete control of the forces of nature and the weather. It also served to demonstrate to his disciples who He was.

Our God is not limited in what He is able to do for us, or through us. The One who is the Creator of the universe is also the same with Him who sacrificed and forgave us our sins. He knows us to the very depth of our hearts. Our God is the One who controls the elements and who works all things for our good and to the good of those who seek Him. Romans 8:28 *"And we know that God causes all to work together for good to those who love God, to those who are called according to His purpose."* Even the storm clouds have an ultimate purpose for good.

Thank you Lord, that You are in control of all the elements of nature. You alone are above the earth, and nothing can happen to us that is not in Your perfect will, Amen!

October 19: Day 292

GOD FORMS A SPIRIT WITHIN US

Zechariah 12:1 "The burden of the world of the LORD concerning Israel **Thus declares the LORD who stretches out the heavens, lays the foundation of the earth, and forms the spirit of man within him,"**

The One who stretches the heavens is the One who created the universe and the earth. Science gives us ample proof today that the heavens are expanding, diminishing any idea of an eternal oscillating universe. The universe had a beginning, and it is winding toward a conclusion. Zechariah reemphasizes the belief in God as the designer, not only of the universe and the world in which we live, but that the spirit of man originates from the hand of God as well. What exactly is our spirit, or our soul; this part of man is still a mystery beyond the scope of modern science.

Many within the science community would prefer to deny the existence of an eternal spirit in any way shape or form. To accept a spiritual reality, would be to acknowledge that natural science is limited and unable to explain many of the realities of our universe. In many ways, we are products of the culture in which we live. Many people live by fear of rejection, or simple ignorance. The believer however understands the reality in which we live. Proverbs 28:5 give some insight: *"Evil men do not understand justice, But those who seek the LORD understand all things."* When we recognize God as the creator of all things, it opens a door of unlimited understanding regarding the universe, this world and the spirit within us.

We acknowledge You God, the creator of all things. You have put an eternal spirit within us. You are the author of our being. Thank you for Your infinite grace and mercy extended to all who believe, Amen!

OUR GOD WAS PIERCED FOR US

Zechariah 12:10 "They will look upon Me whom they pierced."

Though this passage does not directly address God's creative power, it does give us some insight into the purpose of our creation. The essence of this passage points beyond the infinite power of God to His infinite love and compassion for all mankind; a future look at the death and resurrection of the Jewish Messiah. The reference to being pierced is a common Old Testament theme pointing to an individual who endured great suffering. Isaiah 53:5 gives this reference in another context: *"But He was pierced through for our transgressions, He was crushed for our iniquities; the chastening for our well-being fell upon Him."* Our Messiah took our transgressions upon Himself, as a substitutionary atonement.

The promise of a redeemer was given more clarity in the New Testament texts. Even though the Jews have yet to embrace the work of Jesus as their Messiah, the prediction of His being pierced occurred as the Old Testament texts stated; He was nailed to a cross. Any text or theory to have validity must be able to make predictions that come true; here is one example. An additional example is given in Psalm 22:16b *"They pierced my hands and my feet."* The context of this passage reflect the horrors of crucifixion nearly 1,000 years before the New Testament event. God's creative work comes to its pinnacle when Jesus cried out on the cross *"it is finished!"*

Thank you Lord, for the work you finished on the cross by being pierced for our transgressions. We thank you again for continuing Your work of transforming lives throughout the world, Amen!

Malachi

The last Old Testament prophet, acknowledges God as creator. He is unchanging, able to accomplish His purpose to bring all nations under His rule. God will one day restore relationships.

October 21: Day 294

WE ARE GOD'S CREATION

Malachi 2:10 "Has not one God created us?

Malachi ends the Minor Prophets and closes the book on the Old Testament. It will take another 500 years before the Bible is completed through the New Testament writers of the 1ˢᵗ century. Many things took place in the years between the Testaments. We witnessed the rise of the Greek empire and its influence upon the known world. The world would witness the rise and fall of several empires, including the Persian Empire, and the Greek Empire, though its influence continued because of its culture and learning. The brutal Roman Empire takes the stage as they enter into Israel to take control of the land and its people. The battle for control of the land (Israel) continues even up to the present day.

Malachi makes a direct statement regarding God as the One responsible for the creation of life, including Man and civilizations. Malachi is suggesting that the people understand this as a fact, yet they continued in their conflicts and quarrels. We must keep close to our hearts and minds the one fact that ties all men together, God is the one responsible for our existence and all that we see; we are a product of God's creative power. Malachi leaves us with on final promise regarding the coming of Elijah and the Messiah: Malachi 4:6 *"He will restore the hearts of the fathers to their children and the hearts of the children to their fathers, so that I will not come and smite the land with a curse."* John the Baptist is a precursor for Elijah (Matthew 11:14), he prepares the way for Jesus the Messiah. Through Christ's redemptive act, God creates and restores new life within mankind.

Lord God, thank you for all life you have given us. We acknowledge that everything we have comes from You. Restore our hearts OH Lord that we may be ready to meet You, Amen!

New Testament

Like the hand that fits into a glove, so too the New Testament completes the Old Testament closing this chapter of God's creative work while beginning a new one. The New Testament is the culmination of God's promised Redeemer. Jesus clarifies who He is, the Son of God possessing the very essence of God, one with the Father. He is our creator, our Redeemer, our perfect High Priest, and our soon coming King. In the person of Jesus Christ, we have the fulfillment of all Old Testament prophecies regarding the promised Messiah.

Matthew

God's inspired gospel by a tax collector. The Gospel of Matthew is directed at Jews who would understand the significance of Genealogies in connection with the Messianic claims regarding Jesus as the Christ, the Messiah. The omnipotence of God is made clear through the pages of Matthew. God is in complete control of the events and circumstances surrounding His Son and the direction these events would lead.

October 22: Day 295

GOD DRESSED DOWN AND CLOTHED HIMSELF IN HUMAN FORM

Genealogies: Matthew 1

Matthew chapter 1 traces three sets of 14 genealogies leading us to the life of the promised Messiah; these genealogies trace the ancestry of Jesus through three periods of Jewish History. The first set of genealogies traced from Adam to Abraham giving us the Abrahamic covenant. The second set of genealogies goes through King David fulfilling the Davidic covenant with the promise that Israel will never lack a person to sit on the throne. The promise predicted that a direct decedent from David will reign forever. The last set of 14 generations, traces from the captivity up through the birth of Jesus.

New Testament texts were given to demonstrate the fulfillment of the Old Testament promises. Genesis 22:18a *"In your seed all the nations of the earth shall be blessed."* The person of Jesus fulfills the Abrahamic Covenant regarding the promised seed, Jesus. The northern kingdom of Israel experienced coop after coop with no continuity. The division of Israel and Judah was God's working to protect the ancestry of Jesus. Judah was going to war with Israel to restore the united kingdom, but God intervened. I Kings 12:24 *"thus says the LORD, 'You must not go up and fight against your relatives the sons of Israel; return every man to his house, for this thing has come from me."* Matthew's genealogies demonstrate God's faithfulness in preserving Jesus' pedigree amidst many conflicts.

Thank you Lord, that You are in complete control over the affairs of man. You protected Your Son by preserving the promises given of the promised seed of both the Abrahamic and Davidic covenants, Amen!

October 23: Day 296

GOD KNOWS ALL ABOUT US, GOOD AND BAD

Matthew 10:30 "The very hairs of your head are all numbered."

God's absolute knowledge of Man and his ways is brought front and center through this interesting statement demonstrating the exacting nature of **God's creative ability**; nothing is lost or unaccounted for. Everything is purposeful and plays a role in the continuing saga of human history. We can only know in part, **God the creator** knows all things in complete detail. Just as God knows the names of all the stars in the heavens by name. Psalm 147:4 *"He counts the number of the stars; He gives names to all of them."* God knows us more completely than we know ourselves.

We are reminded by this challenging passage that God knows every detail of His creation. It is estimated that we can have in excess of 50,000 hairs on our head. This is only a small fraction of what God knows and understands. God alone can be just in His judgments because He is privy to every detail of our lives, He knows every aspect of His creation; He knows every word uttered by men though-out history. It is also clear that there will be an exact accounting of our lives. Psalm 139:1-2 *"O Lord, You have searched me and known me. You know when I sit down and when I rise up; You understand my thought from afar."* He knows everything about us including the hairs on our head.

Lord we are humbled by the knowledge that You know everything about us, good and bad. Thank you that You do not hold our sins and failures against us by clearing our slate through Your sacrifice, Amen!

October 24: Day 297

OUR CONVERSATIONS ARE BEING RECORDED

Matthew 12:36 "Every idle word that men shall speak, they shall give account thereof in the day of judgment"

Since our Creator God knows everything, be wise in all your speech. Every word is being recorded. God is just in His judgments because He is privy to every detail of our lives, He knows every aspect of His creation; He knows every word uttered by men though-out history. It is also clear that there will be an exact accounting of our lives. From this passage alone, it would be wise to take the advice of this tax collector (Matthew), one who was responsible to the Roman authorities for the accuracy of his books. God is perfect in this regard, His accounting will not only balance the books, He will account for every idle word.

Our Creator God not only knows every detail of our complex universe; He knows everything about each of us, our motives, thoughts, and words. In addition to His ultimate knowledge, He cautions us to use His name with honor and not carelessly. Exodus 20:7 *"You shall not take the name of the LORD your God in vain, for the LORD will not leave him unpunished who takes His name in vain."* God not only wants us to honor His holy name, He will hold us accountable to what we say about others, and how we treat others.

Help us Lord to guard our mouth, to be slow to speak, to speak kindly with those around us, and to think the best about others, Amen!

October 25: Day 298

GENERATIONAL JUDGMENTS

Matthew 12:41 "The men of Nineveh will stand up with this generation at the judgment and condemn it, because they repented at the preaching of Jonah; and behold, something greater than Jonah is here."

Jesus quotes this passage to the Jews to remind them, God cares also for the Gentiles. God is judge of the Jews, and the Gentiles, the living and the dead. He is above time and able to judge across the span of history, attributing responsibility for all wrongs. It would seem that people from different generations would be witnesses against those who would follow. God will hold responsible people whose crimes were committed as a response to their father's wrongdoing. Generational wrongs would appear in conflict with God's statement that each man would be responsible for his own sins. The apparent conflict with regard to this statement would be resolved in light of a greater spiritual reality; only eternity can answer this question.

The people of Nineveh apparently repented at the preaching of Jonah. This seems like a most unlikely group as the Ninevites were extremely evil in contrast to Jewish morality. It was for that reason, Jonah sought to flee when God commanded him to go to Nineveh. The generation of people who repented at the preaching of Jonah must have truly changed. It is unfortunate their children didn't do the same. God would eventually destroy Nineveh as the people returned to their old ways.

The Jews of Jesus' generation were to be held responsible for the death of the prophets. Luke 11:50 *"so that the blood of all prophets, shed since the foundation of the world, may be charged against this generation."* It must be noted, Jesus forgave the people before Him who were most responsible for His crucifixion.

Lord may we not be a stumbling block for others. Thank you for forgiving us of all our wrongs, Amen!

October 26: Day 299

JESUS MULTIPLIES OR CREATES FOOD BEFORE THE MULTITUDE

Matthew 15:36 "and He took the seven loaves and the fish; and giving thanks, He broke them and started giving them to the disciples, and the disciples gave them to the people."

This passage in Matthew shows **Jesus' creative power** as He is able to multiply a small meal sufficient for one or two people to feed many thousands. Jesus can multiply food for the sake of people in need. His multiplying the food to feed four thousand would be a direct act of creation. He multiplied the food beyond what was possible through natural processes. For Jesus to truly perform such an act; it would be a direct demonstration of his creative ability and would act as one proof of his claim to be the Son of God. In this case, the incarnate God in the flesh.

If God is able to create something from nothing (the universe); it is a small step to translate a small meal into a smorgasbord sufficient to feed thousands. If our God is able to multiple through such an event, He is more than capable of meeting all our needs in this life. He alone is the God of creation; He cares about every detail of our life as He seeks a closer relationship with us.

Thank you Lord for Your sufficiency, to multiply small things into large. You are more than able to meet every need in our lives, Amen!

October 27: Day 300

GOD'S REDEMPTIVE SACRIFICE

Matthew 26:28 "for this is My blood of the covenant which is poured out for many for forgiveness of sins."

The most noteworthy aspect of God's creative work is His willing self-sacrifice. He creates an open door for sinful man to enter into His presence. God provides the sacrifice mortal man was unable to furnish. Without the sacrifice of Jesus Christ, man would have been condemned to eternal death with no hope of restoration. God's love for His tarnished creation is made manifest in the pages of the New Testament. The final act of God's finest creative work is soon to be fulfilled.

In addition to God vicarious atonement of sinful man, God is in active participation with man creating a new person within each individual willing to acknowledge Him. I Corinthians 5:17 *"Therefore if any man be in Christ, he is a new creature: old things are passed away; behold, all things are become new."* Man is not left to his own devices as he strives to become acceptable to God. God is continually in the process of restoring man, day-by-day. What man is incapable of doing, God supplies the means to bring man back into a fruitful relationship with his Creator. Man is now given a new and eternal hope of being with his Creator for all of eternity. What the mind could not conceive, God is able to provide. Not only is man given a new life, He is given the hope of a new world, a New Jerusalem and a new universe; one that is completely untarnished by sin or curse.

Thank you Lord Jesus, for giving your life as a ransom for me. You are my Creator, Sustainer, Redeemer, and soon coming King. You are creating within me a new person. You have given me a new hope and a life eternal with You, Amen!

Mark

We are given two specific references to God as Creator. Jesus is shown to be the one in authority over nature, diseases, and all spiritual forces who must submit to Him.

October 28: Day 301

JESUS HAS AUTHORITY OVER ALL REALITY

Mark 4:41 "They became very much afraid and said to one another, Who then is this, that even the wind and the sea obey Him?"

Just like God, the person of Jesus Christ had authority over nature. Several Old Testament references demonstrate God's power over the forces of nature. Jesus demonstrates the same power as He calmed the Sea of Galilee by a verbal command. Jesus showed little concern for the raging sea surrounding Him and His disciples. Jesus gave His disciples a gentle rebuke for their lack of faith; they were not yet privy to the reality of who Jesus was. He along with the Father and the Holy Spirit was responsible for the creation of the wind, the sea, and the natural forces surrounding them.

In addition to the forces of nature, Jesus had authority over all spiritual entities. Mark 5:13 gives us an example of Jesus telling demonic forces what they can or cannot do. *"Jesus gave them permission. And coming out, the unclean spirits entered the swine;"* God has authority over all reality, spiritual and natural. In this case Jesus, the Son of God must give permission for the demonic to enter another entity. According to the biblical text, Jesus is absolute in His authoritative reign. All the spiritual realms must submit; this point is not provable within the context of naturalism. However, for many missions' organizations who deal with such realities, this comes home to real spiritual confrontations.

We are most thankful that You OH Lord are in control, and above all spiritual and natural forces. You are the absolute authority of all reality in the physical and spiritual realm, Amen!

October 29: Day 302

GOD CREATED TWO GENDERS

Mark 10:6 "But from the beginning of creation,
God made them male and female."

We learned from Genesis chapters 1 and 2 that God created man, male and female. The gospel of Mark repeats the same reality. God created man in two separate genders to complement one another. Men and women are different in the way they think, the way they interact, and in their relationships with others. Man and woman are equal before God. Galatians 3:28b *"there is neither male nor female; for you are all one in Christ Jesus."* We however have different roles to play in God's creative plan. While women play the major role in child bearing and nurturing; men being the physically stronger provide, protect, and support the family. These roles often get mixed up and confused in today's culture.

We live in a society and culture today that seeks to confuse the role of men and women. The primary role of men and women is to separate from parents and to become one together. Quoting from Genesis 2, Matthew 19:5 *"for this reason a man shall leave His father and mother and be joined to his wife, and the two shall become one flesh."* Unless physical realities prevent it, a married couple is to come together to procreate and start a family. Genesis 1:28a *"God blessed them, and God said to them, 'Be fruitful and multiply, and fill the earth,"* That commission has not changed even for society today. When families split, children most often suffer the greatest. Pray for our families, our children and for those single parent families needing an extra measure of grace to raise their children.

Lord, You are Lord of the universe. You are the creator of genders, and the roles men and women play. You are the protector of the downtrodden and the lost. You are the One who established the family unit, Lord, protect our families and intervene for our children, Amen!

October 30: Day 303

GOD IS IN CONTROL OF ALL HISTORY FROM BEGINNING TO THE END

*Mark 13:19 "For those days will be a time of tribulation such as has not occurred since the beginning of **the creation which God created** until now, and never will."*

We do not know how this picture will come together in the end, but the fulfillment of the previous passage must be taken more seriously. Mark is clear in this statement concerning God's creative work. New Testament Christians were as adamant regarding God's creative work as the Jews. God is regarded by Christians as creator of all that exists, spiritual and physical. In addition, God is the creator and conductor of time; all events stand before His eternal gaze. No event, past, present, or future is beyond His perfect vision.

The predictions made by Mark give the Gentile peoples a foundation on which to build a faith. Jesus does not make idle claims. What He spoke both to the people of His time, and those who would follow bear witness to Jesus' works and predictions. What He spoke, came true even to this day. We must make ourselves ready for the difficult times to come. When that time comes, we do not know. Mark 13:32 *"But of that day or hour no one knows, not even the angels in heaven, nor the Son, but the Father alone."* Our responsibility is to be ready for that day at any time.

Thank you Father, that You alone are the guardian of the future. All events are in Your powerful hands. You are the creator of all things and all the events in history will come to an end in Your perfect time, Amen!

Luke

The Gentile church: Luke is the only Gentile writer in the New Testament. He alone comes from a non-Jewish culture, being brought up in a Hellenistic world with little or no concern for the big picture of Jewish redemptive rights. Luke is deemed responsible for both the gospel of Luke and the Acts of the disciples. He was perhaps the most meticulous writer of the New Testament. Every proper Name, place and title has been discovered and confirmed by Archaeological evidence.

Little question that Luke is considered the most accurate historian of his day. Refer to: https://www.ichthus.info/Luke/intro.html

Luke gives no direct reference to God as Creator within the pages of His gospel. He does present several sources within the Acts of the Apostles that God was the Creator. Within the gospel of Luke, He gives ample evidence of God's power to heal and restore through the power and words of Jesus Christ. Since Luke was a physician, He would be more a-tune to the healing power demonstrated among the apostles as well as through Paul's ministry.

October 31: Day 304

POWER OVER DISEASES

*Luke 4:39 "And standing over her, **He rebuked the fever**, and it left her; and she immediately got up and waited on them."*

Jesus had complete authority over diseases. If God is the creative Word, he must also be the healer to all diseases. Just as the serpent in the dessert was the designation of healing for those bitten, so too, God is able to heal whom He chooses. John 3:14 *"As Moses lifted up the serpent in the wilderness, even so must the Son of Man be lifted up;"* Jesus' death and resurrection brought us spiritual healing: In this case, Jesus denounced the fever and restored the woman. He in essence commanded the fever to leave, and it left. As Jesus was able to restore health to the sick people, He will someday restore complete order to the universe.

God's healing power was manifested in both word and touch. Luke 4:40 *". . . all those who had any who were sick with various diseases brought them to Him; and laying His hands on each one of them, He was healing them."* Just as Jesus rebuked the fever through his word, His touch also had healing power to restore and order health into the lives of those brought to him. In medical terms, touch is as important as the healing himself. Touching people's lives is part of the process for restoration. In this case Jesus restores that which was lost, their health and vitality. From the New Testament perspective, Jesus is the one who heals all our infirmities, spiritual and natural. Luke 5:13 *"And He stretched out His hand and touched him, saying "I am willing; be cleansed," And immediately the leprosy left him."* The spoken word in this case healed the man. Just as the spoken word created the universe.

Thank you Lord, for Your healing hand. You alone are able and willing to heal both body and the soul. You are the creator of our bodies, and You are able to restore us to health both physically and spiritually, Amen!

November 1: Day 305

GOD REVEALS HIMSELF
TO THE HUMBLE

*Luke 10:21 "I praise You, O Father, **Lord of heaven and earth,** that You have hidden these things from the wise and intelligent and have revealed them to infants."*

God reveals Himself to whom He wishes. God often grants knowledge of Himself to those who honestly seek Him. To the humble, God will often give knowledge. To the wise, they are generally on their own. Unless a man becomes as a little child, they cannot enter the kingdom of God. If a man thinks he knows, he does not know, as he should. Matthew 18:3 *"truly I say to you, unless you are converted and become like children, you will not enter the kingdom of heaven."* We must be willing to humble ourselves, to acknowledge we don't know everything.

God comes to the lowly and humble, as they are the ones who recognize their need for God. Usually it is those who see their need for a Savior who will seek Him. For those who don't see their need, it is often through calamity and hardships that God uses to get their attention. The bottom line is, we all need God and the salvation He offers. Everyone must humble themselves and acknowledge their need for a Savior. Luke 18:14 *"for everyone who exalts himself will be humbled, but he who humbles himself will be exalted."* God reveals Himself to those who see their need for a Savior.

Thank you Father, for revealing Yourself to us. Without Your grace and mercy, we would be lost, Amen!

John

The gospel of John clearly paints Jesus as the Holy One of God; one with God in creation. He is the focal point of all History. Jesus is the only way to God, He is the door to life, the bread of Life, and the light of the world. Jesus shows us the true nature of God, illuminating the way to God, and everlasting life. It is by His perfect life, and sacrificial death on the cross that gives all men the opportunity to enter into a relationship with God, and the hope of eternal life.

November 2: Day 306

GOD'S CREATIVE LOGOS

John 1:1 "In the beginning was the Word, and the Word was with God, and the Word was God."

The theme of a beginning is repeated throughout the biblical text. John gives the reader a different perspective on who is responsible for this beginning. John gives us a more complete picture of God's creative force first presented in Genesis One. The means by which God created the universe was through the Word or Logos of God's Son. He spoke the worlds into existence through the infinite power of His word. Jesus is present here as one with God from the beginning and part of the creative process. John leaves no doubt as to who Christ is and His relationship with God the Father.

The actual identity of the creator comes into clearer focus through the works of Jesus Christ. John 1:3 ***"All things came into being through Him, and apart from Him nothing came into being that has come into being."*** All creation, spiritual, natural, and physical have as their source God. He is our Creator and the originator of all that exists. As part of the God head, Jesus plays an intricate part in the creative process attributed to God. John makes it very clear, God through the person of Jesus Christ is our Creator. Genesis 1:1 *"In the beginning God created the heavens and the earth."* Jesus plays a prominent role in the creation event. He is the master workman spoken of in Proverbs 8:30.

We recognize You Jesus, as one with the Father, and a major participant in the creation of the universe, and all life. Thank you Lord, for the wonders of Your creative power, Amen!

November 3: Day 307

JESUS IS GOD AND MAN

*John 1:12 "But as many as received Him, to them **He gave the right to become children of God,** even to those who believe in His name."*

John was one of three disciples closest to Jesus during His earthly ministry. More than any other gospel writer, John makes a clear distinction regarding the person of Jesus Christ. He is identified as both God, one with God, as well as the one responsible for all creation. God manifests his ultimate creative work in becoming man. As both God and Man, Jesus is able to identify with fallen man. As a result, He is the only one able to make restitution for the sins of the world. No other being in all creation would be able to make such a sacrifice. A perfect God must account for every sin. The perfection of Jesus who was both Man and God was able to satisfy that account.

The Church today is an extension of the life of Jesus Christ. All those who call upon the name of Jesus are declared children of God. Jesus is in the center of God's creative power; He is also at the center of making each of His followers a new creation conforming to His image. The body of Christ is to become like Him, to be a witness to the world of God's saving power though Christ Jesus. Thank you Father for Your Son Jesus, the creator of the universe, and the author of new life. Hebrews 12:2 *"Fixing our eyes on Jesus, the author and perfecter of faith, who for the joy set before Him endured the cross, despising the shame, and has sat down at the right hand of the throne of God."* Jesus' creative power was perfected by His sacrifice on the Cross. John 3:16 *"For God so loved the world, that He gave His only begotten son, that whoever believes in Him shall not perish, but have eternal life."* This was God's most powerful creative work.

Thank you Lord, for adopting us as sons and daughters of God. Our rights are not a result of our work, but derive from the holy and righteous life of Your Son Jesus, who gave Himself for us, Amen!

November 4: Day 308

GOD GIVES ETERNAL LIFE TO WHOM HE WISHES

*John 5:21 "For just as **the Father raises the dead and gives them life**, even **so the Son also gives life to whom He wishes**."*

Life is not an accident, life is a gift of God. We have our life in God and according to this passage, there is no life except it be given by God. Life is precious and has value. God is the author of life and is the sustainer of life. We have our being in Him, He sustains our life. He numbers our days and will dismiss us from this life when our days are complete. God is absolute in His control and purpose. He is the author and creator of life.

Jesus suggests that Moses, the one responsible for assembling the book of Genesis, wrote about Jesus coming. John 5:46-47 *"For if you believed Moses you would believe Me, for he wrote about Me."* Several passages in the Pentateuch could be identified with Jesus. The seed of woman identified in Genesis Three. The plural nature of God is witness to man's original sin. Deuteronomy communicates a future promise that a prophet like himself (Moses) would come. The ultimate implication behind this statement identifies a time when men would doubt the Genesis account. This doubt would lead to questioning his own work on the cross. If Jesus accepted the early accounts of Moses as trustworthy accounts of creation, why wouldn't we?

Thank you Lord for giving us life. All life has its origin from You. The complexities of life are deeper than we can understand, Amen!

Acts

Luke communicates the beginning of the Church and the beginning of God's Kingdom on Earth. God moves the church from Jerusalem out into the world. The Gentiles now become part of the mission field. Luke gives several references to God as the creator of all things.

November 5: Day 309

PETER AFFIRMS, GOD AS CREATOR

*Acts 4:24 "**O Lord, it is You who made the heaven and the earth and the sea, and all that is in them.***"*

Luke references Peter's words as he speaks to the Sanhedrin. Peter speaks to the Jewish leadership regarding God's creative power. All those present would have been in full agreement with that statement. The entire Jewish community in the first century would have consented to God's creative power. Luke however was a gentile believer; most of the Gentile world during this period would have been mixed. Greek philosophy, which had become very materialist, would have held to a completely natural universe.

The materialist or methodological naturalistic philosophy holds sway in today's culture. Our culture no longer considers God as the creator of the universe and all we see. Much of science today gives credit to chance processes to produce all the complexity of our universe, and life. Even though the chances are zero that chance or time had any hand in the creation of the universe we see; nevertheless, these philosophies hold sway in all our institutions of education. The only rational explanation for the existence of anything is the reality of an eternal being. Genesis 1:1 *"In the beginning God created the heavens and the earth."* Luke communicates Peter's words very clearly: God is the creator of all things.

Thank you Lord, for the clarity of Your word. We would have no understanding of who we are, or where we come from, if not for your word, Amen!

November 6: Day 310

GOD CONTINUES TO HEAL

*Acts 4:30 "while You extend Your hand to heal, and **signs and wonders take place through the name of Your holy servant Jesus.** "*

Jesus is credited with acts of wonders, in addition to His power to heal people. During His ministry on earth, many claimed Jesus was a miracle worker. As God's Son, and the essence of God on Earth, Jesus demonstrated His powers through His acts of service. In addition to His works of wonder, He is identified as holy. Jesus is perfect in his character, just as God is holy and perfect.

The power that worked to heal people 2,000 years ago is the same power available today to heal, and change lives. *II Corinthians 5:17 "Therefore If anyone is in Christ, he is a new creature; the old things passed away; behold, new things have come."* God through the person of Jesus Christ and the power of His Holy Spirit is actively changing lives today. In every culture on the planet, God is still the creator, creating changed hearts and lives throughout the world.

Thank you Lord Jesus, for changing our hearts and lives to live more in harmony with You in all our daily lives. Your wonders give proof to who You are, the holy, perfect almighty Son of God, Amen!

November 7: Day 311

EVERYTHING WE SEE COMES FROM GOD

*Acts 7:50 "**Was it not My hand which made all these things?**"*

Luke gives the account of Stephen, the first Martyr of the Christian church. Stephen quotes Isaiah 66:2 *"For My hand made all these things, Thus all these things came into being, declares the LORD."* Like Isaiah before him, Luke gives credit to God as creator of all that exists. Like Peter's defense, the Jews would have been in agreement with this statement, as they stoned Stephen for his condemnation of their hypocrisy. As he was dying, Stephen saw a vision of the Son of Man (Jesus) standing at the right hand of God. As Creator, Jesus himself opened Stephen's eyes to witness his own homecoming before his death. Could this event be an example of near-death experiences shared by many people around the world?

The lone Gentile writer of this New Testament book gives credit to God for the creation of all things. The New Testament writers again leave little doubt as to who they think the creator is. God is reminding us again who the creator is. He alone is able to create something from nothing. No scientific explanation exists that can even begin to show how we came into existence out of nothing. Something must have been eternal. Only a pre-existing eternal God having infinite power could even begin to explain the essential first cause of the magnificent universe we witness today.

Thank you God, that You are far greater than we can even imagine. It is by Your power oh Lord that we exist and live on this complex planet along with all the creatures necessary to sustain our lives, Amen!

November 8: Day 312

GOD OF TIME AND SPACE

Acts 8:39 "the Spirit of the Lord snatched Philip away;"

This passage brings an entirely new perspective to the future Kingdom of God. The power of God rules over time and space; this verse gives us a glimpse into eternity in a familiar sort of way. How would we ever conceive of transporting from one place to another? The idea of a science fiction event would no longer be impossible. For the God of Creation, time and space provide no barriers. So in eternity, could it be possible to move from place to place by sheer thought? This question cannot be answered at this point, but the example of Philip opens many possibilities that go well beyond our understanding of reality.

The God of creation is more than capable of the miraculous. I don't expect to be transported like Philip except on that last day. I Thessalonians 4:17 *"Then we who are alive and remain will be caught up together with them in the clouds to meet the Lord in the air, and so we shall always be with the Lord."* Philip's experience could be a preview of the final rapture event where all of God's saints still living will be caught up together with Christ in the air. The Christian has the hope of a very interesting future where the impossible is possible.

Thank you Lord for the hope of a future where the fantastic becomes reality. You are the God of the impossible who opened the door for finite man to enter into Your infinite holy presence, Amen!

November 9: Day 313

GOD OUR GREAT PHYSICIAN

*Acts 14:15 ". . . turn from these vain things to a living **God, who made the heaven and the earth and the sea and all that is in them**."*

Paul is credited with healing a man in the city of Iconium. The people having witnessed this act, wanted to worship Paul and Barnabas. Paul diverts these accolades back to God, whom he credits with the real power to heal, as well as being the one true Creator. Paul and Barnabas are careful to give credit where credit is due. It is God who heals, not man. God is able to channel His creative power through whoever he wishes, enabling faithful men to perform acts of healing beyond basic medicine. Cases exist today, where people are miraculously healed of diseases through the power of prayer.

We cannot always predict how God will answer our prayers but God alone is able to heal, as He is the one true God who created the world we live in. Consider the glory and majesty of God's creation; He alone has all power and is able to heal and restore to health those who are sick. Let's remember that our God is the Great Physician, and He alone completely understands how we were made for He is our Maker. Matthew 14:14 *"When He went ashore, He saw a large crowd, and felt compassion for them and healed their sick."* Our Creator God is also the one who heals us.

Thank you Lord, for creating all things and for being our Great Physician; for You heal us from not only our sicknesses and diseases, but from the consequences of our sins, Amen!

November 10: Day 314

ALL THINGS ARE UNDER GOD'S CONTROL

*Acts 17:25-26 "nor is He served by human hands, as though He needed anything, since **He himself gives to all people life and breath and all things; and He made from one man every nation of mankind to live on all the face of the earth,** having determined their appointed times and the boundaries of their habitation,"*

Paul is speaking to the materialists of his day while conversing with the Greek philosophers in Athens on Mars Hill. He is seeking to explain to them the nature of the unknown God as the God of creation. He was putting a face on their object of worship, of which they were unaware. God as the creator of all men and all nations is also the One who determines man's time on earth. God alone possesses the keys to life and death; our days were numbered before we were born. God knows our limits and determines our influence.

This passage more than any other within scripture communicates the complete power and control of God over the affairs of nations and men. Our existence, our life and breath, as well as our futures are firmly held by God's compassionate hand. He knows our end from our beginning, and is the One directing the events of our lives. The future of mankind and the eternal destiny of every person on earth rests solely in the arms of our Creator God. Psalm 31:15a *"My times are in Your hand;"* God's power is not limited to creation, but extends to every detail of our lives.

God, You are greater than we can imagine. You alone are in complete control of the affairs of mankind. You are the guide and protector of our lives. Thank you for caring about Your creation, Amen!

Romans

The Apostle Paul is the author of Romans. Earlier he had been the one responsible for the early persecution of the Church. He later learned that he was in reality working against God. He was driven back to God through the witness of Jesus Christ and became the chief evangelist and witness for the Christian faith.

November 11: Day 315

EVIDENCE OF GOD'S CREATIVE POWER

Romans 1:20 **"For since the creation of the world His invisible attributes, His eternal power and divine nature, have been clearly seen, being understood through what has been made,** *so that they are without excuse."*

God's eternal attributes are on display in His creation. The size and grandeur of the universe and the complexities and diversity of all life, point to a powerful creative force. For man to claim autonomy flies in direct conflict to what man already knows. Without God, there is no universe; there is no reality, there is nothing. Man possesses enough evidence for God through the marvels of His creation, all people are accountable for that knowledge.

Huge advances in current science have revealed a universe of incredible size and complexity. We marvel at the images of vast star and galaxy systems at extreme distances. We wonder at the complexities and diversities of life, trying to discern how they could have come about through blind random processes. Time and chance have no power to create or organize anything. Man today, is even more accountable to the words of scripture, having no excuse for a creation infinitely more complex than Paul himself understood. Psalm 19:1 is still true today: *"The heavens are telling of the glory of God; And their expanse is declaring the work of His hands."* The vastness of the universe is declaring the glory of God even today.

Thank you Lord, for Your magnificent creation. Your universe is vastly larger than we can conceive. We are humbled by Your greatness and power to create such a wonderful reality, Amen!

November 12: Day 316

WORSHIP THE ONE TRUE GOD

*Romans 1:25 "For they exchanged the truth of God for a lie, and worshiped and served the creature rather than the **Creator**, who is blessed forever. Amen."*

We ourselves must also avoid the deceitfulness of sin that resides in our own hearts. Jeremiah reminds us or our condition. Jeremiah 17:9 *"The heart is more deceitful than all else And is desperately sick; Who can understand it?"* We can all be self-deceived and must be on guard against foolish tendencies. God has given us the Word as a filter to correct our ideas. We have another problem as presented by Paul: we can be willful in our disobedience, choosing to go against what we know to be true. This deception is of our own making; may we all learn to be faithful to the truth.

All men are accountable before God and responsible for their life's choices. God reserves all worship for Himself as the Creator; God alone is worthy of our worship and praise. Man tends toward gullibility in his understanding of reality and truth. What is plain before their eyes is often missed because of the deceitfulness of sin. No one is immune to this condition, as all men are sinners. Romans 3:23 *"for all have sinned and fall short of the glory of God."* Don't be deceived, acknowledge your condition and seek God with all your heart.

Thank you Lord, that You have given us Your Word, that we might understand the truth, and avoid the pitfalls of deceptiveness that surround us, Amen!

November 13: Day 317

CREATION WILL BE RESTORED TO ITS PRISTINE CONDITION

*Romans 8:19-20 "**For the creation was subjected to futility**, not willingly but because of Him who subjected it, in hope that the creation itself also will be set free from its slavery to corruption into the freedom of the glory of the children of God."*

Creation is under a curse and subject to futility (having no purpose) until redeemed, because of Him who subjected it, being God. God's perfect creation was put on hold because of Man's sin. The curse was put in effect as a judgment to demonstrate the futility of sin, and to bring man back into a right relationship with God. Pain and suffering became a part of life as a result of this curse, Genesis 3:17. *Cursed is the ground because of you; in toil you will eat of it all the days of your life.* The problem of evil and suffering is explained in part by this passage. The bigger question as to why do good people suffer to some extent is still a mystery. God however works on a much higher plane.

The futility of man's condition before God is apparent, God opens the door to the solution by sending His only Son. In like manner, Abraham was willing to sacrifice his own son out of obedience to God. replace with this sentence – God's request for Abraham to sacrifice his son was difficult. However, this event was an illustration of what God was going to do through the sacrifice of His Son Jesus on the cross for our sins. God's willingness to become man, illustrates God's ultimate love for His creation, and His desire to intervene in our behalf. God loves His creation enough, to pay the debt owed to Himself because of our sins.

Thank you Lord, for subjecting creation to futility to push us into realizing our need for You. You set us free from the bondage of sin by Your sacrifice on the cross, Amen!

November 14: Day 318

GOD'S RESTORATION IS COMING

*Romans 8:22-23 "We know that the whole **creation** has been groaning as in the pains of childbirth right up to the present time. Not only so, but we ourselves, who have the first fruits of the spirit, groan inwardly as we wait eagerly for our adoptions as sons, the redemption of our bodies."*

Paul presents the hope that one day, all creation will be restored into right fellowship with God. Creation is not as it should be. Men and women who place their hope in God as their Creator expect one day to see all creation restored, to its former glory. For the naturalist, there is no such thing as evil; they say we live in a world that exists, and there is no other. However, to question why there is evil is to assume the presence of a higher standard regarding right and wrong.

We see death and dying today all around us. We have wars, and famines, along with crime. Our leaders often fail us as we seek to live our lives unhindered by the restraints of governmental controls. Everything breaks down in time, so our cars and the roads on which we drive need constant repair. The list of bad things that happen could go on and on. However bad things become, God has promised us to be there to help us along the way. Romans 8:28 *"And we know that God causes all things to work together for good to those who love God, to those who are called according to His purpose."* God is still in control of this world through the good and the bad as He continually seeks to redeem lost souls to Himself.

Thank you Lord, for the gift of Your Spirit. We trust You to eventually restore all things to their original pristine purpose. We ask also that You restore our broken bodies to Your likeness by Your power, Amen!

November 15: Day 319

OUR PART IN HIS-STORY IS ALREADY WRITTEN

*Romans 8:29 "For those whom He foreknew, He also predestined **to become conformed to the image of His Son**, so that He would be the firstborn among many brethren."*

God's knowledge is not limited to time. God knew us before the creation of the world. Romans 8:30 *"and these whom He predestined, He also called; and these whom He called, He also justified; and these whom He justified, He also glorified."* We learn a difficult reality: from God's perspective, the story is complete. We are running behind the reality. God has completed the story of history. He is the Creator, the Writer and the Author of all history, both recorded and yet to be recorded. We can only see parts of history as recorded by historians; even those are extremely incomplete. We can see only glimpses of the reality surrounding us.

We are called to take part in the saga of God's historical drama, to become a major part, to the extent we believe His claims. Every time we doubt God's claims, we take a lesser roll. According to this passage in Romans, our story within history is already written. Our part is to trust Him and to follow His prompting. Our God is the script writer for everyone's part in History. We do well to trust Him with our parts since He knows the end from the beginning. Whether we like it or not, we are part of God's historical drama. I Peter 1:2 *"according to the foreknowledge of God the Father, by the sanctifying work of the Spirit to obey Jesus Christ and be sprinkled with His blood: May grace and peace be yours in the fullest measure."* We can have confidence in the future, for our Creator God holds the future as well as the past, in His hands.

Thank you Lord for making us a part of Your historical drama, a completed history only You could write. You knew us before the creation of time, and in You we have the hope of an eternal future with You, Amen!

I Corinthians

As Paul communicates to the Corinthian Church, he clearly presents God as the source of all growth, all structure and purpose in this world. Our existence and being come from God alone.

November 16: Day 320

GOD BRINGS SALVATION

*I Corinthians 3:7 "So then neither the one who plants nor the one who waters is anything, but **God who causes the growth**."*

All productivity comes ultimately from God. God is the source of all growth, materially, and spiritually. We learn from Paul in this passage, we are workers with God bringing salvation to all people. We are fellow laborers, though we plant and reap, it is God who provides the increase. We have no power to save anyone, only our obedience to the command to go will result in fruit, our failure to obey would be synonymous to our refusal to plant a crop. No planting, no fruit, according to this passage, spiritual realities operate on the same plane.

This lesson applies to our everyday lives. In order to be productive, we must do our work. All things in God's creation are kinetic, in motion. We must plan, prioritize, and do the work we are called to do. Winning souls to Christ requires the same diligence. Proverbs 24:27 *Prepare your work outside, Study God's word daily.* Pray committing all your work to His glory, finally, show by example a faithful life; being ready to share with others the hope within you. I Peter 3:15 *"but sanctify Christ as Lord in your hearts, always being ready to make a defense to everyone who asks you to give an account for the hope that is in you, yet with gentleness and reverence;"* We must do our work in preparing the ground and plant, it is God alone who can produce the fruit of saved lives.

Thank you Father, for the privilege of sharing the hope within us to others. May we be faithful in the task of living a righteous life, and sharing the good news as God provides opportunity. You alone produce the fruit of salvation in people's lives, Amen!

November 17: Day 321

WE EXIST FOR GOD'S PLEASURE

*I Corinthians 8:6 '**Yet for us there is but one God, the Father, from whom are all things and we exist** for Him; and one Lord, Jesus Christ, **by whom are all things, and we exist through Him**."*

God is referenced in this passage as our Father. We derive our existence from Him. Our existence is by God's will and by His design; in addition, we were created for His pleasure. Meaning in life derives from God, our failure to acknowledge God will only result in a purposeless reality. As we serve God in the capacity He created us, we will find our purpose, and will discover our pleasure. Find out what you love, and what you are good at, do it unto God, and you will be a success.

The earth belongs to God along with all that is in it. Though man may hold power for a season, though he may have material possessions in large quantities, the final title of ownership belongs to God. I Corinthians 10:26 *"For the earth is the Lord's, and all it contains."* In addition to our property, our lives belong to God, not as servants, but as children of the **Creator**. God is the ultimate landlord of everything that exists. Our primary responsibility as part of His creation is to use the gifts and talents He gave us to honor and serve Him.

Thank you Lord, for our existence. Our lives exist because of Your creative power. Our continued existence is dependent upon Your infinite grace, Amen!

November 18: Day 322

PRO-CREATION IS GOD'S DESIGN

*I Corinthians 11:12 "For as the woman originates from the man, so also the man has his birth through the woman; and **all things originate from God**."*

Men and women were created by God. It was by God's design that men and women could, through their union, create new life. The birthing process is not the result of an accident. It required a great deal of precise structure. Pro-creation is pleasurable for a very specific reason, to maintain the continuation of life. The extreme complexity of the creation of a new life can only be attributed to an intelligent designer.

The concept of life's origins is clearly spelled out in the Bible. The functions of life are unimaginably complex. The origin of man is clearly given to us; there is little ambiguity in this passage, God is the originator of all things, living and innate. God designs everything for a purpose; in this case, the woman was designed to give birth, through procreation with the man. We all have a mother who gave birth to us, but God is the ultimate arbitrator of life.

God created the process which brings life into the world. Though our mothers give birth to us, it is a tag team operation between the man and the woman. God designed sex as a good thing to unite, and marriage to establish a safe environment to raise a family. God is the Creator and originator of life, we all have our being ultimately from God. Genesis 2:22 *"The LORD God fashioned into a woman the rib which He had taken from the man and brought her to the man."* God brings all things full circle, for as woman was created through man, man has his being through woman.

Thank you Lord, for the beauty of pro-creation. You have given to man and woman the ability to create new life through their union together. You have given us order and purpose for life now and for eternity, Amen!

November 19: Day 323

EVERYTHING IS SUBJECT TO GOD

I Corinthians 15:27-28 "All things are put in subjection, it is evident that He is accepted who put all things in subjection to Him. When all things are subjected to Him, then the Son Himself also will be subjected to the One who subjected all things to Him, so that God may be all in all."

Paul gives the same message as earlier New Testament writers: all things fall under God's care and protection. God's plan for this world and this creative order is made clear within the context of these verses. Even though sin (evil) entered the world and tarnished God's perfect creation, it is His plan to bring everything back into harmony and order. All people who submit to Him will again be put into a right relationship with God along with His creation.

Everything in God's creation has a purpose and a place. Each person is different, given different abilities and aptitudes. Paul continues as he illustrates how the stars in the universe are different. I Corinthians 15:41 *"There is one glory of the sun, and another glory of the moon, and another glory of the stars; for star differs from star in glory."* Science confirms Paul's statement that stars differ in size, brightness, and color. Everything in God's creation is subject to His ultimate control, including man.

Thank you Lord, for the diversity of Your creation. Each of us has a different purpose as all Your creation is and will be in subjection to Your perfect plan, Amen!

II Corinthians

Paul appeals to the church in Corinth littered with sin issues. The church was in need of a spiritual renewal or revival as sin issues were prevalent. Paul however never suggests the church is a failure or weak, rather Paul simply encourages and strengthens the church in the state they existed.

GOD IS OUR ETERNAL DESIGNER

*II Corinthians 5:1 "**we have a building from God**, a house not made with hands, eternal in the heavens."*

The building from God referenced by Paul is a new and spiritual body which all those who believe on Him will one day possess. This points to a future spiritual reality created by God that will never end. God is not only the Creator of the physical world, our home here; He is also the Creator of all the spiritual realm. The human race is given the promise of a greater home and reality beyond what can be seen through our physical eyes. This building from God is a new body that will endure forever in heaven with God.

The hope this passage brings us is of a future reality that is more real than the world we live in now. We have the hope of receiving a new, eternal body that will never grow old. The longer we live in this world, and the older we become, it becomes more apparent that we were never meant to live here forever. We want to think that this life will never end as science stretches life spans by a few years. But reality will sink in, this life we now enjoy will soon come to an end; an eternal future waits for us on the other side.

Thank you Lord, for the promise of a new body that will live forever in Your presence. You have given us the hope of eternal life with a body that will never grow old, Amen!

November 21: Day 325

WE ARE BECOMING A NEW CREATION

II Corinthians 5:4-5 ". . . what is mortal will be swallowed up by life.
Now He who prepared us for this very purpose is God who gave to
us the Spirit *as a pledge."*

Paul again refers to a life beyond this mortal existence. Paul gives a perspective on God's creation that transcends the one we now see. A higher purpose exists giving man a reason for optimism. For those who seek God, there is a purpose and a future. For those who do not seek God, there is an effort to seek another solution for the dilemma of humanity. They look for another way to explain the reality we see apart from a Creator God. Regardless of what man thinks, God's way will still be accomplished.

God is the creator of our mortal as well as spiritual lives. We were created not by accident, but for a purpose to which each of us is accountable. For those who will accept God's offer of pardon, God's own spirit will be supplied as a token of His faithfulness. He does not leave us to travel through the rest of our lives alone. He accompanies us in our effort to accomplish the purpose for which He called us. I John 4:13 affirms the same: *"By this we know that we abide in Him and He in us, because He has given us of His Spirit."* God is faithful to see us through to the end of this life and into the next.

Thank you Lord, for giving us of Your Holy Spirit and a new life through Your Son Jesus, Amen!

THROUGH CHRIST WE ARE CHANGED

II Corinthians 5:17 "Therefore if anyone is in Christ, he is a new creature; the old things passed away; behold, new things have come."

We are changed into a new creation through the power of Christ in us. He is the source of our conversion into His image. Through His example and life, we are given the opportunity to throw away our old self, and to become a new creation. He does not ask us to do this difficult task through our strength, but by His example and the power of His Holy Spirit. Philippians 4:13 *"I can do all things through Him who strengthens me."* Our God is the source of our change, as we draw nearer to Him, we become more like Him. Our old self becomes less and less important.

As the Creator of all the universe, God is the source of all that exists. He is also the source of all that is new. He enables His people to change into new creatures, putting away the old habits, and old life styles that we are not proud of. He alone is able to open our hearts and minds to bring about the changes that create within us a new person in the image of Christ. Romans 8:29 *"For those whom He foreknew, He also predestined to become conformed to the image of His Son, so that He would be the firstborn among many brethren."* We are His creation, made in His likeness for the purpose of helping and winning others to Him.

Thank you Lord for rescuing us from our old self, for creating within us a new person in the likeness of Your Son. You have given us a new life and a purpose for living that we can serve You by helping others, Amen!

November 23: Day 327

GOD IS CREATING A HARVEST OF NEW LIVES THROUGH US

*II Corinthians 9:10 states: "Now **He who supplies seed to the sower and bread for food** will supply and multiply your seed for sowing and increase the harvest of your righteousness;"*

God is the source and provider of all our food. We celebrate Thanksgiving at the end of our harvest season to remember God as the One who provided the increase. The sun and the process of photosynthesis are complex creations from an all-knowing God. All the nutrients in the ground, even the minerals in our fertilizers along with the rainfall, are gifts and provisions from God. God provides all we need to produce a harvest of food.

The ability to produce a harvest hundreds of times over permits us to feed the world. Our produce from the harvest provides the seed necessary for the next planting. The ability for those seeds to germinate is an astounding process. The replication of genetic material is very complex and the product of a powerful designer. Matthew 6:26 *"Look at the birds of the air, that they do not sow nor reap nor gather into barns, and yet your heavenly Father feeds them. Are you not worth much more than they?"* If God can provide food for the birds in the field, He can certainly provide food for His people, created in His image.

Thank you Lord, for the harvest of new souls along with all the provisions that makes a great harvest possible, Amen!

Galatians

Christ is being recreated in everyone who submits to Him. God is in the process of creating within us a new creation.

November 24: Day 328

GOD'S NEW CREATION

*Galatians 6:15 "For neither is circumcision anything, nor uncircumcision, but a **new creation.**"*

Paul gives us a view into God's new work in the world. God is in the act of creating today as He is establishing a new way of life, to bring all people together. What matters is how one lives for Christ, and gives his glory and success to God, recognizing his authority and Lordship. Our old life is passing away, we are becoming a new creation. Galatians 2:20 *"I have been crucified with Christ; and it is no longer I who live, but Christ lives in me; and the life which I now live in the flesh I live by faith in the Son of God, who loved me and gave Himself up for me."* When we let Christ control our lives through the power of the Holy Spirit; we will live in harmony with God and will accomplish the purpose for which we were created. We have a new birth, a new life, in a new covenant, and the promise of a new creation that will last for eternity.

God is actively building His Church today in the world. Those who have come to faith in Christ Jesus are part of that church. He is actively restoring all those who have called upon His name to be saved. God is actively seeking to save all people and to bring them into a new and restored relationship with Him.   I Timothy 2:4 states, it is God *"who desires all men to be saved and to come to the knowledge of the truth."* God is actively seeking to draw people to Himself that He might create that new life in all His creation. II Corinthians 5:17 *"Therefore if anyone is in Christ, he is a new creature; the old things passed away; behold, new things have come."* God is continually in the process of creating within His people a new creation.

Thank you Lord, for seeking and saving us by giving your Son, and endowing us with Your Holy Spirit, that we would become a new creation in You, Amen!

Ephesians

We are created in righteousness. God created a job and a purpose for every person on earth to complete.

November 25: Day 329

GOD'S REVEALING LIGHT

*Ephesians 3:9 "and to bring to light what is the administration of the mystery which for ages has been hidden in **God who created all things.** "*

The Old Testament prophets give us a hint into the creative power of God. In the person of Jesus Christ, God reveals His plan to redeem mankind into a renewed relationship with God Himself. After the fall of Adam in Genesis 3, Mankind was estranged and separated from God, without hope, and under the curse of death. But God did not leave man in a state of lostness; He sent His own Son in the person of Jesus Christ, the author of all things to restore us.

We have the hope of a new life through God's redeeming grace. We are not recipients of a reward for anything we did; it is by the grace and mercy of almighty God that we can come before Him, restored and whole. Our Creator God, who created all things, is able to create within each person a new heart (a passion to know God and to serve Him). Our perfect God required a payment for our debt of sin; since we were unable to pay for our misdeeds, He died in our place to pay that debt for us. Ephesians 3:20-21 *"Now to Him who is able to do far more abundantly beyond all that we ask or think, according to the power that works within us, to Him be the glory in the church and in Christ Jesus to all generations forever and ever, Amen."* By His own power, God balanced our account, and redeemed us back to Himself.

Thank you Lord, for paying our debt that we were unable to pay. You have finally made known to all mankind Your redemptive plan by giving Yourself in our behalf, Amen!

November 26: Day 330

CREATED IN RIGHTEOUSNESS

*Ephesians 4:24 "And put on the new self, which in the likeness of God **has been created in righteousness** and holiness of the truth."*

God is actively at work today, creating within each person the capacity to be righteous. This righteousness is not of our own making. God is creating a new life within every man and woman willing to submit to His corrective spiritual surgery. We are under the knife in a spiritual sense, as God works a miracle in the lives of all those who have submitted to the procedure of this transformation, into the image of Christ. We however must be willing to allow God to work on a daily basis; this sanctifying process will take the rest of our lives, even into eternity.

Living the Christian life does not depend upon a one-night stand, a one-day confession of faith with no further action required. We must daily submit to God's cleansing work as we continually submit to the teachings of His word. Ephesians 5:26 clarifies in reference to the church: *"so that He might sanctify her, having cleansed her by the washing of water with the word."* We must allow God to continue His work in us, that we might be transformed and live the righteousness of Christ in our lives.

Thank you Lord, for creating a new life, and for providing me with Your righteousness. Help me to continue in Your transforming work, that I might remain on the table until Your work in me is complete, Amen!

Philippians

God is in the process of transforming and creating a new people. God's people will be in harmony with one another and with Him.

GOD WILL BRING US TO PERFECTION

*Philippians 1:6 "For I am confident of this very thing, that **He who began a good work in you will perfect it** until the day of Christ Jesus."*

Paul sees a new world coming, one we as yet cannot comprehend. For perfection to have any meaning in this case, there must be a perfect being; One who is lacking nothing, having all knowledge, all power, and all sufficiency. For us to become perfect, unlikely in this world, there must exist a perfection with the means of pulling off the impossible, making flawed man perfect. This is a predicted future event, not of this world, but of the new creation that is coming.

No man living today can claim to have any part of perfection. Even the Apostle Paul acknowledges this shortcoming for himself. Philippians 3:12 *"Not that I have already obtained it or have already become perfect, but I press on so that I may lay hold of that for which also I was laid hold of by Christ Jesus."* God is actively creating and conforming a body of individuals into new creations. The promise in this passage, is that God's active work will not be thwarted, regardless of the obstructions our culture and world brings upon people of faith, God will see his work through to the end. II Timothy 1:12 *"He is able to guard what I have entrusted to Him until that day."* God is faithful and can be trusted to complete His work in the lives of all believers.

Thank you Lord, for Your faithfulness in rescuing lost people. We trust Your word, that You will accomplish Your work in the hearts and lives of people through to the end, Amen!

November 28: Day 332

GOD IS ACTIVELY WORKING IN THE LIVES OF BELIEVERS

Philippians 2:13 "for it is God who is at work in you, both to will and to work for His good pleasure."

Man is in no way autonomous; God equips man to become righteous. Philippians 3:9b *". . . not having a righteousness of my own derived from the Law, but righteousness which comes from God on the basis of faith."* We are in a process of maturing into the image of God's Son, Jesus Christ. The New Testament gives us a blueprint for this life. As we follow that plan, with the help of the Holy Spirit, we become more like Christ in our lives. God is continually at work, creating that image in us as we become willing participants with Him.

Transforming man to be more like God is not achievable in our own strength. Philippians 3:21 *"Who will transform the body of our humble state into conformity with the body of His glory..."* It is not in us to change or start acting more righteous. As we seek God or become closer to God, God strengthens us through His Holy Spirit to be able to conduct ourselves in a more righteous and holy manner. He is the source of our change; we however must continually seek His presence and help. As we change to be more like God, we honor and please God with a life that reflects His presence.

Thank you Lord, for enabling your people to change, and to become more like You. May we honor and please You as we become more obedient to Your will, Amen!

Colossians

Jesus Christ is the glue of creation. By Him all things were created, and by Him all things hold together. God sustains this creation by His power. Without His sustaining power, all things would immediately fly apart.

November 29: Day 333

BY GOD'S SPIRIT AND THROUGH HIS SON, ALL THINGS WERE CREATED

*Colossians 1:16 "**For by Him all things were created**, both in the heavens and on earth, visible and invisible, whether thrones or dominions or rulers or authorities—**all things have been created through Him and for Him.**"*

Paul affirms Christ's role in creation. He is the creative power behind the material world and, the immaterial along with all spiritual realities. All reality is subject to His control and power. If all things are created through His creative power; this would also include any alternate realities, though speculative in nature. If there were an infinite number of realities, as suggested by the science community, they would also require a creative power. Paul suggests that regardless, God is the Creator of all things.

We must wonder at God's creative design. Every creature has been gifted along special instincts by Gpd which enable them to survive. The harmonious relationships in the animal kingdom enable all life to thrive with numerous symbiotic relationships. The human mind has its ability to think, communicate, and create. We are given the power to pro-create to sustain the human race as with all species of life. The complexities of DNA and the cell defy all efforts to naturalize any explanation. By God's power and design, all things material, mineral, and living were created.

We can all praise You, God for the wonders of His creation. We would not be here if not for Your plan and purpose for our lives, here and into eternity, Amen!

November 30: Day 334

GOD HOLDS THE UNIVERSE TOGETHER

Colossians 1:17 "He is before all things, and in Him

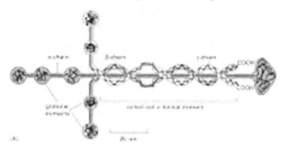

all things hold together."

Paul identifies Christ as the one responsible for holding all matter together. Laminin is a molecular binder that holds biological matter together. For Christ to be the creator and sustainer of life, it seems proper that the binding substance of our lives would resemble the cross. This symbol illustrates the consistency of how the biblical and physical realities merge together in the most unique ways. This molecular structure gives us a hint into God's sustaining power.

As believers we know that He is faithful to complete what He began in us. Philippians 1:6 reminds us *"For I am confident of this very thing, that He who began a good work in you will perfect it until the day of Christ Jesus."* The One who saved us by His sacrificial death on that cross, is the same one who maintains His creation. The writer of Hebrews reaffirms this. Hebrews 1:3 *"And He is the radiance of His glory and the exact representation of His nature, and upholds all things by the word of His power. . ."* For the believer, we can have confidence that Christ will keep the lights on until His work is finished.

Lord, You are ultimately responsible for maintaining the entire creation including every star, galaxy, and planet in the universe. Thank you for sustaining us until all Your work is completed, Amen!

December 1: Day 335

GOD RENEWS HIS PEOPLE

*Colossians 3:10 "and have put on the new self who is being renewed to a true knowledge according to the image of the **One who created him**."*

We were created for a purpose, with a task to fulfill. The problem of sin however has rendered every human being that has ever lived, an outcast before almighty God. God in His absolute holiness and perfection cannot and will not allow sin or corruption into His presence. For this reason, God through His Son, suffered in order to pay the debt we owe. The one who created us is the one who also redeemed us through the death and resurrection of His Son.

We are now given the tools necessary to put away sin and begin the process of becoming new people in Christ. The new self is the result of God, through His Spirit entering into our lives and changing us into a new person, and a new self that is continually being renewed. The goal of this renewal is to change us into a person like Jesus Christ, and how He lived on this earth. II Corinthians 3:18 demonstrates the process of becoming like Christ. "*But we all, with unveiled face, beholding as in a mirror the glory of the Lord, are being transformed into the same image from glory to glory, just as from the Lord, the Spirit.*" God is actively creating, inside all who believe, a new person in the same likeness of Himself and His Son Jesus.

Thank you Father God and Your Son Jesus, for new life. You have enabled us to enter into Your presence by the conforming power of Your Spirit. We are in the process of becoming new people in Christ, Amen!

I Thessalonians

It is by God's great power and His Holy Spirit that we are made right and acceptable to enter into His presence.

December 2: Day 336

BY GOD'S POWER WE ARE CHANGED

*I Thessalonians 1:5 "for our gospel did not come to you in word only, **but also in power and in the Holy spirit** with full conviction; just as you know what kind of men we proved to be among you for your sake."*

The first cause of creation (God) is one and the same with the one causing each person to grow in response to God's eternal grace. I Thessalonians 3:12 "***And may the Lord cause you** to increase and abound in love for one another, and for all peoples, just as we also do for you;"* Our Creator God is the means and the avenue by which we grow into conformity with Christ. We cannot become righteous or good; by our own efforts. Only God is good. God alone possesses the power to change lives. We can become a new creation by the power of God's Spirit. He knows our hearts. As we open ourselves to Him, He changes us, inside out.

God is continually at work changing lives by the power of His Holy Spirit. He is at work changing us and completely conforming us into His complete image. Even in creation, we were created in the image of God. God is now at work cleaning us from the effects of sin so that we can be a clear reflection of His image. Thessalonians 5:23 *"Now may the God of peace Himself sanctify you entirely; and by your spirit and soul and body be preserved complete, without blame at the coming of our Lord Jesus Christ."* At that time, all those who confess Him will be ready to meet Him. May God bring all men into a right relationship with their Maker.

Thank you Lord, for the power to change our lives, and to conform us into the perfect image of Your Son, Amen!

II Thessalonians

God knows each person, and the intentions of our hearts, even from the beginning of creation.

December 3: Day 337

GOD CHOOSES US

II Thessalonians 2:13 "God has chosen you from the beginning."

God was present from the beginning. He was the One responsible for the creation of the world. God not only created you in time, from this passage, we learn that **He knew you from the beginning of creation**. He had a plan for each of us from the first light of creation. We are not an accident; regardless of our background, we were part of God's plan. We have value to God as He knew who we were from the dawn of time.

The concept of predestination can be a stumbling block for many people. Can people have a choice to follow Christ if we were already destined? It would appear that we are either compelled to follow, or on the other hand condemned from the beginning. Do we have a choice in the matter? The ultimate reality may well be that God knows the end from the beginning. From our end however it is clear, each of us has a choice to follow, or reject God's plan in our life. Joshua 24:15 makes that choice clear. *"If it is disagreeable in your sight to serve the LORD, choose for yourselves today whom you will serve:"* Each of us has that same choice today; only God knows our ultimate outcome. Let's trust God who chose us, even when we were still in our sins. II Thessalonians 2:16 *". . . God our Father, who has loved us and given us eternal comfort and good hope by grace,"* God desires that each of us choose to follow Him.

Thank you Lord, for Your creation, for choosing us, and drawing us to Yourself. We are the product of Your grace and mercy, Amen!

I Timothy

Paul encourages his disciple Timothy to remember, all things created by God are good.

December 4: Day 338

EVERYTHING CREATED BY GOD IS GOOD

*I Timothy 4:4 "**For everything created by God** is good, and nothing is to be rejected if it is received with gratitude;"*

Paul makes it very clear in this passage, that the original creation of the world and all the universe was good. It was not at the beginning, tarnished with sin or corruption. All of our food, and the provisions that enable life on this world to continue, is from God. Even the events in life along with trials have a good purpose, to draw us nearer to God, or to expose evil. Paul reminds us in Romans 8:28 this principle, *"And we know that God causes all things to work together for good to those who love God, to those who are called according to His purpose."* God ultimately seeks our good in this world.

Our attitude is a key element in how we receive God's gifts. When we recognize God as the ultimate creator of all things, we should orient our perspective with an attitude of gratitude. God seeks to give good to all mankind, but so many reject God. I Timothy 2:4 is a reminder of God's greater purpose for man: *"who desires all men to be saved and to come to the knowledge of the truth."* We sometimes fail to recognize God's provisions, and we often make poor choices and must suffer the consequences. God cares about His creation and seeks to give us good things. Paul exhorts Timothy to remember who God is: our Creator, and the One who gives us every good thing. I Timothy 1:17 *"Now to the King eternal, immortal, invisible, the only God, be honor and glory forever and ever."* Our God is good, and worthy of our praise.

Thank you Lord, for every good gift that comes from You. All Your creation is good; even though we have contaminated it with our sins. With the sacrifice of Your Son, You have made all things good again, Amen!

396

II Timothy

God is the guardian of life, He gives life purpose and meaning. To all His people He gives the power to live life to its fullest.

December 5: Day 339

GOD IS THE SOURCE OF PURPOSE & POWER

II Timothy 1:7 "For God has not given us a spirit of timidity, but of power and love and discipline."

God provides men who seek Him the ability to serve. It is assumed, Timothy was inclined toward an insecure demeanor. A timid spirit would not disqualify Timothy from serving God effectively, however, Paul was reminding Timothy that God gives gifts to those who seek Him. God was both willing and able to grant a renewed power to serve Him with love and discipline. Our Creator God's resources are infinite, and He is willing to give to all people the ability to rise above their circumstance.

II Timothy 1:9 reminds Timothy that God will give purpose and direction to his life. Our God *"who has saved us and called us with a holy calling, not according to our works, but according to **His own purpose and grace** which was granted us in Christ Jesus from all eternity."* God has a purpose for each one of us; God designed a specific work for each of us to fulfill from the beginning. God alone grants to us the sufficiency, the grace, and the will to accomplish all things for which He designed us. It is God who gives us life, for now and into eternity. II Timothy 1:10 *"... **and brought life and immortality to light** through the gospel."* God provides all the resources to live a successful life for now and into eternity.

Thank you Lord, for giving us life, purpose, and all the resources necessary to be successful in life, Amen!

Titus

Titus is continually reminded of God's ever persistent grace to provide him and us with all that is necessary to overcome and enter into eternal life. God's promises are true and can be counted on to be fulfilled.

December 6: Day 340

GRACE AND PEACE COME FROM GOD

Titus 1:2 "in the hope of eternal life, which God, who cannot lie, promised long ages ago."

Assurance comes in knowing God and trusting that His promises will come to pass. For the believer, who is the recipient of God's special grace, peace becomes the outcome. Titus 1:4 continues this theme: *"Grace and peace from God the Father and Christ Jesus our Savior."* God's grace is a necessary condition to being saved. God's promise to extend grace is available to all who are willing to accept it. It comes by an act of faith in Christ Jesus' redemptive work.

Our willingness to accept the conditions of God's redemptive work will result in our justification. Justification according to God's plan is the act by which God **created** a new condition for man. According to this condition, all mankind is up for parole bringing with it a full and complete pardon. Even though all people are guilty before a Holy and Perfect God, God grants us this pardon through His grace, if we are willing to accept it. The ultimate result of this pardon of grace, is eternal life. Titus 3:7 *"...so that being justified by His grace we would be made heirs according to the hope of eternal life."* God is willing to extend His grace and peace to any and all who are willing to accept it.

Thank you Lord, for extending grace to a wicked and fallen people. You have given us a full pardon from our sins and a new hope in eternal life with You, Amen!

Philemon

This letter spesaks of eternal relationships. We are no longer slaves, but free in Christ.

December 7: Day 341

GOD RESTORES US BACK INTO A RIGHT RELATIONSHIP WITH HIM

Philemon 1:15 "For perhaps he was for this reason separated from you for a while, that you would have him back forever,"

Slavery is an evil that came upon the world. Western civilization abolished slavery in the 1800s leaving the slave trade being conducted primarily in the Middle East and Asia. Unfortunately forms of slavery still exist all over the world, such as sexual trafficking, and unjust child labor. In spite of modern man's perspective on slavery; slavery had a necessary role in the order of civilization in the times of antiquity. It was a means of providing to those who are destitute and in need. A slave however must be able to work. The harsh treatment of a slave in our more modern history is another story. The slave trade in the new world was a wicked abuse of another human being.

Paul was restoring back to Philemon his servant who had run away. Onesimus had run away from his master for some unknown reason. During this time, Onesimus had become a Christian. How was he to deal with his master Philemon? Through the ministry of Paul, Onesimus was restored to His Master and into a right relationship as a free slave who honored his master. The Old Testament recognizes slavery. Proverbs 27:18b *"And he who cares for his master will be honored."* We too are to enter a new relationship with our Creator as free slaves; giving ourselves whole heartedly in service to our Master, Jesus Christ, who redeemed us. We are no longer slaves, but brothers. Philemon 1:16: *"no longer as a slave, but more than a slave, a beloved brother,"* God restores us to Himself. Not as slaves, but as sons and daughters.

Thank you Lord, for restoring us back to Yourself as more than slaves or servants, but sons and daughters, beloved brothers and sisters, Amen!

Hebrews

The writer of Hebrews makes it clear that God is the creator of all things. Jesus Christ is our spiritual high priest.

December 8: Day 342

GOD SPEAKS THROUGH HIS SON JESUS

Hebrews 1:2 "...in these last days (God) *has spoken to us in His son, whom He appointed heir of all things,* **through whom also He made the world."**

The writer of Hebrews gives credit to Jesus as the Creator in much the same vein as the apostle John. As the Son of God, Jesus and the Father work together in the process of creation. They complement one-another, at the same time being one together. The mystery of the Godhead still defies our ability to understand or comprehend God. Genesis 1:2 includes the Spirit of God in the creative process. "*the Spirit of God was moving over the surface of the waters.*" The paradoxical nature of God (the Trinity) transcends any attempts at placing God into any box, He is much larger than our thoughts or conceptions.

Another passage confirms the active roll God plays in keeping our world and this universe together. Hebrews 1:3 "*And He is the radiance of His glory and the exact representation of His nature,* **and upholds all things by the word of His power***. When He had made purification for sins, He sat down at the right hand of the Majesty on high.*" Our God is the maintenance director of our world. It is by His power that we exist and have our being. Without our God, we would be nothing, and this reality would not exist. The power that created our world, is the same power that upholds and maintains our existence.

Thank you Lord Jesus, for the wonders of this world and your creative power. You are worthy of all praise for keeping us and sustaining us by the power of Your word, Amen!

December 9: Day 343

ALL THE HEAVENS ARE HIS CREATION

*Hebrews 1:10 "**The heavens are the works of Your hands.**"*

From the vantage point of the ancients, the heavens were the sky, the stars, the sun and the planets. They had a very limited understanding of the full nature of the universe. Yet they still looked with wonder at the heavens, seeing them as the product of creation at the hands of an infinite God. Modern man is challenged today with the same awe as he gazes at a universe much larger in scale and complexity. Through the tools of science, we perceive a nearly infinite universe; this revelation corresponds much nearer to the infinite God described within the pages of the biblical text.

Today's secular view prefers answers without addressing the creative work as a product of a Grand Designer. The task is formidable and littered with inconsistencies. Though many questions may yet bring answers, the grand questions of existence and life most likely will never be answered from the platform of modern science. II Timothy 3:7 *"Always learning and never able to come to the knowledge of the truth."* We can speculate until the end of time, but we never come to any concrete conclusions through man's wisdom until we recognize the existence of a much higher reality in our Creator God.

Thank you Lord, for the world created by your hands. By Your power the heavens exist; You alone are the Creator and Designer of this magnificent universe, Amen!

December 10: Day 344

GOD THE MASTER BUILDER

Hebrews 3:4 "For every house is built by someone,
*but **the builder of all things is God.**"*

In this passage, God is referred to as a builder; one who constructs from raw materials. In the case of God, there were no raw materials (Ex nihilo); it is from His hands that we have the raw materials from which we can build. Since we are created in God's image, we can design, build, and construct magnificent structures. In the same way, God designed, and built the magnificent world and universe we can see today. This is not a case for Intelligent Design. It is a case that gives God full credit for the power and order we see in the universe along with the complexities of life.

Since man was created in the image of God, we are endowed with specific skills and abilities to design, build and create structures using the resources God have given us. Genesis 1:28 reveals God giving humans a commission to *". . . Be fruitful, and multiply, and fill the earth, and subdue it:"* Man was given the task of making this planet a beautiful habitation to live in. God the ultimate builder gave Man the ability to build and create in similar manner.

Thank you Lord, for the gift of creation. You are the most powerful
Creator, having made the universe and our world from nothing by the
power of Your Word. You endowed man with the ability to create using the
resources You provided, Amen!

December 11: Day 345

PRIEST FOREVER

Hebrews 7:3 "The Son of God is eternal." Vs. 21 "You are a priest forever."
Vs.28 "A Son, made perfect forever."

Each of these verse segments provides a glimpse into the nature of Christ (God's Son). His eternal nature is presented in verse 3 where He is acknowledged as God's Son and with it possessor of God's eternal attributes. Verse 21 shows us His priestly position as one that has no end. As a priest, Christ is the mediator for mankind, to present us as spotless before the Father (God). Verse 28 gives us another attribute to His nature, that of perfection. He makes no mistakes. His creative workmanship is on trial as well when we gaze upon His creation. As the workman of God over this creation according to John 1:1, *"In the beginning was the Word, and the Word was with God, and the Word was God."* He is responsible for the creation of all things.

The origins of time and space cannot be explained within the context of this time space guppy bowl we call the universe. It must have originated from an eternal Designer. Since matter cannot create itself from nothing, even science submits to the concept of an eternal particle. This view however does not explain the order and organization of the universe nor the origins and the extreme complexities of life. Our God is the eternal Designer that explains those complexities and order. Our God exists in eternity future, giving us hope for a future with Him. Hebrews 1:12 *"Your years will not come to an end."* As our high priest, He intercedes for us that we may experience an eternal future with Him.

Thank you Lord, for paying our debt of sin and being a faithful high priest on our behalf. It is by Your eternal existence that we exist and have hope for eternal life in paradise with You, Amen!

407

GOD'S BUILDING BLOCKS ARE TOO SMALL TO SEE

*Hebrews 11:3 "By faith we understand **that the worlds were prepared by the word of God**, so that what is seen was not made out of things which are visible."*

God is the ultimate designer, engineer, and has made all things with excellence and beauty and with form and incredible function. His cosmos is no exception. God is our Creator and has done so with beauty and magnificence. The Apostle Paul stated clearly in Romans 1:20 *"For since the creation of the world His invisible attributes, His eternal power and divine nature, have been clearly seen, being understood through what has been made, so that they are without excuse.* The Scripture is accurate in this description of God's magnificent reality.

We cannot see all the things happening around us but we can operate on a level of faith in the power of God to keep the engines of this universe working until the end of time. Science can give us many models that explain the function of the world we see and the world we don't see. They are helpful to develop many technologies we can use to make our lives better. The ultimate reality of life, lies within a relationship with Jesus Christ. We have God's Word as a guide to help us maneuver through many of the difficulties of life. Even the unseen particles of matter are held together by the power of God.

We are thankful to You Lord, that You keep our world in order. It is by Your power we exist and live our lives. We know by faith that You keep all things working together, Amen!

James

James, the earthly brother of the one claiming to be God incarnate, acknowledges Him as his Lord and Savior. In His early ministry, the family of Jesus questioned His sanity and did not believe Him to be the Jewish Messiah. To turn one's intimate family member into a believer is to suggest a miracle in its own right. James affirms, God is the creator of all that is good, even recognizing Jesus as his Lord and Savior.

December 13: Day 347

GOD IS AUTHOR OF ALL THAT IS GOOD

*James 1:17-18 "**Every good thing given and every perfect gift is from above**, coming down from the Father of lights, with whom there is no variation or shifting shadow."*

James does not address God as the Creator directly in this verse, but he does give God the credit for being the source of all things good. For James, all that God gives is perfect. Perfection needs no more refining or adjusting. God is sufficient and complete, just as are all His gifts. However, men became corrupted by sin, having separated themselves from God. God is in the process of restoring man back into a right relationship with Him. Though we were originally created in His image, that image was distorted by sin resulting in the fall.

Everything that is good comes from God. The original creation was called *"very good"*. Genesis 1:31 *"God saw all that He had made, and behold, it was very good."* When the rich man called Jesus 'Good Teacher', Jesus responded. Mark 10:18 *"and Jesus said to him, 'Why do you call me good? No one is good except God alone."* God is the originator of all that is good, and is in the process of restoring His creation to its original perfection.

Thank you Lord that You are good. May we learn to be more like You in all that we do. Help us to do good for others in Your name, Amen!

December 14: Day 348

OUR CREATOR AND JUDGE

*James 3:9 . . . men, who have been **made in the likeness of God**;"*

James is in complete agreement with Genesis 1:27; mankind is made in the likeness of God. *"God created man in His own image, in the image of God He created him: male and female He created them."* This verse leaves little question as to who the Creator is. James gives us a clear message that we are valuable because we are created after God's likeness. We have potential for great things as we have God's mark of identification. Our greatest value is that we have God's likeness stamped on our entire being. Having been created in His likeness, God expects us to produce fruit in our lives. James 1:18 *"In the exercise of His will He brought us forth by the word of truth, so that we would be a kind of first fruits among His creatures."*

Having this great potential, also puts us into a position of great responsibility and accountability. James 4:12 *"There is only one Lawgiver and Judge, the One who is able to save and to destroy; but who are you who judge your neighbor?"* Even though we have judges and lawmakers, we are to judge others lightly. We must remember who the grand Lawgiver is and that we too, one day shall stand before Him as a product of His creation, made in His likeness. We are responsible for all our actions in that God is an exacting accountant of each person's life. He expects us to produce fruit from our lives and to help others.

Thank you Lord, that we were created in Your likeness with great potential. May we be found faithful bearing much fruit from the gifts and abilities You gave us, Amen!

I Peter

Peter was the most prominent disciple of Jesus during His ministry on earth. Peter was the one who launched the Church movement by his sermon on the day of Pentecost in Jerusalem. Peter gives us clear examples of God as our Creator. Peter was said to have been the Apostle to the Jews to whom he sought to bring the gospel message. Peter was later crucified upside down for his faith, as he was willing to die for the belief that Jesus was the Christ.

December 15: Day 349

GOD'S GIFTS OF SERVICE

I Peters 4:10 "As each **one has received a special gift**, *employ it in serving one another as good stewards of the manifold grace of God."*

Each one of us has special gifts from our Creator God for the purpose of serving one another. God does not ask us to do something in respect to service without giving us the will and the ability to do that service. Special gifts can take several forms: some have a commission to serve others through gift giving, others by baking or cooking and, others may do acts of service through mechanics or home repairs. A compassion for others is a gift from God for the purpose of serving others. To others He gives the gifts of teaching and the ministry of the Word of God.

For those who know God, they will have a passion or a burden to see needs and have willingness to reach out, finding ways to meet those that are hurting. God will instill within His people a compassion for others and the ability to reach out to them. Many are spiritually lost, hurting, or lacking basic needs. Matthew 15:32 *"I feel compassion for the people, because they have remained with Me now for three days and have nothing to eat."* May we recognize and have compassion for helping others as God gifted us to serve and help others.

Thank you Lord, for giving us Your gifts of compassion to help and serve others, Amen!

December 16: Day 350

ENTRUST YOUR SOUL
TO OUR CREATOR GOD

I Peter 4:19 "Therefore, **those also who suffer according to the will of God shall entrust their souls to a faithful Creator** *in doing what is right."*

God is absolute in His creative order; He is above time and space. He knows the beginning from the end, as well as the final product of His creation. We are told, God knew us before we were born. Romans 8:29 *"For those whom He foreknew, He also predestined to become conformed to the image of His son,..."* There is an ultimate purpose for our lives. We are all part of His creative plan. We are recipients of an eternal inheritance through Jesus Christ, who made it possible for us. I Peter 1:4 *"...to obtain an inheritance which is imperishable and undefiled and will not fade away, reserved in heaven for you,..."* When we receive an inheritance, it is because we are part of a family.

Though we are promised an inheritance, that road is often a hard road of difficulties and suffering. Matthew 5:10 *"Blessed are those who have been persecuted for the sake of righteousness, for theirs is the kingdom of heaven."* God loves each of us with a perfect love; He will bring us through any suffering we may face. He designed us from the beginning of creation to walk in relationship with Him. He knows us from the very beginning and created each of us for a specific task. Revelation 22:13 *"I am the Alpha and the Omega, the first and the last, the beginning and the end."* Our Creator God will see us through to the end.

Thank you Lord, for knowing us from the beginning, and giving us life and purpose, with the hope of eternal life with You. Strengthen us through the difficulties of life and bring us safely home, Amen!

December 17: Day 351

GOD IS FAITHFUL THROUGH OUR SUFFERING

I Peter 5:9 "But resist him, firm in your faith, knowing that the same experiences of suffering are being accomplished by your brethren who are in the world."

We acknowledge our Creator God as faithful, One in whom we can confidently put our trust. Those willing to suffer will eventually understand the purpose for their pain and will one day be rewarded for their perseverance and patience. Our suffering can be seen as a badge of honor, having the privilege of identifying with and suffering for Christ. Acts 5:41 *"So they went on their way from the presence of the Council, rejoicing that they had been considered worthy to suffer shame for His name."*

God will preserve our souls because he cares for us. I Peter 5:6-7 *"Therefore humble yourselves under the mighty hand of God, that He may exalt you at the proper time, casting all your anxiety on Him, because He cares for you."* It is God who has the ultimate power and authority. I Peter 5:10 *"After you have suffered for a little while, the God of all grace, who called you to His eternal glory in Christ, will Himself perfect, confirm, strengthen and establish you."* God's authority is real and above all earthly rulers. He will reign on into eternity when this world's rulers and authorities are gone, and this world order is completed. God's eternal nature is able to preserve the soul of everyone who places their hope on Him.

Thank you, God, for being with us even in our suffering and difficulties. You Lord are our faithful redeemer and preserver who will keep us now and into eternity, Amen!

II Peter

God's coming judgment on this creation. Peter recognizes God as Creator,. This creation, however will soon come to an end and God will judge it.

December18: Day 352

DON'T BE FOOLED, THERE IS AN END COMING

*II Peter 3:4 "...For ever since the fathers fell asleep, all continues just as it was from **the beginning of creation**."*

The continuity of Life gives man a measure of confidence for each new day. Man is a creature of habit. We establish routines that enable us to succeed in life. These patterns of life have existed from the very beginning of creation and will most likely continue well after we have passed away. Yet this routine will not continue forever. God has set a day for judgment of the world. This world is scheduled for extermination by fire. II Peter 3:7 *"But by His word the present heavens and earth are being reserved for fire, kept for the Day of Judgment and destruction of ungodly men."* The world offers no real security.

Every beginning must have an end. We are told so by the writers of both the Old and New Testaments. We live in a world with a shelf-life that is soon coming to an end. We must remember, at some point, we will stand before God. Hebrews 9:27 *"And inasmuch as it is appointed for men to die once and after this comes judgment,"* We must be diligent to secure safe passage into the open arms of our God who cares about us. I Peter 5:6-7 *"Therefore humble yourselves under the mighty hand of God, that He may exalt you at the proper time, casting all your anxiety on Him, because He cares for you."* Our God provided a way of escape into His loving arms through the sacrifice of His Son Jesus. Let's keep this perspective of the song writer: "This world is not my home, we are only passing through."

We give You praise almighty God, that You are in complete control of this world from its beginning to its end. May our hearts be ready to meet You when that day comes, Amen!

December 19: Day 353
ALL KNOWLEDGE LEADS ULTIMATELY TO GOD

II Peter 3:5 "For when they maintain this, it escapes their notice that **by the word of God the heavens existed** *long ago and* **the earth was formed out of water** *and by water."*

By the power of God's word, the heavens and the earth have their existence. Peter looks back to Genesis to remind us how it is possible to have something from nothing. The answers to man's greatest questions about our existence are revealed in scriptures. The Bible is written with sufficient proofs, offering mankind a clear and unobstructed pathway to God. The only condition, we must want to find it. Whether through ignorance or self-deception, modern man is having a difficult time finding his way to God. It is one of the responsibilities of the church to help clear the road of the obstacles preventing many from seeing the big picture of God's creative purpose.

Man cannot prove with any certitude the age of the earth. Speculation based upon natural premises seems to be the normal guide. However, no man was living during the creation event; God alone knows His creation. One proof is that we have evidence of water found on the moon, and Mars. Comets are made up primarily of water, the so-called building blocks of our wonderful Planet. By faith and through God's revealed word, we know that the heavens were created by His hand. We refer back to the writer of Hebrews to see the necessity of faith. Hebrews 11:3 *"By faith we understand that the worlds were prepared by the word of God, so that what is seen was not made out of things which are visible."* Let's not forget, you can't get something from nothing; the existence of matter, the complexity of life, and order in the universe cancels both time and chance as creative possibilities. Genesis 1 reminds us: *"In the beginning God ..."* We can have confidence, the world we live in was created by a powerful and loving God who created an environment suitable for our habitat.

Thank you Lord, for our protective planet, Amen!

December 20: Day 354

GOD WILL DESTROY
THIS CORRUPTED CREATION

II Peter 3:10 " "But the day of the LORD will come like a thief, in which the heavens will pass away with a roar and the elements will be destroyed with intense heat, and the earth and its works will be burned up."

God has set a time for the eventual destruction of His creation. The basic building blocks of the universe will come apart creating what appears to be a nuclear reaction. From this description, we can assume the structure and organization of the physical universe will return to its primeval state. The intense heat could exceed millions of degrees Fahrenheit, far hotter than the surface of the sun.

The good news: God will create a new heaven and a new earth. The new creation will be restored. Romans 8:21 *"that the creation itself also will be set free from its slavery to corruption into the freedom of the glory of the children of God."* The present earth will have accomplished its purpose, God will give the earth and mankind a new beginning.

Thank You Lord that all corruption will be destroyed, and a new creation will come, restored to perfection, Amen!

I John

John's epistle to the Church. The Apostle John gives us a second look at his perspective on God's power and character. His reflection on God's attribute of light demonstrates His power and timelessness.

December 21: Day 355

GOD'S OMNIPOTENCE, OMNIPRESENCE, AND OMNISCIENCE

I John 1:5 "This then is the message which we have heard of him, and declare unto you, that God is light, and in him is no darkness at all."

The message of God's light takes on a new meaning in I John 1:5. Light is a form of energy that consists of both matter and energy. Photons though not clearly understood seem to mimic matter while the energy of light transcends physical limitations. Energy is not only a physical entity, but it also encompasses a degree of power and energy that stays in motion. This kinetic reflection on light gives us some insight into God's progressive interaction with His creation.

Light has other unique qualities that reflect the character of God. Light travels at incredible speeds, slightly more than 186,000 miles per second. However, for any matter to reach such speeds, would require all the energy in the universe. God alone possesses all the energy of the universe reflecting His omnipotence. Just as light permeates the entire universe, so too God's presence is everywhere showing His omnipresence. God's light reflects His goodness, while chasing away all darkness.

John adds one more aspect to God's character. I John 3:20 *"God is greater than our heart and knows all things."* Our God knows us and everything about us. He knows what is in our hearts, just as light permeates everything, God knows everything. This demonstrates God's omniscience. He alone possesses all the characteristics necessary for the creation of all things.

Thank you Lord, for Your incredible attributes. Your light and goodness chases away all wickedness and evil. May we learn to reflect your light which is in our hearts, Amen!

December 22: Day 356

WE ARE GOD'S NEW CREATION MADE PERFECT

I John 4:17 "By this, love is perfected with us, so that we may have confidence in the day of Judgment; because as He is, so also are we in this world."

By the One who is perfect, **we will be made perfect.** John continues to explain the process toward perfection. I John 4:18a *"There is no fear in love; but perfect love cast out fear."* The love of God brings the believer into harmony with God, removing all fear. Having been made in the likeness of God, the believer is now conforming to the likeness of God in spirit. Romans 8:29 *"For those whom He foreknew, He also predestined to become conformed to the image of His son."*

The perfection of the believer is preceded by God's New Creation that will be one without corruption or end. I Peter 1:4 *"To obtain an inheritance which is imperishable and undefiled, and will not fade away, reserved in heaven for you."* The promise is given by the One whose promises are true. All God's promises come true, in time. We may not always see the results in our lives here and now; God's works transcend the here and now. We are currently in the process of being perfected by the only one capable of completing that task. Our Creator God, who is perfect, is able to equip all those who seek Him to enter into His perfection by His power, and by His strength. God will ultimately complete His work in the lives of all those who call upon Him.

Thank you Lord, that You are perfect and all Your ways are perfect. We look forward to the time when we will experience Your perfection in us for eternity, Amen!

II John

God is eternal Truth.

December 23: Day 357

GOD'S TRUTH IN US

II John 1:2 "for the sake of the truth which abides in us and will be with us forever."

God is greater than our desires, He knows the hearts of all men. God ultimately places His truth within our hearts. He will conform our hearts to bear the image of truth. God knows all about us. He knows our coming and our going. He knows how many hairs are on our head. He knows the number of days we will live on the earth. We are completely known by Him, He knew us before the creation of the world. We are part of His greater plan. He is continually in the process of conforming us to reflect His image, the image of truth and holiness.

God is often presented as synonymous with truth. God's omniscience is again on display in this passage. Truth is a key element in understanding God. Our God is often identified as truth; John 8:32 *"and you will know the truth, and the truth will make you free."* God is the representation of what is true: Psalm 119:160 *"The sum of Your word is truth, And every one of your righteous ordinances is everlasting."* Truth will never pass away, just as the eternal nature of God endures forever. Every word of God can be counted upon to be true. The clear implication is God's perfect truthfulness and holiness will be perfected in all those who call upon Him. He will never lie, we can depend upon Him to be truthful in all His Word.

Thank you Lord, that You are the perfect embodiment of truth. You are truthful in all your words. You can be trusted to fulfill all You have promised, Amen!

III John

Good versus Evil. God is the creator of all that is good.

December 24: Day 358

ALL THAT IS GOOD, COMES FROM GOD

III John 11: "Beloved, do not imitate what is evil, but what is good. The one who does good is of God; the one who does evil has not seen God."

Good and evil are contrasts; there is a distinct difference between good and evil. There is no such thing as an absolute good or evil without an absolute authority. A Creator who is a standard for right and wrong must exist before a substantive basis for right and wrong to exist. Our God is perfect and true; He is characterized by goodness. He is our standard for how to live, what is acceptable, and how we differentiate between good and evil. God has put within each person a sense of right and wrong called a conscience.

Without God, we would not know or understand what good is. God is the originator and creator of all that is good. We have that standard to help us live our lives. God also gives us His Holy Spirit to guide us. John 14:16-17 *"...He will give you another Helper, that He may be with you forever; that is the Spirit of truth..."* Evil characterizes everything that is outside of God. We would do well to keep our focus on God and all that is good. Let us thank God for making known to us the difference between good and evil and how we should live our lives in line with His standard.

Thank you Lord, for giving us a standard to live by, and Your Holy Spirit to guide us. We would not know the difference between evil and good if not for the example of Your Son, and Your Living Word, Amen!

Jude

Jude was another half-brother of Jesus on earth and bond-servant to His Lord and Savior. God is the possessor of all power. He has given His Son Jesus all dominion and authority on earth.

December 25: Day 359

NO MORE FAMILY FEUDS

Jude 25 "To God our Savior, who alone is wise, be glory and majesty, dominion and authority, before all time, now and forever. Amen."

Jude along with James was the half-brother of Jesus. Jude however identifies himself not as a brother to Jesus Christ, but as a bond servant. He understood his place as one who serves much as Christ did with his disciples. Jude does clarify his relationship with his brother James who was martyred for his faith. Though not as prominent as James, Jude still recognizes his half-brother Jesus as the one who saves and justifies. Jude does not mention specifically God's role in creation, however he does give credit to God as the One having all authority. He sets God apart as the only being possessing wisdom, implying that He alone would be capable of control over the vast universe.

Jude acknowledges God's role as our wise and powerful Savior. God's power and dominion are not only real and absolute. His power will see no end, because he is the One who is above time and space, as the One who now exists in power, For Jude, the absoluteness of God's power and control is never in question. Jude has given us this example of family harmony, linking it to Jesus and His saving role of mankind.

Thank you Lord, that You are in control of all Your creation. We are wholly dependent upon You for our life, breath, our salvation, and for the hope of eternal life, Amen!

Revelation

The conclusion to God's creative work. The new creation is the primary theme of God's work on this earth. God will bring a restored relationship between Himself and Mankind. He will establish a new heaven and a new earth.

December: 26: Day 360

GOD FINISHING HIS-STORY

*Revelation 1:6 "...and **He has made us to be a kingdom, priests to His God and Father**- to Him be the glory and dominion forever and ever. Amen.*

The story of humans on Earth and also the story of God's creative work are coming to a close. As Genesis brings us a front row seat to the beginning of God's creation, Revelation gives us the ending chapter to this historical narrative. God as the Creator will complete the project with a new creation, yet to be revealed. The New Heaven and the New Earth continue God's creative work on into eternity. Man is not privileged to see what this new creation will be like as yet; only that it transcends the old. God's perfect work is given more than a face-lift; it is a whole new creative work. We will see God completing His greatest work without sin or the curse to hinder; all things will become new.

Judgments

God's judgments are also complete and final. There is no recovery from the final verdict as man's opportunity to change and recover comes to its conclusion. Man will then be fixed into whatever state he was in at his time of death. The nations are also judged as to how they treated their people. God is the protector of the poor and innocent. At this point, all wrongs are accounted for. Some nations are brought to a close, while others continue on. God's kingdom is established on earth and God's glory is finally revealed to man. All men will eventually witness the power and glory of God, some to eternal glory while others will enter eternal separation. The final chapter of Earth's history will then be complete. Heaven and eternity will move on in disregard to time and space.

Thank you Lord, for revealing to us Your conclusion to History. We do not need to fear any cosmic accident. You are the One preserving our planet until Your work is completed, Amen!

December 27: Day 361

GOD'S KINGDOM IN HEAVEN

*Revelations 1:6 "...**and He has made us to be a kingdom, priests to His God and Father**- to Him be glory and dominion forever and ever. Amen."*

People play a major role in the kingdom to come, for man is to serve and minister both to God and to others. It is hard to imagine how we could be priests unless God's creation extends far beyond what this world provides. Going back to Paul, I Corinthians 13:*12 "For now, we see into a mirror dimly, but then face to face;"* We have glimpses into eternity, but we can only see in part now. For the believer however, God has wonderful things in store.

Jesus talked extensively about His coming kingdom. This kingdom however would start within the hearts of those who would believe on Him and learn to follow and serve Him. Luke 17:20-21 *"The kingdom of God is not coming with signs to be observed; nor will they say, 'Look, here it is!' or, 'there it is!' for behold, the kingdom of God is in your midst."* God's kingdom begins with the hearts of faithful believers who have learned to trust in Him. This kingdom will continue on into eternity with God.

Thank you Lord, for the privilege to know You. You saved us and gave us the right to become your children. You have the power to make us priests through Your Son Jesus, Amen!

December 28: Day 362

THE GOD OF BEGINNINGS

Revelation 3:14 "The Amen, the faithful and true Witness, the Beginning of the creation of God, says this:..."

God is recognized as Creator directly in this passage. The idea of a beginning is consistent with current scientific knowledge. Science however is subject to change and is not a great determinant for ultimate knowledge. Change necessitates improvement and structure; God will bring all things to ultimate perfection. No further change or improvement will be necessary or required. God's ultimate creative work will be perfect.

The original creation was declared good in Genesis One, Genesis 1:31 *"God saw all that He had made; and behold, it was very good."* The new creation will be perfect and without blemish; all sin will be eliminated. Man will live in a perfect state before God. Even though this world, this universe, and all life had a beginning, God's ultimate creation will have no end. What God creates will be eternal, all corruption will be ended. God will reign in perfect harmony with His creation.

Thank you Lord, for the beginnings of all Your creative work. We thank you again that You will bring all creation including Your people into perfect harmony with You, Amen!

December 29: Day 363

GOD REVEALS HIS PURPOSE FOR CREATION

*Revelation 4:11 "You are worthy, O Lord, to receive glory and honor and power; for **You created all things, and by Your will they exist and were created**."*

Due to His creative power, God alone is worthy of all praise. John gives us a direct reference to God's creative work. All creation is in existence by God's will. His purpose and plan are at work. God's purpose is revealed, man is to give God the glory and honor for His work of creation as well as for His redemptive plan. People are subject to God because He created us. We are the products of His Divine plan and God is worthy of that honor.

Rev. 5:13 brings home the reality for which we are created. *"And every created thing which is in heaven and on earth* (Give Praise). . . *'To Him who sits on the throne, and to the Lamb, be blessing and honor and glory and dominion forever and ever."* We are given a glimpse into the future, we will behold God and the Lamb of God, Jesus. We will desire nothing more than to give praise and honor to Him. The delights of heaven will transcend beyond anything we could imagine. Our purpose and existence will be made clear: to praise the One who gave us life, and meaning.

Thank you, Lord God, Our Lamb, the One who redeemed us from our sins. We can do no other than to give you all praise, honor, and glory, Amen!

December 30: Day 364

CREATOR OF HEAVEN AND EARTH

Revelation 10:6 (The angel in verse 5) *"swore by Him who lives forever and ever,* **who created heaven and the things in it, and the earth and the things in it, and the sea and the things in it.***"*

The One who created all things is nearly finished with His revelation. It is He who inspired the biblical prophets to reveal to mankind the creative power of God. All that exists both in the physical and spiritual realms were created by God's power. The biosphere, with all its diversity of life and all the variety of plants, and animals living in a symbiotic relationship along with the delicate balance allowing all life to exist, originates from God's hand; plus, everything that exists on earth, including all the many resources necessary for building societies. All life, all talents and all skills given to men and women were gifted to mankind. With these abilities men and women were able to think, communicate, build and create many things, including many great structures and beautiful cities.

This revelation is the final revelation of God. He is nearly finished at this point. God has made Himself known to mankind. All those willing, have accepted His pardon and will be made complete. Those who have rejected God's provision for salvation will now be condemned. God's purpose and His Kingdom will have been established. He will now reign in complete harmony with His creation.

Thank you Lord, for revealing Yourself to us and for Your provisions of grace and mercy. You have made it possible for ordinary man to enter into Your presence as righteous and acceptable in Your sight, Amen!

December 31: Day 365

NEW HEAVENS AND A NEW EARTH

*Revelation 21:5 "He who sits on the throne said, "**Behold, I am making all things new**."*

The One who created the heavens and the earth of Genesis I, will be the One who gives us a New Heaven and a New Earth. Revelation 21:1 *"then I saw a new heaven and a new earth; for the first heaven and the first earth passed away,"* Verses 5 and 6 gives credit to God for being the originator of this new creation. He is referred to as the Alpha and Omega, the beginning and the end. God is our eternal Creator. The One who was there in the beginning, before anything existed, is the One who is there at the very end of time.

God's creative work continues with His revelation of the New Jerusalem. Revelation 3:12 *"...the new Jerusalem which comes down out of heaven from My God..."* The New Jerusalem will be a magnificent city. God will continue His creative work as He begins with a New Jerusalem to be the center of worship, only this Jerusalem will be without a temple in that Christ will reside Himself with mankind. Man will have no further need of a place to worship. The new city of Jerusalem is described as a cube of 1,500 cubic miles. That's an unimaginable size when compared with our current earth. This raises the question as to what this new earth will be like. It will be beyond anything we can imagine. As Christians, we have a future hope that transcends anything in our current reality.

We have so much to be thankful for Lord. You are our Creator God who loves us so much, You were willing to sacrifice Yourself to restore us into right fellowship with You. We have the hope of eternal life in Heaven within a city of unimaginable size and beauty. Thank you Lord God, for all You have done and will continue to do. In Jesus name we pray, Amen!

FINAL THOUGHTS

Genesis One set the foundation for our understanding the universe, our planet and the nature of life. Man is the highest order of God's creative work. We must see our reality in light of God's creative order. Our failure to do so will only result in more suffering and wrongs. The Bible from beginning to end paints a picture of God's creative work. It is an ongoing portrait of God's handiwork amidst the suffering of the world. It is an intimate look at God's concern for man in spite of his disobedience. God is reaching out to a world, who has forgotten who they are, and the purpose of their being. As man seeks to understand his place in the universe, apart from this revelation, he will only find confusion amidst the insane complexity of life. How can he translate this conflict into an orderly understanding? He can only speculate as to what is true, he can know very little without the revelation of God's Word.

The portrait of God presented in these pages represents a being, passionate for His creation. He not only created the universe for the sake of man, to reveal His grandeur, He is in a constant state of creating a new kingdom on earth through the work of His people.

All societies depend upon the diversity of skills and abilities each individual offers. God has instilled that diversity for the sake of maintaining civilization. All our skills and talents are gifts equipping each man and woman with the ability to serve others. God is at work directing the hearts of men for a greater purpose. God's ultimate gift is though His identification with man by becoming man in the person of Jesus Christ. It is through His work as a healer, teacher, and redeemer in which Christ presents a picture of God that demonstrates His love and compassion for His people (the Jews), and for all peoples in the world. God willingly took the suffering of an entire world upon himself. He paid the debt owed to Himself, setting men free of their obligations. Man is now free, to pursue a relationship with all mighty God, without fear.

From the biblical context we learn the purpose of mankind. We are given insight into why the universe was created; we are given the reason for suffering and evil in the world. The answers to all man's greatest questions are answered. Though we don't understand all the details of life's suffering. We understand enough to know, God has a greater good that is yet to be shown. Trust is a difficult commodity to earn. The Bible demonstrated through the person of Jesus Christ, God's concern for lost man. Romans 5:8 *"While we were yet sinners, Christ died for us."* God's compassion for man overrules all wrongs, He sets the record right, He brings Man back into full fellowship with Him. We need only to reach out and accept it.

As the Psalmist said 3,000 years ago, *"Create within me a clean heart O God, and renew a steadfast spirit within me."* Psalm 51. God is at work creating a new kingdom within the hearts of millions around the world. It is God's passion to instill within man a new creative work, to renew and right the ship of man's heart, and to heal the hurts of all suffering. Amidst the pain and frustration of life. God is ever at work creating His Kingdom within the hearts of men who seek to know, and honor Him. God is revealing Himself through the lives and works of His people. A new kingdom, and a new world, is being created in the midst of the confusion. Peace, order, and purpose begins with our Creator God. A new world is coming, as God is at work preparing the hearts of men, to fellowship with Him in that new everlasting world.

www.ingramcontent.com/pod-product-compliance
Lightning Source LLC
Jackson TN
JSHW060703050525
83719JS00009B/7